Brand Warriors China

Fiona Gilmore

Fiona is one of the two founding partners of Springpoint, a leading brand strategy and innovation consultancy with offices in Shanghai, Beijing and Hong Kong, headquartered in London.

She has spent the last 20 years directing brand positioning, migration strategy, innovation and identity programmes for international clients such as Vodafone, Unilever, Lloyd's and Giorgio Armani, as well as local brand leaders in China. She has also been responsible for developing brand strategies for countries and regions all over the world including Britain, Wales, Northern Ireland, England, the Blue Mountains and Hong Kong.

Fiona is a regular speaker on brand positioning and innovation and has participated in TV programmes including *The Money Programme* and *Question Time*, and has also judged the BBC Design Awards.

Her books *Brand Warriors* and *Warriors on the High Wire* are also available from Profile. *Brand Warriors China* was published in Mandarin in January 2003, selling over 25,000 copies in the first six weeks.

Fiona is a Trustee of Wateraid and a Fellow of the Royal Society of Arts.

Serge Dumont

Serge Dumont is non-executive chairman of Springpoint and is a board-level strategic adviser to large multinational companies and major firms in the communications industry.

He is a noted expert in the communications industry in Asia, where he has lived for about 20 years, and is recognized for his expertise in the field of public affairs as well as corporate and issues management in the PRC.

Over the years, he has advised organizations such as Unilever, Mars Incorporated, Eastman Chemical, ABB, Nike, Kodak, UPS, LVMH, IBM, Intel, Mobil, Nortel, Bank of Boston, Texas Instruments, ING Insurance, Ericsson, the New York Stock Exch-  McKinsey & Co, KFC, Christian Dior, KLM, Northwest Breweries, Rolls-Royce, Richemonde, Dupont, Saatchi & Saa Procter & Gamble, the Chicago Board of Trade, Tetra Pak as ernment organizations.

Serge is actively involved in philanthropic and artistic activi of the provisional Rotary Club of Beijing for the year 2002-2 ...man of the advisory board of the Beijing Music Festival and the vice-president of the China Heritage Society.

He is fluent in French, English and Mandarin Chinese.

Brand Warriors China

CREATING SUSTAINABLE BRAND CAPITAL

Fiona Gilmore and Serge Dumont

PROFILE BOOKS

First published in Great Britain in 2003 by
PROFILE BOOKS LTD
58A Hatton Garden
London EC1N 8LX
www.profilebooks.co.uk

10 9 8 7 6 5 4 3 2 1

Typeset in Janson and Ellington by MacGuru Ltd
Printed and bound in Great Britain by
Clays, Bungay, Suffolk

A CIP catalogue record for this book is available from the British Library.

ISBN 1 86197 699 2

Contents

Acknowledgements   viii
Contributor's Biographies   ix
Foreword by Fiona Gilmore   xvi
Foreword by Serge Dumont   xxi

Introduction: Fiona Gilmore   1
  Brands: the new gold   1
  The counterfeiters' legacy: greater emphasis on substance and
  real quality   6
  The value of brands   7
  Beyond awareness building   10
  Macro-trends matter   14
  Innovation in everything: an attitude of mind   17
  Each positioning and accompanying benefits and substantiators
  form a possible brand strategy   21
  From the inside out   24
  International brands and the banana skin slip-ups   25
  Nation and region branding   27
  The new calibre of entrepreneurs   29
  China's innate creativity   31
  Conclusion   31

1   **China Mobile**: Preparing to Capitalize on its Customer Base   35

2   **Shanghai City**: Spectacular Shanghai   51

3   **Haier**: Dancing and Competing with the Wolves   63

4   **SINA**: Brand Shifting™ for a Connected World   79

5   **TCL**: Going Deeper with the Brand   89

6 **Tong Ren Tang**: A National Treasure, Not Just a Brand   101

7 **CITIC**: In the Front Line of Reform   111

8 **Broad**: The Benefits of an Idiosyncratic Culture Inspired by Ideals 125

9 **Legend**: Championing the Value Perception of 'Made in China' 137

10 **AsiaInfo**: Setting Standards in Corporate Governance   153

11 **Erdos**: Valuing the Origins of a Brand   167

12 **Yanjing Beer**: Choosing the Right Path for Growth   181

13 **Yue-Sai**: Influencing the Course of Social Change   195

14 **Phoenix TV**: Becoming the Media Brand King   207

15 **Wall's**: Global Brand Capital, Local Application   217

Index   226

For my sons, Dan, Alex and Eddie. I hope you all get a chance to stay in China, enjoy the experience like I have done and learn to speak Mandarin better than your mother.

Fiona Gilmore

For all my Chinese friends, from Beijing to Taipei, Shanghai to New York, Hong Kong to Pingyao, who for the last twenty years have helped make my life so interesting.

Serge Dumont

Acknowledgements

Deadlines have been tight and there are many many people to whom we owe not only our thanks, but ultimately our sanity as well.

First we would like to express our gratitude to our publishers, both in London and China, who consistently provided excellent editorial guidance and maintained a positive outlook throughout this whole process – Andrea Chu, Pan Yan, Wang Bin, Andrew Franklin, Martin Liu and Penny Daniel – thank you.

The book could not have been completed without the contributors and interviewees: Su Fang Wen, Zhou Yun Jie, Li Da Chuan, Wang Ying, Bai Li Hua, Zhu Guang, Zhang Er Jing, Jin Yong Nian, Roger Uren, Stella Chen, James Ding, Li Dong Sheng, Lu Xiang Dong, Peter Ter-Kulve, Wang Lin Xiang, Wang Jun, Yue-Sai Kan, Zhang Rui Min, Zhang Yue, Daniel Mao, Yang Yuan Qing, Liu Chang Le, Li Fu Cheng and Zhou Hanmin who have been a delight to interview, even if the surroundings were, at times, a little surreal.

Special thanks are due to our translators, Sunny Sun, Penny Li, Roger Pua and Ge Lei whose professionalism, enthusiasm and energy have been inspirational. Also invaluable was Alan Liu, our project manager in Beijing, who single-handedly co-ordinated the entire interview schedule with diplomacy, patience and the stubbornness of a mule.

We are also indebted to our colleagues at Springpoint Asia who provided unfailing support, in particular Sherry Tang and Michael McComb who, bleary-eyed, accompanied us to far-flung corners of China at the drop of a hat and usually at the crack of dawn. Our thanks, too, to our colleagues in London – Peter Smith and Laurence Lassalle, for their creative input and to Laura Mazur for weaving her editorial magic.

Very special thanks go to Penny Lo Wai Pek and Becky Rumens without whom this book could never have got off the ground – their research and editorial contribution have been truly remarkable – and to Cherie Keith, a wicked angel, who has had the unenviable task of looking after Fiona during this whole exercise.

Finally, we would like to thank Fiona's children Dan, Alex and Eddie for their understanding when Mum was in China and should have been at home.

Contributor's Biographies

Liu Changle

Liu Changle is the founder and chief executive officer of Phoenix Satellite Television. During its early years Phoenix had only one channel, the Phoenix Chinese Channel, but under Liu's direction it has expanded rapidly into five channels and can be seen in Australasia, North America, and Europe as well as East Asia. Phoenix went public in 2000 and is listed on the Hong Kong Growth Enterprise Market.

Liu was born in Shanghai in 1951. Like many of his generation, his education was disrupted by the Cultural Revolution, which broke out in 1966 and during which he served in the People's Liberation Army. At the end of the Cultural Revolution he joined the Central People's Radio Station as a reporter. Leaving to study at the Beijing Broadcasting Institute, he then returned to Central Radio in the early 1980s, working in a variety of journalistic positions.

In 1988 he moved to Singapore, where he began trading in petroleum and other products. By the mid-1990s he had a commercial base that was sufficient to allow him to consider establishing a Chinese-language television broadcaster that would be politically neutral and use modern technology to broadcast to Chinese around the globe. As a result, in March 1996, Liu formed a joint-venture partnership with News Corporation's Star TV and established Phoenix Satellite Television.

James Ding

One of AsiaInfo's co-founders, James Ding has served as president since January 2001 and as chief executive since May 1999. He has been a member of the board since the company's inception in 1994. Before becoming chief executive, Ding served as vice-president of business development and chief technology officer from 1997 to 1998, and as senior vice-president and chief technology officer from 1993 to 1997. He holds an MSc in Information Science from the University of California in Los Angeles.

Li Dong Sheng

Li Dong Sheng has been chairman of the board and president of the TCL Group since 1996. After graduation from senior high school in 1974, he went to Huiyang's Ma'an Farm to become a machine operator. Three years later he enrolled at Huanan Technological University to specialize in wireless communications.

After graduation in 1982, he joined TTK Home Appliance Co. Within three years he became general manager of TCL Communication Equipment Co. In 1986 he joined Huizhou's Industrial Development (main branch) as a department head but returned to TCL in 1989 as first assistant general manager. Six years later he was appointed general manager of TCL's Electrical Group before taking up his current position.

He was born in 1957 in Guangdong's Huizhou province.

Li Fu Cheng

Li Fu Cheng is the chairman and general manager of the Beijing Yanjing Brewery Group Corporation. Established in 1980, the brewing company now has total assets exceeding 10 billion yuan.

Li Fu Cheng was appointed as general manager in 1989. Since then he has focused on building a strong and sustainable business through a strategy based on continuous innovation, quality, employee motivation and keeping a close watch on market dynamics. As a result, the brewing group now ranks number one in the Chinese market, with output in 2001 reaching 1,700,000 tonnes. Li Fu Cheng has also successfully led the company into the public domain, with a listing on the Hong Kong Stock Exchange to further the long-term development of the company. Since 1999, the company has also acquired and merged 12 companies, as well as acquiring shares in several high-tech companies.

Li Fu Cheng's achievements have been recognized in a number of ways. For example, he has been awarded the titles of 'Outstanding Entrepreneur' and 'Outstanding Manager', along with other accolades.

Born in 1954, Li Fu Cheng's background is in economics. Along with his business success, he was elected a member of the 15th national congress of the Communist Party of China and the ninth NPC.

Lu Xiang Dong

Lu Xiang Dong has been vice-president of China Mobile Communications Corporation and vice-chairman of China Mobile (Hong Kong) Group Limited since 2000.

His first job was as a technician with the New Technology Center of the Fujian Microwave Station, which was followed by an engineering post at the Fujian Administration of Posts and Telecommunications. After four years, he was promoted to director and chief engineer of the Fujian Bureau of Radio Communications. In 1997 he was made vice-director general of the Mobile Communications Bureau of the Ministry of Posts and Telecommunications. This led, two years later, to an appointment to lead the preparatory group of the China Mobile Communications Corporation as vice-head. In 1999, he became vice-chairman of China Telecom (Hong Kong) Group Limited.

His degrees include a BSc in Radio Communications from the Beijing University of Posts and Telecommunications and an MSc in Telecommunications and Electronic Systems from the China Academy of Posts and Telecommunications, part of the Ministry of Postal and Telecommunications.

He was born October 1960 in Fujian province.

Daniel Mao

Mr Mao was appointed SINA's chief executive officer in June 2001, taking charge of the company's Technology-Media-Telecommunications (TMT) business strategy and its execution. He joined SINA as chief operating officer in April 1999, looking after global business integration and co-ordination and the setting up and management of business operations and business development.

Before joining SINA, he was vice-president of Walden International Investment Group (WIIC), overseeing investments in technology-based companies in the US, China and Hong Kong. Of the more than US$1 billion investment fund managed by WIIC, close to $100 million was invested and managed by Mr Mao in over 20 companies in the Internet, technology, building materials, home appliances, medical equipment and other industries in China. The investment in Stone Rich Sight Information Tech. Co. Ltd in 1997, in particular, was a well-publicized venture capital investment in high technology in China. Mr Mao was also the main overseer of the merger in 1998 between Stone Rich Sight and the former Sina.com to form the present SINA.

He holds an MSc in engineering economic systems from Stanford University and a BSc in computer science from Shanghai Jiao Tong University.

Peter Ter-Kulve

Peter Ter-Kulve has been with Unilever since completing his MA in Business Administration and Economics at Erasmus University in Rotterdam.

The initial years of his career were spent building up his marketing skills in various brand management jobs within Unilever. He then moved to Prague to head up the marketing department of Unilever's ice-cream subsidiary. For the next five years Peter lived and worked in Central Europe, holding both national and regional roles. For three of those five years, he held the position of general manager. In 1999 he became chairman of the Greater China Ice Cream operations for Unilever. His assignment involved turn-around management as well as the building of a powerbrand in China for Unilever.

Born in 1964 in the Netherlands, Peter has a broad and eclectic range of interests, from sculpting, political history to endurance sports and good food.

Wang Linxiang

Wang Linxiang has been president of Erdos Cashmere Group since 1995, and chairman of the board of directors since 1999.

Wang Linxiang has won numerous awards over the years in the fields of management and economics. For example, in 1996 he was named one of the 'Top Ten Outstanding Businessmen Supporting the Worker Class' by the China Labour Association. He is also an enthusiastic participant in many public and professional services and charitable organizations, such as the China Brands Association, Inner Mongolia's Youth Development Foundation and the Inner Mongolia Youth Liaison Group.

After gaining a university degree in economics, he began his career in cashmere production in 1970 when he joined Yimeng Cashmere Factory. In 1980 he was appointed vice-head of the Development and Installation Department, followed by promotion to vice-head of Yimeng Cashmere Factory a year later and, in 1983, to head of the factory. From 1991 to the present, he has been president and party committee secretary of the Erdos Cashmere Group.

He was born in 1951 in Baotou, Inner Mongolia.

Yang Yuanqing

Mr Yang Yuanqing has been the president and chief executive of Legend Group Limited since 2001. Under his leadership, Legend has been transformed into a 'self orientated, high-tech and international Legend'.

He has worked for the company since 1989, becoming general manager in 1994 at the age of only 29. Under his leadership, the market share of Legend brand PCs has increased consistently to the point where, in 1996, it became the top seller in the Chinese market for PCs – a position it still holds today.

Mr Yang is a member of the National Youth Committee and a visiting professor at the University of Science and Technology of China. His outstanding contribution to China's information industry has won him many accolades. For instance, in 1999 Mr Yang was selected as one of the 20 'heroes' who promote Asia's development among only two representatives from mainland China. In June 2001 Mr Yang was chosen by *Business Week* magazine as a runner-up in the Stars of Asia.

Mr Yang was born in November 1964 in Zhejiang province. After he graduated from the Department of Computer Science in Shanghai Communications University in 1986, he continued his studies at the University of Science and Technology of China before joining the Legend Group in 1989.

Yue-Sai Kan

Yue-Sai Kan is one of China's most beloved and respected entrepreneurs and personalities. She founded Yue-Sai Kan Cosmetics in 1992 and in 1997, in a joint venture with Coty, opened a $20 million cosmetics factory in Pudong, Shanghai. In 2001 she launched the Yue-Sai Doll in China and in the US.

In her previous career as a broadcasting journalist in the US, she made notable contributions to the popular culture of China. Her programme, *One World*, was the first television series ever produced and hosted by an American on China's only national network, CCTV, introducing the outside world to China. Her documentary *China Walls and Bridges* (ABC) received an Emmy Award in 1989.

She is also the author of *One World* and Yue-Sai's *Guide to Asian Beauty*. Her latest book on modern etiquette, entitled *Where Does Charisma Come From?*, is currently a bestseller in China. She has also completed a video series, *Doing Business in China*, which is being distributed by the International Institute for Learning.

For her dedication to linking East to West, Yue-Sai has been presented with a number of honorary doctorate degrees, Women of the Year Awards, Lifetime Achievement Awards and countless humanitarian awards. As a UNICEF Ambassador, she concentrates on education and children, including the establishment of many scholarship funds for outstanding students in China and the US.

Born in Guilin, China, she grew up in Hong Kong in the 1950s and 1960s. Yue-Sai Kan currently divides her time between Shanghai and New York City. *People* magazine dubbed her 'the most famous woman in China'. *Time* magazine, *The New York Times*, *Newsweek*, the Asian *Wall Street Journal*, *Cosmopolitan* and *Le Figaro* are among the many publications that have profiled her career and efforts in the cosmetics industry.

Zhang Ruimin

Zhang Ruimin is chief executive of one of China's best-known and most popular conglomerates, Haier. He began his rise to prominence in Haier's home base of Qingdao, Dalian, where he was credited with rescuing a local refrigerator factory from bankruptcy. Today Haier, under his leadership, is one of the most successful companies in China and a significant player in the electrical appliances market worldwide. The company's products are now exported to over 160 countries and territories.

Much of the company's success has been attributed to Zhang, who has been applauded both at home and abroad for his creative leadership and corporate management practices. He believes that the group's rapid growth will continue to rely on an internationalization strategy, especially with the development of the Internet economy and China's entry into the WTO.

His business expertise has been recognized internationally. For example, in 1998, Harvard University invited him to give a lecture based on Haier's experience, which has since become part of Harvard's business case study collection. He has also given a lecture on Haier's management and innovation capabilities at the world-renowned business school, IMD, in Lausanne. In 2000 he was ranked by the *Financial Times* as 26th on a list of the world's 30 most prestigious business entrepreneurs.

Zhang Yue

Zhang Yue, chief executive of Broad AC, founded the Broad Air Conditioning Company in 1988 with his brother, Zhang Jian. Subsequently, he was responsible for developing the first generation of vacuum boilers in China. In 1992, he oversaw the successful development of another major product, the direct-fired lithium-bromide absorption chiller/heater, which is now the company's main product.

At Broad, Zhang Yue still devotes most of his time to working with his engineers on technology development and environmental research. In addition, he attends key world summits such as the World Economic Forum. He also gives speeches and lectures on a wide range of subjects such as enterprise management, environment protection, energy policy and air-con technology.

Born in Changsha in 1960, Zhang Yue started off his career as a fine arts teacher, first at Leiyang Normal University and then at the Professional School of Chenzhou. When he was 24, he resigned from teaching to start his own business, the South Construction Material Company. His business success provided him with his first taste of management.

Zhou Hanmin

Zhou Hanmin is presently serving as the Chinese delegate to the Bureau of International Expositions, vice-chairman of the Shanghai World Expo 2010 Bidding Office and also as the deputy chief commissioner of Shanghai Pudong New Area People's Government. He is the former vice-president of Shanghai Institute of Foreign Trade and dean of its law school and was formerly chief editor of *Focus and Research on WTO*, the first journal in China to cover this topic.

Other positions include deputy to the Shanghai Municipal People's Congress, decision-making consultant for Shanghai Municipal People's Government, member of the American Policy Advisory Committee MOFTEC, WTO legal consultant to MOFTEC, WTO's vice-chairman of law, China Law Society and also executive director of WTO Shanghai Research Centre.

For the past two decades, Professor Zhou has devoted himself to the research and teaching of international economic law, international trade law, GATT/WTO, Sino–US relations and the development and opening up of Pudong Area in Shanghai. He has participated in the editing of a range of publications, as well as publishing more than 200 essays about these subjects.

Foreword

FIONA GILMORE

A few months ago my family spent an agreeable weekend at one of my favourite retreats, Ackergill Tower, a castle situated on the most northeasterly tip of Scotland, just south of John O' Groats. Looking over Sinclair Bay where the Gulf Stream warms the waters, it lifts the spirits, even on a day when skies are leaden. We saw and heard the lark ascending over the loch as Jimmy the Ghillie[1] gave us a spot of fly fishing tuition.

Aside from the festivities of the local highland games – where, in the tug of war, the Castle of Mey 'Bravehearts'[2] vanquished the Ackergill Tower 'Flower-pot men'[3], presided over by Prince Charles and Camilla[4] – I set all the other castle guests a game: each person was asked to hunt through their clothes, as they were packing and note down any article of clothing that was manufactured in China, including the brand name. I also asked them to recall if they had anything at home that was Chinese branded. Everybody joined in, largely incentivized by the prize bottle of sloe gin. The results were collected over the breakfast porridge. The good-hearted competitors, who hailed from the UK, Austria, Germany and the US, discovered much to their amazement that they had a 'shed load' of things manufactured in China. Interestingly, most people had not studied the labels before and were not aware of the country of origin. On realizing that many of their belongings were made in China they were not disappointed, because they felt that Chinese manufacturing today must connote a certain quality stamp, but not at the level of Japan, Germany or the US.

The brand names however were really intriguing because they covered such a broad spectrum from mass-market all the way through to up-margin haute couture: a Jaeger silk dress, Facconable shirts, Callaway golf shorts, Tommy bahama pants, Billabong Australian boardies, M&S underwear, a Musto country jacket, Debenhams sweatshirt, Planet trousers, Pastimes dressing-gowns, Monsoon children's beaded trousers, Uniqlo children's polo shirts, Titleist golf shoes, John Lewis lingerie, GAP leather belt, Racing Green polo shirt, Ted Baker shirt, Adidas trainers, Next boxer shorts, Peter Storm linen coat, Warehouse linen suit and a French Connection wet weather jacket and hat. People had also noted a Morphy Richards travel iron, a Nokia mobile phone battery and charger, a Psion palmtop computer, Clinique make-up bag, Conair curling irons, voltage adaptors from Sony – and these were just the things they had packed in their cases; so imagine how many more branded products had been manufactured in China at home. Not a single person could recall any thing they had that was Chinese branded and indeed the majority of people struggled to think of a single Chinese brand name, not even being able to recall Haier or Tsingtao.

What was most interesting for these people was the fact that they had not realised how much of the manufacturing universe was now centred in China.

Arguably the greatest success story of the last 20 years in China has been its remarkable ability to grow its export manufacturing industry. In the 10 years prior to 2000 exports nearly quadrupled from $72 billion in 1991 to $249 billion in 2000. Today the chances are that any one of us is wearing at least one article of clothing that has a 'Made in China' label. The actual manufacturing process is increasingly sophisticated and products such as toys where the complexity of assembly involves very often electronic and mechanical devices, as well as memory chips, passed from initial sketches to full production line implementation in just a few weeks. This export manufacturing industry is growing so dramatically that one can imagine a day in the near future where the majority of all processed products will come from China.

One of the dilemmas for the Chinese government today is how they can spread this new found wealth more broadly amongst the Chinese population. Many of these export manufacturing businesses are actually run by Hong Kong and Taiwanese businessmen. They benefit from a cultural and linguistic affinity and they have done extremely well in the last few years in building hugely successful businesses out of China. There are the very famous millionaires and billionaires who have made their fortunes in the last 20 years – men such as Allan Wong from V-tech the computer equipment and toy company, Frank Lowe the brassiere emperor and Clifford Pang who manufactures computer disk drive heads. What is painfully clear to many Chinese is that they could be making more money, if they not only manufactured these goods but also promoted them under Chinese brand names, thereby benefiting from the added value margins. This is perhaps the greatest challenge for China in the next 10 years and one of the reasons why I was curious to put this book together. I wanted to see how Chinese brands were starting to develop and the kinds of challenges that people in China were addressing in a country where there has been little commercial brand building in recent history.

I first went to China in May 1987 when I was invited by Michael Peters and Jim Fleury to speak at a conference dedicated to the subject of brands. The conference took place at the Great Hall of the People in Tiananmen Square. It was entitled The Third World Advertising Congress. The combination of subject matter and location was a first and the historical significance was not lost on anyone (the student protests took place two years later). I vividly remember the experience where, after presenting our paper, young Chinese executives and students clamoured to find out what books they should read, where they could find out more information and how could they transform their products through brand innovation. Never before and never since have I seen such hunger and enthusiasm for knowledge. At the time the title of the conference struck me as a little bizarre – it suggested that advertising was going to be the panacea, the complete solution for building brands in China and that every other aspect of brand building was subservient to advertising.

To this day I have a photograph hanging in my office of all the delegates and speakers at this conference, well over 500 people. In the front row the speakers are arranged in order of importance; in the centre are one or two people whom I did not know then, but who have since become friends, people like Yue-Sai (who in those days was one of the most famous television presenters in China). I was captivated by China when I visited Beijing those 15 years ago, not only because I found the people so open to new ideas and inquisitive but also, as I toured the country for a week's holiday with my husband, I realized the social and economic changes that were taking place were of such great magnitude, requiring courage, imagination and belief.

Europeans have always been seduced by China. The love affair goes back over many hundreds of years. There is something quite extraordinary about the scale of this country, something intriguing in the history of a civilisation that was progressive, outgoing and sophisticated for many, many centuries. It is thanks to the Chinese that, between the eleventh- and fourteenth-century, Europeans acquired the skills to make magnetic compasses, gunpowder, the escapement – a key component of clockwork – and many other critical technologies for modern day living. Then, 500 years ago, China appeared to take a back seat. Given China's recent history it is surprising for foreigners to discover that the Chinese were wise to the benefits of branding and creating mystique earlier than most.

Over 2000 years ago, the western world first became fascinated by a product that still fascinates people today – silk. Not only did Cleopatra, mistress of Julius Caesar and Mark Anthony, Queen of Egypt, enjoy wearing silk dresses but today every woman aspires to having a silk dress in her wardrobe. The 'Silk Road' was the West's first encounter with the trade between China and Europe. The legend of the Silk Road has gained in mystique over centuries. Even Marco Polo and Christopher Columbus were beguiled by the aura surrounding this commercial enterprise and misjudged the extent of the actual trade. What is clear is that silk was for China a great source of wealth and in its own way became a precious brand.

One of China's greatest treasures following after the success of the Silk

Road was its ability to produce the greatest porcelain in the world. It was the Chinese who were the supreme alchemists or more specifically arcanists – they were the ones who managed to discover the perfect formula for transforming clay into translucent, brilliant china. As a Frenchman wrote in 1716 '*Allons à cette porcelaine, Sa beauté m'invite, m'entraine. Elle vient du monde nouveau, L'on ne peut rien voir de plus beau. Qu'elle a d'attraits, qu'elle est fine! Elle est native de la Chine*'[5]. Until the eighteenth century when a young European apothecary Johanne Frederick Böttger, struggled to realise the alchemist's dream and managed remarkably to find the formula for producing exquisite porcelain, the Chinese owned uniquely this 'white gold'. While silk was perhaps the first known great Chinese brand, its greatest successor was Chinese porcelain, unique, premium priced, mesmerizing Europeans for centuries.

In a sense, what some Chinese entrepreneurs are now looking to do is return to some of these roots. Qualities such as craftsmanship, creativity and care, as well as innovation, are central to the future success of many brands. It was these very qualities that made Chinese silk and porcelain two of the earliest successful brands, albeit in the days when the brand name was simply the source or provenance, in this case 'China'.

It is hard to find many brands today, that have been unique for so long, enjoying such long life cycles and commanding such huge premiums.

China can now look forward to making *brands* their new gold: acquiring the skills to create sustainable advantage through brands will significantly influence the next 20 years of economic, social and political development in China. Brand arcanists will be as welcome in China as the inventors of the products and services themselves.

Management consultants and advertising agencies first came to China some 15 years ago. Consultants, notably McKinsey, have already established great credibility here. Large multinationals were not slow to recognize the opportunity to bring international brands, such as Coca-Cola and McDonald's, to China; the advertising agencies, unsurprisingly, wanted to keep their clients' company. When we consider what the local Chinese brands need at this time, it is strategic advice on brand positioning, brand architecture (portfolio management) and brand innovation. Local Chinese companies are now realizing that there is no point advertising a generic product if they do not have a clearly positioned brand and differentiated product or service performance.

We decided to set up a brand strategy and innovation consultancy in China and opened our first office in Shanghai in March 2002.

Serge Dumont, Springpoint Asia's non-executive Chairman, suggested putting together a book about the issues emerging brands in China are having to address. By undertaking this project Serge and I would be able to explore the progress already made, and also gain insights into the extraordinary trans-formation of a country by meeting people in their workplace, eating in the factory canteens, sleeping on campus, seeing and hearing for ourselves stories that one could not have imagined even 10 years ago. Serge did not need to work hard to convince me. We embarked on this new venture the following month. Over the last six months, we have visited many parts of China, con-trasting in landscape, people and culture. We have received a genuinely warm welcome from each contributor and their people. They have also been a little curious, partly due to the make-up of our team: a charming Frenchman and a determined English woman (so they say), accompanied by Sunny our diligent Shanghainese interpreter and Alan, a suave PR man originally from Changchun. With the looks of an Armani model, Alan has excelled at smoothing the path throughout this whole investigative journey.

We set ourselves an intensive work programme in order to publish this book in 2003. We wanted the stories to be fresh and topical. We are fortunate that so many people have chosen to share with us their experiences and philosophies. Our one disappointment is that a number of companies could not participate in the book at this moment in time because they are busy changing their business model and brand; it is premature for them to talk about it. We hope they will be in the next book.

I want to take this opportunity to thank Serge for being my partner in this venture. Having spent 18 years in China, Serge is described as 'the father of Public Relations in China'. For me, Serge is a gutsy orchestrator as well as an entertaining friend. Even at 6am in the morning at one of the many airports in China when we would meet to take a flight, there he would be, wearing his signature dark glasses with a big smile on his face, a bag of fragrant lychees in hand, purchased from one of the airport market stalls (one of the things Western airports have yet to discover) and newspaper cuttings ready for us to peruse on the plane ride. Merci, Serge.

FIONA GILMORE, LONDON

Notes

1. Gillie is the Gaelic term for professional 'keeper' (hunting, fishing, shooting). On this occa-sion we were learning to catch 'broon troot'. The Gillie is a 'threatened' species in the UK, owing to political pressures to kill off some of these traditional country pursuits.
2 The film *Braveheart* famously encouraged comparisons between the courage of Scottish war-riors versus the English 'fainthearts'.
3. Term chosen by the Scottish ladies to characterize the pale-faced, slightly built Englanders.
4. The castle of Mey was the Queen Mother's holiday home in Scotland and thus a well -known 'brand'.
5. *Embarras de la Foire de Beaucaire en vers burlesque*

Foreword

SERGE DUMONT

When Fiona and I discussed the concept of this book, little did we realize the amount of time and energy it would take us! But it was an eye opening experience which we both enjoyed tremendously.

We travelled to some remote corners of China and met with an amazing breed of entrepreneurs – emerged from throughout this immense country as a consequence of its closer integration with the world community.

It was a deeply emotional personal experience as well: when I decided to move to this part of the world from France to start the first independent public relations firm in China at age 25 (against the advice of all the reasonable people I knew) China was a very different world.

China had just emerged from over 30 years of diplomatic isolation, central planning and some periods of violent internal turmoil. China was determined to build a better life for its citizens. It was the time when new slogans like 'to get rich is glorious' appeared, a sea change from those of the previous era.

I was privileged to witness China's breathtaking economic and social changes from the late seventies until now. It was fascinating for instance to see the speed at which China was able to integrate new concepts and the latest technologies, leapfrogging from a state of having virtually no telephones to becoming the largest market for mobile phones in the world.

My role as one of the forefathers of the Public Relations industry in China allowed me to be involved in most of the biggest events that have marked China for the last two decades and to be associated with some of the leading Fortune 500 companies in their entry in to the Chinese market. These early days offered some unusual challenges.

When we launched some of the LVMH brands like Christian Dior, Hennessy and Louis Vitton, the concept of luxury had to be introduced into a market that was not prepared for it in any way! When we organised the first visit of the Chairman of the New York Stock Exchange to China, it was not just an ordinary visit, but the introduction of an entirely new way of thinking that was quite alien to some of the most conservative senior leaders.

And when I advised Beijing on its first bid for the Olympic Games in the early nineties, the very concept of branding a city was entirely unknown to most of the officials I was dealing with. How much progress has been made in less than a generation!

China is now a full member of the WTO and an increasingly active player on the diplomatic scene. Beijing has won the Olympics bid and is building the most modern opera house in the world – the Grand National Theatre. Shanghai meanwhile, has developed into a bustling modern metropolis and won the battle for World Expo 2010.

Writing this book allowed us to have insightful conversations with this new breed of Chinese CEOs and entrepreneurs. Their history, their vision, the way they go about building their businesses and their brands are all truly inspiring and lets one foresee a future that few would have imagined only a few years ago.

In a world where so much energy is spent on futile and deadly conflicts, it is heartening to see how much a country can achieve when it focuses on its economic development.

Fiona and I hope you will find as much pleasure reading the following pages as we had writing them. I want to thank all the contributors who have graciously given us a lot of their time, as well as the people who have made it possible for us to write this book. And thank you Fiona, for being such an entertaining, perceptive and charming partner. Working with you on this project has been a true pleasure!

SERGE DUMONT, BEIJING

Introduction

FIONA GILMORE

Brands: the new gold

The manufacturing industry in China has burgeoned over the last 20 years. In particular, the export manufacturing industry has grown remarkably rapidly to the extent that we now have a world in which we can expect at least one of our articles of clothing that we are wearing at any point in time to be made in China. While the label 'Made in China' may not historically have given the quality reassurance Westerners look for, there are now signs that this has changed for ever, particularly in the last few years. Today, the sophisticated supply chains, the efficient logistics industry and the quality of the machinery itself have all contributed to making the production of goods in China superior to many other countries. The speed and efficiency with which manufacturing now takes place is one of China's greatest achievements. This fact is evident in many of the case studies in this book – for example, TCL believe that it is increasingly able to beat Japanese and Korean manufacturing in their markets, both in terms of speed of delivery and efficiency.

However, China recognizes that it cannot be complacent and stop there. In order to achieve the wealth creation for its people that the government has talked about, it is crucial that, in the next 20 years, real brand capital is established in China itself. Everyone knows and understands the value of intellectual capital and human capital. What is perhaps less clear is the value of brand capital. Our definition of brand capital is the sustainable value that the brand can generate as a result of the differentiated tangible and intangible benefits it provides and which therefore justifies a premium price positioning. This capital can accrue over many years and provide the money to invest further in R & D as well as in other innovation developments. Superiority in product or service performance is, of course, increasingly difficult to achieve. However, the benefit of finding and protecting real indices of superiority in performance will deliver exponential benefits. Broad has invested in technology, in particular its unique environmentally-friendly air-conditioning systems. Such investment should deliver a tangible benefit for the end user – in this case, a quieter, more environmentally-friendly air-conditioning system – and the guarantee of future business orders is firmer thanks to such investments.

One of the biggest tasks for Chinese companies in the future will be to find these ways of differentiation and transform them into business reality.

People are always happy to be associated with positive exponential outcomes. The single most compelling equation for business today is to maximize the value of intellectual capital, human capital, supply chain efficiencies and brand capital value. These factors should then be multiplied together in this way:

$$\text{Intellectual capital} \times \text{human capital} \times \text{supply chain efficiencies} \times$$
$$\text{brand capital} = \text{more (less) customer satisfaction} =$$
$$\text{positive (negative) exponential outcomes}$$
$$\text{for brand share, profits and shareholder value}$$

It is a multiplicative equation, not additive. Each of these constituent elements impacts on the others.

The really successful businesses are those where each of these elements are a positive and where they are factored together to give more customer satisfaction and therefore a significant positive exponential outcome. If, however, one of these elements is a negative, then it impacts negatively on everything. For example, if the human capital is not positive – that is, the staff are not motivated and are not really connected or engaged with the brand ideology – the whole business will suffer and brand capital will be undermined.

Brand capital is a very central part of this equation and something that we are discussing from many different perspectives in this book.

There are other benefits to building true sustainable brand capital. For example, the company itself has more power to control its own destiny, to determine whether to focus on its core businesses or to diversify; it also has more ability to reward its employees and train them to be better skilled to meet the needs of the future. A company with significant brand capital will attract and retain the best people, and this means that the human capital value is enhanced accordingly.

A good finance director will support mid-term brand investment planning because he or she will understand the links between brand capital and shareholder value (see Figure 1).

Chinese companies have had little experience of valuing brand goodwill. We are encouraging companies to explore ways of valuing this in the future, as it represents a significant part of the total brand capital. The intangibles are an important element of the brand's cultural understanding. How one feels about a brand, one's relationship with that brand and one's ultimate loyalty to

Figure 1: **The relationship of brand capital to shareholder value**

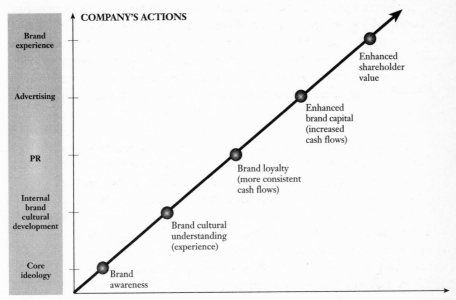

that brand all contribute to these intangibles. In the West, we are aware that building a brand is not simply a question of increasing brand awareness and, in China today, more and more business managers are realizing that they need to go deeper with their brands. Some so-called brands in China are not in fact brands, they are trademarks, often with a high awareness amongst certain target groups.

Strong brands, however, have substance and resonance. Each stakeholder group has a cultural understanding about the brand. This means that customers' responses to the brand are not just rational, but also emotional, and indeed can even help fulfil certain spiritual needs. The implications for all aspects of brand building are enormous. It is not simply a question of having an up-to-date and memorable advertising campaign.

The world's ten most valuable brands are mainly American in origin, with the exception of Nokia. In the next ten years (not the next 20) there will be a few brands from both Europe and Asia in that top-ten list – and at least one Chinese brand.

In this book we have quite consciously set out to select companies that are leaders in their fields, which have pioneered in their own ways, broken new patterns and have been successful. A smorgasbörd of tastes or perhaps, more appropriately for this book, the full Chinese banquet menu is on offer, with some companies clearly experiencing difficulties at the first few hurdles and other more mature and advanced companies likewise having to address new challenges. The case studies included here do not show a perfect world, because there is no such thing. Some of the companies are much more profitable than others, some more transparent, some more socially responsible, some more innovative. It is for the reader to take out of each story, particular lessons relevant to their own individual situation. Often it is what people leave unsaid that is most revealing.

The first task for many companies in China today is to become strong brands within the national context. This has been one of the goals for all the brands discussed in detail in this book. Today Yue-Sai is the number two cosmetics brand in Shanghai, Legend is China's largest PC manufacturer, Haier is number two in China's refrigerator market and number one in the air-conditioning market, and each of these brands demonstrates that it can hold out defiantly against foreign competition.

The timing of this book coincides with the news of China's entry into the WTO. No longer can China's companies be considered in geographic isolation. In the future, the growth of all these brands is likely to be affected by world economic and capital market trends. Brand development can, amongst other things, help strengthen companies' growth and mitigate negative economic trends. The majority of these companies are publicly quoted companies in China (and, in some instances, also in the US and Hong Kong) or have subsidiaries that are quoted. In this respect, they have shown the desire to tap capital markets for growth, and brand development can be seen as a strategic tool in this context. Issues such as corporate transparency and governance will become more salient as the spotlight falls on these companies. Brands, by definition, seek the limelight and they therefore inevitably have to become more accountable and more responsible if they are to survive.

The companies highlighted in *Brand Warriors China* are expected to become even more profitable in the next few years. The toughest challenges exist in the technology and media sectors. Growth in profitability may slow down in the near term, due to many factors: world economic climate, increasing foreign competition, or the implications of China's WTO membership for the company concerned. Many of these companies have net cash positions on their balance sheets, which is ideal for expansionary policies. In some instances they are also backed by strong shareholders – the state as well as red-chip companies. Some have decided to break into foreign markets, some choosing to compete in developing countries, while others such as Haier and Beijing Yanjing Brewery Group choosing to enter what is arguably one of the most aggressive markets in the world, the US. As Haier says, 'we have to become a wolf to dance with the wolves. If we position ourselves as sheep we will be left with one possibility – to be swallowed by the wolves.' The task of becoming a strong national brand is, however, big enough in its own right to be a major preoccupation for many. Mergers and acquisitions are routine as the more aggressive predators seek to provide a countrywide distribution. For example, one beer company has acquired 36 regional breweries. Its goal is now to rationalize those 36 down to a single coherent brand. The name change is the easy task. The greater challenge will be to convince the regions that they should have one national brand because, whilst there are economies of scale to be derived from having one brand, local tastes are important. Unifying cultural understanding will take time and considerable effort and skill.

It is unrealistic and also not imperative for every brand to have international aspirations. Unlike the Swiss Swatch brand, Dutch tulips or Irish Guinness, most of these Chinese brands have enough potential consumers in their home country to keep them busy for a long, long time. Nonetheless, as Yue-Sai Kan Cosmetics has discovered, an international reputation can help build a local one.

Until the 1980s many Chinese companies were restricted in their distribution internally within China. Export markets were limited for Chinese brands, and many companies were forced to sell via export companies on an OEM (Original Equipment Manufacturer) basis, as in the case of Erdos. The market context and restrictions meant that some of these companies had their hands tied and were not able to operate as freely as companies in other countries.

Some of these companies have been forced to be imaginative in the creation of new distribution opportunities. Erdos, again, is an example: following a decision to set up its own retail chain stores, it opened 200 boutiques and used teams travelling throughout the country in luxury buses during the peak season of cashmere sales to give fashion shows to consumers. Wall's has opened a chain of ice-cream parlours in the Shanghai area on a test basis. These are examples of companies that have chosen to try to control their own destiny and to obtain more direct access to their consumers in order to build those relationships at a deeper level. Through the Internet, the technology brands such as Sina.com and AsiaInfo are able to get closer to their customers and through user-experience research they can refine and fine-tune the services offered.

The Chinese companies featured in this book all have an understanding of the benefits of building their brand. They have many different ways of describing what a brand is. Legend, TCL, Haier and Erdos all talk about the brand not only bringing the company intangible assets but also representing and reflecting well on their country's image and power. For this reason, Erdos argues that the brand should receive protection and affection from the state.

The counterfeiters' legacy: greater emphasis on substance and real quality

Beijing's Silk Market is the most crowded shopping street that I have ever come across. The slick, super-modern shopping malls boasting the presence of Versace, Prada, Gucci and other premium designer brands are virtually empty; yet Silk Market is a bustling, heaving, throbbing hive of enthusiastic traders and bargain hunters. High-income earners jostle shoulder-to-shoulder with blue-collar workers, all eager to cut the best deal.

The sheer thrill of the negotiation and final outcome probably exceeds the reward of the actual product. Three long-sleeved Ralph Lauren polo shirts are on offer for a third of the original asking price, just a snip at £12 (156 RMB) for the lot. They may not be the real thing, but the quality of fake goods is getting better. These shirts will not fall apart, at least for some time, but do not try to wash white shirts with one of the blue fake polo shirts. Pirated DVDs are traded openly on Beijing's main streets and wealthy professionals are gaily filling the DVD rogues' coffers.

Many fake goods are being sold at virtually the same price as the genuine article, and – horror of horrors – some cheeky counterfeiters have chosen to trade at a premium price to the original.

Yue-Sai has written a book on modern etiquette which recently went on sale at 23 yuan; numerous fake copies of this book have been found and, in addition, two unauthorized 'sister' books have since been published. One of them sells for 28 yuan! No wonder that worried marketers talk about the risk of devaluing real brands.

Yet, arguably, the Silk Market culture is reinforcing the appeal of the brand. Certainly, it boosts awareness levels. In Shanghai and other cities, Burberry have become ubiquitous.

Perception, we are told, is all. In the light of second-generation higher-quality counterfeit goods, we are reappraising this assertion. 'Faking reality' is judged to be cool. The definition of a true brand experience is debatable.

Ultimately, it is in China's interests to promote the importance of added-value brands. The integrity of a true brand experience can still be desirable. However brand builders are going to have to work harder than ever to justify their price. Substantial points of difference and real quality in product and service delivery are essential.

The world is a more diverse and entertaining place. The impish imitators are reinforcing the tenets of a capitalist society: we have free choice to make our own decisions on how and where we spend our money. We now have brands, mock-brands, private own labels and generics.

Intellectual property is an issue for Chinese companies striving to enhance sustainable brand capital. Erdos and TCL are worrying about these dilemmas just as, hundreds of years ago, the Chinese porcelain makers tackled the threat of European imitators.

The value of brands

Branding is ultimately about securing the future of a company, its products and services by building loyalties using emotional, as well as rational, values. Such values matter because they are exchanged for cash in the marketplace and affect the perception of a company's products and services, as well as its ability and its freedom to manage its future.

The companies that are rated by marketers as the rising stars for the future are those with very clearly positioned, confident corporate brands. These companies deliver through their core competencies and, more importantly, have a coherent core value and emotional brand proposition for the consumer.

A brand is inclusive. It is the tangible and intangible benefits provided by a product or service: the entire customer experience. It includes all the assets critical to delivering and communicating that experience: the people, the product, the service, the environment as well as the reputation, the name, the design, the advertising, and the distribution channel.

Sometimes the marketing hype overshadows the economic advantages of branding, but as *Brand Warriors China* shows, branding survives because it enhances the present value of future cash-flows. This simple economic value comes from the price premium justified by effective branding, the maintenance and growth of the market, and from the building of brand loyalty which deters new entrants and substitutes, thereby making future earnings more secure.

In pure financial terms, the importance of brands is clearly shown by the price that companies have been prepared to pay for them. Nestlé, for example, paid £2.5 billion (more than five times the book value) to win control of the Rowntree group in 1988. Similar acquisitions can be seen in Figure 2. Virgin only came to realize the value of its brand over the last few years – when it wanted to break into the financial services market. A new partner was willing to put up half a billion pounds to Virgin's half million – for only 50 per cent of the company!

Branding is *the* differentiation strategy. The cost of differentiation must naturally be less than the perceived value, but we need to be alert to the temptation to erode differentiation by cost-cutting, or other short-term tactics.

Good business leaders set about the nurturing and caring inherent in good brand management because they know it pays off. Yet, this makes investment bankers and other financial professionals uneasy because, even though the

Figure 2: **Examples of goodwill payments**

Acquirer	*Target*	*Goodwill (% of price paid)*
Nestlé	Rowntree	83
GrandMet	Pillsbury	88
Cadbury Schweppes	Dr Pepper	67
United Biscuits	Verkade	66

Source: Greig Middleton & Co. Ltd

cost of differentiation can be quantified, its benefits cannot: shutting an inefficient factory is easier to justify than introducing more cost into a product improvement or a significant investment in marketing.

The economic arguments against brands might be characterized as the 'cost fixation' versus 'art' schools of management: to the cost-fixated, branding adds cost of uncertain value, so it is driven out and joins the other downsizing initiatives. Renting a brand share encourages brand promiscuity, where a customer shows little loyalty.

Most, if not all, consumers like choice. In many other product categories, consumers like the intrinsic or extrinsic reward of branding. After all, who buys trainers without an explicit brand name? The secret, surely, of good brand building is to understand customers' underlying motivations, their deep psychological needs and moods. For this reason, it is dangerous to assume that 'mystique' per se is still credible or relevant. Today's customer cannot be bought so easily. *Brand Warriors China* shows that there needs to be a true psychological contract between customer and company.

The raison d'être for Disney is to make people smile. The raison d'être for Starbucks is to give people that third space, an oasis between the office and home. Coffee and feature films are core products, but not brands. The premium price that Starbucks can command is much higher than the actual cost of making a cup of coffee. The premium differential above cost is at least US$2.00.[1] The two schools of management – 'cost fixation' and 'art' – illustrate the company director's perennial dilemma. How do you strike an appropriate balance between the two sides? Careful benchmarking of where your brand *really* is, rather than where you have convinced yourself it should be, is central to this process. Successful brands operating in aggressively competitive markets have acquired these disciplines out of necessity. Brands that have flourished in monopolistic environments have greater difficulty in coming to terms with self-criticism. Whilst companies will never achieve perfect sufficiency in both product delivery and soft values, *Brand Warriors China* confronts the dilemma.

The economic arguments are more difficult for the 'cost-fixated' manager. Branding needs the sustenance of investment. It is easy to see that successful brands command a premium price and that their branding creates a volume demand, which can provide scale economies in procurement, manufacturing, distribution, R&D and even marketing. Plus, critically, once these are achieved, they are *real* barriers to entry.

Cost-fixated managers, even if they are not comfortable with the art of branding, ought at least to know about the risks of high sunk costs in market entry caused by better-scaled branded competitors. The final nail in the coffin of the cost-fixated view is the inexorable temptation to reduce price. The quickest way of eroding profits is to reduce prices; and it is very hard to raise them again. The more progressive Chinese companies refuse to participate in price wars, even though this is difficult. China Mobile, for instance, has quickly realized that its brand 'is both a shield that protects as well as an effective weapon that [it] can use in price wars'. One of the key legs of China Mobile's brand strategy involves abolishing any management thinking that is price-focused. The company's solution is to rapidly increase the quality of its services and products so that it can raise the profile of its brand. This allows the company to explain how it is superior to competition and why its brand justifies premium pricing in the market.

Low cost and differentiation are not alternative strategies. Most of the greatest branded businesses have always pursued both with vigour, exploiting all possible economies of scale to deliver lowest cost and differentiating via product, service and branding. This combination is the key to superior returns, higher profit margins and less likelihood of disruption by other entrants.

Short-term pressures on performance have destroyed the Procter & Gamble paradigm of 'brand manager as managing director of the brand'. Today's brand manager is often the custodian of tactics to maximize short-term profitability, not the custodian of brand positioning and brand values. In these circumstances, the custodian of brand positioning and brand values clearly needs to be the CEO with the support of the team. Many Chinese CEOs recognize that they need to champion their brand. Only they can balance the short-term/long-term trade-off. *Brand Warriors China* illustrates the importance of not getting distracted from managing the brand.

The custodian's role should not be underestimated. Brands need a lot of love. Fred Smith, founder and chairman of FedEx, has a clear view about his role: 'maintaining (the FedEx) reputation and its brand image is a top priority for me, since it is one of the most valuable things the company has.' Allan Wong, chairman of VTech, admits that many companies in the Far East are only now starting to appreciate the importance of developing a brand: 'being too focused on cost and not nurturing and investing in the brand has been typical of many companies in this region. Perhaps people here are very good merchants but are not necessarily also good at building brands.'

Beyond awareness building

Take, for example, Sony's strapline 'go create'. This is a hugely powerful message for many people who are personally looking for greater individualism and creativity in everything they do. Sony is seizing the high ground in advance of its competitors. Over the next few years as the Sony offer broadens and consumers use their digital televisions, laptops, MP3 players, DVDs, palmtops, cell-phones, digital cameras and other multifunctional devices which we cannot even begin to imagine today, Sony will be there giving the user the opportunity to individualize everything. Whilst this is potentially a generic proposition, Sony will make sure that, over the next few years, it puts its stamp on it and owns it, in the knowledge that it has tapped into a very big consumer desire. Samsung is doing the same, but with a democratic philosophy, and its claim 'everyone's invited' is designed to convey a less elitist offer than Sony's.

Along with other Chinese companies hoping to compete against Sony, Samsung and the rest, TCL will need to be as intelligent and thoughtful in the way it goes about finding a positioning that is engaging and compelling. This is new territory for many Chinese companies. Trying to find a core ideology that focuses on the end benefit, not just for the individual customer, but also for the collective, will be one of the fertile areas for concept development.

Some Chinese enterprises have a very loyal following but there is an opportunity to add a new dimension to that loyalty with more explicit emotional and rational benefits for customers. Traditionally, corporate messages have reinforced size and stature and this strategy has given reassurance and strengthened the trust values. Whilst to Western eyes some of these claims might seem somewhat indulgent, size and stature have historically been important criteria for many customers, and therefore some of these stories reinforce the company's credibility. Take, for example, the awards won by Yanjing Brewery. They are an index of quality.

A myriad of mixed messages compounds the communications problem. The more sophisticated companies are exacting in their development of consistent messaging, all originating from a single conceptual idea. Legend, for example, has decided to concentrate on communicating a more focused message so that equity in its brand can accumulate over time.

Ideally, the chosen positioning incorporates rational, emotional/spiritual and sensory benefits. An emotional benefit or a rational benefit per se has never been enough. A brand positioning melds these benefits together. A good test of whether the core proposition is compelling is to conduct focus groups or one-to-one research to explore in some detail the relative merits of a range of proposition ideas. Sometimes a proposition will focus on meeting the needs of a specific stakeholder group. Increasingly these target markets are defined not by socio-economic groupings per se, but also through attitudinal clusters. Explorers, statists, DIYers, laissez-fairers, hedonists and puritans are just some of the attitudinal type profiles. We can be all of these things, some of the time, depending on the day of the week, time of day, context and mood we are in.

A rigorous approach for defining the core ideology and brand positioning is crucial. There are four influencing factors that help judge the relative merits and demerits of the various positioning options. These factors are:

- Which future macro-trends are likely to influence the behaviour patterns and the responses of your primary stakeholder group?
- What are the company's core competencies and capabilities? Are we building on these?
- What are the competitive gaps? Where are the real market opportunities?
- What are the particular consumer insights that help create greater empathy?

Taking time and reflecting on the consequences of your chosen positioning is a worthwhile exercise. There is no point in spending money promoting the wrong messages. Looking back over the years, brand propositions have become more focused on specific psychological need-states. When brands first originated, companies such as Procter & Gamble and Unilever focused very simply on using brands to provide a stamp of quality. The earliest brands, such as Unilever's Sunlight soap, benefited from this simple statement of quality. Today it is as important as ever to ensure that we do not ignore the need to give quality reassurance. This is where the indices of performance play a role. Just as Procter & Gamble historically signalled superior performance through an index such as 'see the difference in five days' for an anti-acne cream, or 'washes whiter' for a detergent brand, so today service brands can equally find such indices. A particularly motivating index of performance for cell-phones is the claim made by one of the market leaders that all the emergency services – that is, ambulances and fire engines – use their particular service network.

Indices of performance play a critical role in any differentiation strategy. They are no longer uniquely concerned with efficacy. For an enterprise brand, these indices may engender greater affection and respect by touching on some of the initiatives concerned with progress on 'responsibility' issues, be they environmental, community or human rights. Anita Roddick's Body Shop is one of the best-known 'principled' retailers, which purchases many products from local communities in developing countries. Indeed, Anita Roddick pioneered the notion that principles matter. Large corporations are now choosing to promote these 'indices', but whilst avoiding the hype. Unilever has a very progressive responsibility programme, incorporating a whole range of initiatives. For example, the company was one of the architects of the Marine Stewardship Programme. The Marine Stewardship Council (MSC), an independent accreditation system that encourages sustainable fishing practices, was established by Unilever in association with the World Wildlife Fund for Nature (WWF) but operates independently from them. Its mission is to harness the power of consumers, businesses, governments and international institutions to secure the future of fish stocks.

The MSC's principles and criteria for sustainable fishing were compiled following wide-ranging international consultation. Fisheries can volunteer to be assessed against its standards, and independent MSC accreditation bodies will certify whether the fishery complies effectively. Companies that process or sell fish from these fisheries will then be able to carry the MSC logo on their products and consumers can buy clearly labelled fish in the knowledge that they come from sustainable sources.

As one of the world's largest buyers of frozen fish, Unilever is committed to sourcing all fish from sustainable fisheries by the year 2005. In addition, the company is enabling some employees to take a year out to work on NGO projects in developing countries. Unilever believes that the local management should work closely with the local communities to determine how such voluntary work can provide real benefit.

Motherhood and apple pie values, such as 'professional', 'friendly', 'tried and trusted' are no longer assumed; a company needs to explore its cultural heritage to appreciate the very roots of its success and understand what particular values differentiate it from others. Enron's 2000 Annual Review referred to some of these motherhood values, such as 'sincerity' and 'consistency'. But being hoisted by your own petard is everyone's nightmare. Companies will now become more circumspect and their claims may become more modest.

Social ideology has always been an important ingredient of every Chinese state owned-company's culture. The benefit to the collective has been a well-debated concept. In the West, more and more companies are looking to integrate corporate social responsibility policies into the fabric of their business, and they are attaching more importance than ever before to their corporate social responsibility (CSR) activities. The problem is that, for many of these companies, CSR is not an integral part of their brand ideology but an appendage. The cynics are publicly denouncing as hypocrites many of the companies who appear to be adopting new social causes with such evangelical zeal.

The majority of Chinese companies routinely consider social ideology as a central part of their core ideology and ensure that their actions, as well as their words, are aligned with this ideology. Most of the companies interviewed were able to cite examples of initiatives which provided significant benefits to the local community or another community in China. Some of these projects have been initiated by the grassroots rather than imposed by senior management, which means that they are more likely to have a lasting impact as people will be enthusiastic and keen to make a difference. Many projects in the West have been initiated by senior management, often in response to the question 'How can we give something back?' Yet this question suggests that the company must have taken something in the first place and that therefore there is a need to return something. In fact, these words imply collective guilt.

An alternative way of thinking about social responsibility is to think of the concept of sharing. This is more readily understood in countries such as China where collective work within campus communities is common. As in the case of Legend, each employee can influence a company's performance through his or her own sense of individual social responsibility in working to drive economic progress in the country.

In future, more and more brands will choose to espouse a social cause or issue as part of their mainstream activities and promotional campaigns. Recent Shell advertising, for example, examines human rights issues. Ultimately this has got to be good news for everyone concerned. With the advent of consumer activism, whether it be patient activism (such as purchasing Viagra on the web) or DIY financial services activism, whatever market he or she is in, the customer is going to make choices between brands, where on every other level the brands have parity. The decision to buy one brand versus another on the basis of respect will become more commonplace, so it is not surprising that fuel companies, such as Shell and BP, are exploring their own responses to this issue. At times, it looks in the West as if you have to be bad to be good because it is very often the companies which are dubbed as the 'baddies' that spend time and money doing some really useful things. The more transparent a company can be in describing its policies and social charter relating to wide-ranging issues including the environment, equal opportunities and community sharing, the more respect it will earn. Consumers will be seeking to know whether a company has employed child labour, how much of its bottom-line profits it is sharing and whether it is

plundering the planet. The new generation of students will shortly be one of
the most influential customer groups and they are far less ignorant than previous generations on such matters. No company can afford to sideline these
questions. Governments in European countries are encouraging companies
to take on more social responsibility tasks because they cannot afford to
provide the social welfare benefits expected from a growing middle-class,
greying population. Pension support is a huge issue for many countries and
therefore new initiatives, resulting from co-operation between government
and private enterprise, are springing up every day. For example, Caravan is a
charity established to assist low-income earners in the grocery industry to
prepare for their retirement and other welfare issues. The major retailers and
food and drink manufacturers are endorsing and funding Caravan.

The opportunity is there for Chinese companies to jump ahead of some
Western companies by adopting more progressive social policies and thereby
meriting the reward of greater consumer loyalty. Despite Milton Friedman's
famous words, 'the social responsibility of companies is to make profits' the
conventional business model may not be appropriate for every Chinese
company over the next few years. Many companies may have to sacrifice a
level of profitability in order to carry out their work in a socially responsible
way, providing employment opportunities as well as delivering real benefits to
customers. Establishing the right core ideology with the appropriate social
charter could be a higher priority than achieving maximum profitability in
these early critical years of brand development for some Chinese enterprises.
In the early stages of a market economy, Tong Ren Tang has adhered to its
principles and earned high degrees of trust amongst its customers. Nevertheless, worthy, self-righteous messages could alienate. Adopting a low-key
approach, in which individual real-life stories engage people in some of the
difficult issues, will be more appealing than self-congratulatory assertions.

We recently conducted a piece of research in the UK exploring senior
managers' views on CSR and found that only one in three UK companies do
anything around 'activities to promote and protect human rights'. One of the
big questions for all companies is centred around this equal opportunities
issue, and here, once again, there is scope for Chinese enterprises to forge
ahead of the others in thinking through some of the solutions to this problem.

Macro-trends matter

Awesome or not quite so awesome macro-trends will inform future brand
positioning and innovation. Moreover, the pace of change in today's society,
particularly in China, but also across the world, is breathtaking.

At a recent dinner, a friend who is a very young 72-year-old ex-commodore of our local sailing club, confessed that he had 'lost the plot'. He went on to explain how the technology revolution and the speed of product obsolescence had left him behind. In China there are many elderly people who are in a constant state of shock and awe at the changes taking place around them. On the other hand, such have been the historic milestones in China over the last 50-odd years that, overall, the Chinese elderly population is curiously more sanguine than might be expected.

Some of the demographic predictions are causing people to pause and reflect. China will soon be home to an increasingly aged population. By 2011, 15 per cent of the population will be over 60 years old, that is, 195 million greys. Men outnumber women by 18 per cent in the countryside. These kinds of statistics pose questions relating to everything from pension schemes to birth control policies.

The revolution in the life cycle is another trend that is deeply interesting to us, as the authors of this book, because, as the French express it in such a perfectly concise way, we are 'un homme et une femme d'un certain age'.

Whilst even just 20 years ago this would have been a horrifying thought, in the new millennium people have become used to the fact that the whole shape of the life cycle has been fundamentally altered. Puberty arrives frighteningly early (9-year-old girls are developing breasts and pubic hair); middle-class 28 year olds still want to be (and act) ten years younger; most 40 year olds are still ambivalent about whether they are fully grown-up; middle age is no longer an accepted concept; and the fifties and sixties are now completely new landscapes of life. The demographic predictions are extraordinary. 'A girl born in the US today has a one in three chance of living to 100.' Gail Sheehy's *New Passages* proposes the concept that 'the day you turn 45 is the infancy of another life.'[2] Her perceptive account of real-life stories illustrates the importance of developmental stages during which different parts of our personality can be lived out. In each passage, we enjoy a 'heightened potential for making a real stretch of growth'. Brand thought leaders are exploring the implications of some of these life-cycle step changes and realizing how dangerous it is to use conventional age groupings to determine a target market. The anthropological study of changes in behaviour and attitude patterns gives clues to new business and brand opportunities, as in the cases of SMS messaging, home snacking and home entertainment.

Post 9/11 (which has become a branded historic event in the same way as the Holocaust) or, as some prefer to say in plain English, after September 11, behaviour and attitude patterns changed quite dramatically in the US and to a lesser extent in other parts of the world. Many Americans refocused on some of the more basic needs of safety and security for family (a significant step down in Maslow's hierarchy of needs).[3]

Concepts that have assumed new significance for Americans in the year 2002 include the following:

- The collective (that is, the local community or however it is described) is a more respected concept.
- The search for authenticity (beyond Martha Stewart and other homemaker gurus) has assumed more importance.
- Ideas and ideals are valued greatly.
- Word-of-mouth/grapevine recommendations have more validity than 'interruption' marketing (such as conventional advertising or sponsorship).
- People are making more intense and regular hedonistic forays (the most overused sentiment of the year 2002 was 'I've only got one life').

These particular trends have different slants in China where people are now focused on making money. What we define as hedonism in Europe and the US is still vastly different to what most Chinese would consider as hedonism. Even amongst progressive, middle-class Shanghainese babes, it is a little embarrassing to discuss self-indulgence beyond the innocent pleasurable moments of drinking a Mexican beer out of a bottle, kissing your boyfriend in public (a very new phenomenon), dancing to pop music on your own in the park on a Sunday afternoon in front of the passing crowds and so on. The difference between the output from a creative workshop amongst city women from China and the UK is still quite dramatic. A group of New York or London City girls, as the soap operas testify, are so liberated that it is hard for any workshop discussion to shock. Sexual fantasies are discussed openly and the idea of self-restraint is quite alien to certain types of urban predators (as they are now dubbed). In Chinese culture on the other hand, open discussions of a sexual nature are discouraged and individuals are taught to hide their true emotions or feelings in public.

Tribal behaviour patterns across the globe are converging as the media brings the latest concepts to new emerging middle-class populations. The Shanghai edition of *Elle* gives identical tips and gossip to fashion-conscious ambitious girls as the Parisian edition (only the models and some of the ads are different). Small, trend-setting groups are springing up in urban centres. Sub-cultures are emerging in the performing arts, crafts and other creative fields. It is only as a result of these vibrant sub-cultures that rich and dynamic cultural centres are established. After all, what would London or New York be without their Sohos?

Shanghai is the most sophisticated, cosmopolitan, 'hip' city in China. For this reason, companies such as Wall's are locating their marketing and consumer knowledge teams there. The city is often used as the testing ground for new product or service launches.

The Confucian concepts of self-discipline and responsibility to family and community are so profoundly embedded in the Chinese culture that it is hard to imagine how quickly or to what degree some of these hedonistic drivers will influence behaviour. The one-child per family principle has certainly led to a new breed of young adolescents who are more self-centred than ever before; throughout their young lives they have enjoyed huge amounts of attention and material gifts.

Dietary trends are changing rapidly in China. For example, children's snack eating habits are closer to Western kids' eating patterns. Chinese toddlers enjoy chocolate and fast food, whereas most of their parents have not developed a great liking for chocolate. With higher disposable incomes the Chinese are eating meat, children are drinking milk and the height and general build of today's adolescents is not surprisingly very different to that of their parents.

Traditionally, the Chinese have had a very good sense of balance in their diets. Quite understandably, the Chinese government is now concerned that the Western influence of fast food – particularly junk food – does not impact too greatly on dietary habits. For the first time obesity is looming as an issue.

These few snapshots suggest that every enterprise will need a trend observer and interpreter. Graduates in social anthropology should be in demand.

Innovation in everything: an attitude of mind

There are many different interpretations of what the word 'innovation' means. The dictionary definition refers to the meaning 'to change or alter', coming from the Latin root *innovare*. My own personal definition comes from a particular understanding of what innovation can do, not just for a brand but for every aspect of business. Douglas Adams,[4] the author of *The Hitchhiker's Guide to the Galaxy,* used to live above our flat when my husband and I were first married. We had the garden flat with a long thin strip of land and, at the very tender age of 22, I enjoyed being middle-class and middle-aged long before my time. At weekends I would be gardening and designing flowerbeds with lines of tulips and daffodils. In those days I lacked the confidence to create my own personal oasis; whilst I was engrossed in my neat and tidy garden, Douglas Adams was bearing witness to these earnest green finger endeavours and probably chuckling to himself. He was caught up in a much more worthwhile exercise, writing about the universe. When I started to read *The Hitchhiker's Guide to the Galaxy* I was completely shell-shocked. Here was a man who had a remarkable way of seeing things – he was a genius of our time.

The universe jumped, froze, quivered and splayed out in several unexpected directions.

Douglas not only broke patterns in his use of the English language, but also broke patterns in the way that he regarded the universe. His views have now influenced thousands of people, if only in terms of leading them to question their prejudiced assumptions. The chaos theory is something discussed in my first book, *Brand Warriors*, and I keep returning to this theory as I realize that we will always live in uncertain times and, rather than being nervous about the uncertainties, we should accept chaos and see how we can use it to our advantage. Whether we are talking about distribution patterns, consumer purchasing patterns, consumer behaviour patterns, communication patterns, whatever patterns we are talking about, the challenge is there for us to break those patterns and create new ones in their place. This philosophical approach to brand innovation is fundamental to building successful business today.

The whole concept of differentiation – standing out from the crowd, being different – has been antithetical to many people's beliefs and cultures. It is not always a comfortable option. On the other hand, it is only through creating useful differentiation that we can seek to build sustainable brand advantage.

Some of the games and exercises we use in our workshops are designed to encourage people to try to see things differently. Taking an alternative perspective is to be encouraged so long as there is a useful outcome.

Innovation processes need to be determined and as much thought should be given to the way in which new ideas are generated as to the stages of control. Today there are very few brand strategy and innovation consultants in China. Advertising agencies, PR consultancies and management consultancies all offer advice, but many of the fundamental issues today are concerned with brand innovation. Without more focus on product differentiation and more real indices of differentiated performance the risk is that many Chinese brands will simply be commodities. Without doubt, more emphasis on techniques designed to create innovation throughout the whole organization will impact significantly on the potential future success of Chinese brands. Here, we are not just talking about technology advances but, importantly, exploring opportunities for innovation in every aspect of the business.

The catalyst for real step change often comes from an insight into a new way of understanding customers' needs. The development of the Wall's Viennetta ice-cream product was a major innovation. Although it was the food technologist, Kevin Hillman, who produced the solution, the consumer insight that triggered the chain of development was crucial: consumers were looking for ice-cream desserts that they could eat at home that represented a small treat for the family or for invited guests – something that looked out of the ordinary and that everybody would like. The step change in innovation came from transferring the idea of a Viennese patisserie into an ice-cream offering. Its intricacy of design is impressive: paper thin layers of chocolate interspersed with waves of vanilla ice cream are indeed something out of the ordinary.

Innovation is often simply the way someone looks at things – differently. One of 3M's researchers had produced a particular kind of adhesive that provided only a weak attachment to surfaces. Another 3M researcher had an idea for bookmarks that stayed in place, yet were easily removable without damaging his books. As a result, Post-it® notes were created and immediately fulfilled a huge consumer need. Today, Post-it® notes are one of the top five selling office products available. The need was immediately understood by customers, the technology was a simple advance and, again, there was a clear competitive gap. 3M has gone on to extend the Post-it® brand to more than 250 office and home communications products, such as tape flags, easel pads and many others.

Such innovations do not always spring from R&D but often from listening to what consumers are saying, either through conventional focus groups or through observational behaviour research. The technical experts did not predict young people's remarkable take-up of SMS. This is a new phenomenon, which was only spotted through user experience research, notably in Japan where teenagers were very quick to take up text messaging. They became such experts so quickly that they do not need to take their cell-phones (if you can still call them that) out of their pockets to text message – they are so adept that they can do it without even glancing at the keypad.

The kinds of people who are useful in this kind of brand innovation thinking are more likely to be amateur or professional psychologists and social anthropologists. Searching for insights can be a more fruitful exercise if proven diagnostics systems are used. They have to be tailored because there are many choices of research. Combining the appropriate elements of a research programme requires considerable skill. Good qualitative research is still hard to find in China. Within the next few years there will be more qualified and experienced research moderators but, until then, it makes sense for the brand managers and brand consultants to get close to the consumers for themselves.

When you see the chief executive of a company attending focus groups and observational behaviour research sessions, you can feel reassured that everyone all the way up to the top of an organization is passionately involved in the search for new insights and ideas. We feed our brands by exploring the implications of these insights and applying the thinking in practical ways. This is surely one of the highest priorities for any CEO.

One of the biggest challenges is helping teams of people to think freely. University graduates have been encouraged by the education system to be very logical and linear in their thinking: they have been rewarded for finding the right answer to the question. However, in the world of brand development, there often isn't just one right answer to a question; there are 20 possible answers, all of which may fulfil a need or a desire.

Encouraging people to be creative and use their imagination in the fullest sense is, in its own right, one of the biggest challenges facing businesses today, wherever they are in the world. China is not alone in having to address this challenge. Education systems have historically emphasized the pursuit of information gathering and learning. In the Charles Dickens novel *Hard Times*, Mr Gradgrind preaches accordingly '*Facts, facts, facts ...*' In today's world, thought leaders are encouraging a very different philosophical approach to Mr Gradgrind's – developing the individual's sense of curiosity, the yearning to explore and discover new things, seeing things differently, creating new patterns ... As Mr Zhou Hanmin says in Chapter 2 about Shanghai, 'breaking the neck of the bottle will release creative energy'.

The practice of encouraging teams of people within an organization to have the space to exchange ideas in relaxing, yet stimulating, environments is now something well recognized by some of the most successful companies in the world. Getting some of the team to take a few days away from the normal office environment to engage in a completely different activity whether it be sailing, mountain climbing, heli-hiking, kayaking through the jungle, trapezing, or whatever activity your team may want to pursue – finding a new physical, mental and spiritual challenge that people can all tackle together – is often a good starting point for some of the more wide-ranging discussions that lead to new ideas.

Over the years we have developed certain games that we use to release people's imaginations. One such game is DreamStorm®. People are not allowed to come to a DreamStorm® session as themselves. The night before, they are given a piece of homework in which they are asked to act out a different character, often of a different age, with a different lifestyle, or even a different gender. In these DreamStorms® everyone is invited to create their own dream or fantasy about a particular product or service or region and imagine the character they are playing in a context where they are enjoying that 'brand'. Unconstrained by normal habits and behaviour, one can conjure up wild, crazy ideas more readily. At one such DreamStorm® in which we were exploring possibilities for the branding of a Pacific Island, a series of DreamStorm® workshops were conducted at the actual location, the purpose being to explore the deeper emotional associations people have with their home country and how these can be harnessed to create a compelling point of difference for all stakeholders.

Participants included representatives from the local community, the business community and the tourist industry. The technique helped establish the unifying historic story flowing through the people, which informed the identification of the emotional and sensory propositions and core values behind the brand. Future 'dreaming' established the aspirational values that were necessary for this island to achieve its aims for economic independence and social well-being. Various other techniques encouraged participants to think creatively and project into the future (using concept and image boards, music, objects designed to stimulate the senses of taste, touch and smell and dream creation).

These workshop sessions were also videotaped so that a documentary could be made to help build support, participation, understanding and a shared sense of pride in the efforts to enhance the quality of life for the whole population of the island. The insights uncovered using DreamStorm® led to the creation of candidate brand positioning options that captured the spirit of the island and its vision for the future.

Each positioning and accompanying benefits and substantiators form a possible brand strategy

DreamStorm® is a game that we also use in product and service industries, where very often it is only through finding absurd, funny and ridiculous situations that teams discover answers to problems that have been eluding them for many years. People are also encouraged to draw pictures of how they feel when they are using a particular product – at its worst and at its best. Sometimes, in pictures, people suggest things that they have never thought to articulate verbally. In China, research respondents are not accustomed to drawing pictures to describe their feelings. As an alternative, participants are asked to form collages out of pictures torn out of a magazine.

My favourite technique, *psychographic drawing* as we call it, came out of a research group I conducted some years ago, just after the *Exxon Valdez* disaster. A female respondent was participating in a group discussion where we were exploring the difference between various leading brands of fuel and was asked to draw a picture of how she felt about her favourite brand of fuel. Her picture encapsulated some of the most positive, elemental things one could ever hope to draw – the blue sea, fish leaping in the water, blue sky, sunshine – and when I asked her the meaning of her picture she said 'this is Shell, this is my favourite brand, and I have this happy picture in mind. These fish, yes they are leaping.' And yet in the same group discussion half an hour previously, when we had asked the respondents to draw pictures of how they felt about using cars and fuel, many pictures depicted black skies, a sun-baked earth, dirty seas, dead fish and dull colours. There was nothing positive or optimistic in these pictures. This kind of game allows us to dig deep to elicit underlying motivations, responses and the power of the brand.

To a certain extent, brand innovators are just like miners; we are searching for a new treasure, a nugget of new-found wisdom. Without doubt, the most exciting insights have generally come from this kind of research game in which we encourage people to articulate their subconscious thoughts and ideas. This is often through the use of metaphors, found in the pictures they draw or the stories they tell. These metaphors are the lifeblood of brand creation.

One of the exciting things about China is that people think naturally through metaphors. The language uses metaphors where single characters very often have two or three layers of meaning. The language itself, in this respect, feels like a treasure trove of codes and symbols. Chinese words are also pictorial. 木 means wood or suggests trees because it looks like one. The character for three 三 signifies the trinity (mind, body, spirit). Perhaps that is why many Chinese brands have employed the use of metaphors, whether it be through logos or through the choice of the name itself. Take, for example, the reason why Liu Changle chose the name of Phoenix for his TV station. The phoenix is a symbol of inspiration and vision, always flying in front of the other birds and leading the way. In my previous book, *Brand Warriors*, I talked about two Hong Kong brands, OOCL and the Mandarin Oriental Group. OOCL chose to use a very unusual symbol in the logistics business, the plum blossom, and the Mandarin Group chose to use a fan: again, these were two metaphors for the kind of proposition that they were offering people – two completely different industries offering satisfaction and delight and they chose two relevant metaphors. One of the most evocative metaphors for fresh food is the dewdrop on the green leaf captured at dawn. This was the insight into some conceptual development for communicating the notion that frozen peas are fresher than fresh peas that have been degrading in quality for days prior to purchase. These kinds of metaphor are timeless and can become very powerful, valuable communication equities for a brand. Sometimes, such metaphors influence more than just the promotional communication behind the brand; they can be inspirational signals to set in motion new patterns of thinking on any aspect of the business. For example, we developed metaphors for airport experiences, describing good and bad journeys. A good experience (such as in Hong Kong and Singapore) was likened to the feeling of being Aladdin on his magic carpet, cruising through. A bad experience was brought to life through the metaphor of 'walking on coals'. (The name of the airport will not be disclosed on this occasion!)

These positive communication equities (CEqs™) enhance the brand and

Figure 3: **Investing in brand communication equities (CEqs™)**

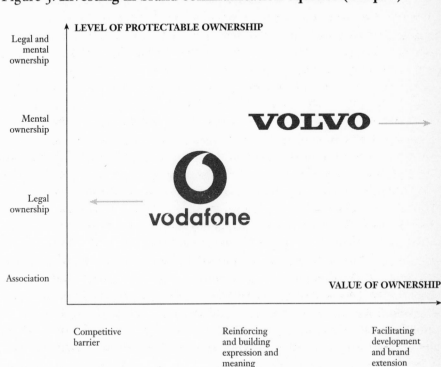

grow in value over time and, by investing in them, a company is crediting their bank of brand capital. That is why enlightened companies continue to invest in promoting their brand and deepening consumers' understanding of these CEqs™ even during the toughest recession.

Chinese companies can augment the value of these equities, if they consciously make connections between their core ideology and the words, icons, music, environment and the associated brand promotional elements. Chinese companies now have an opportunity to harness these communication synergies and reap the benefits in the way that international companies have done for years.

Volvo's core ideology centres around the concept of 'safety'. The design of their cars, the advertising and their visual language across all their communications reinforce the brand essence.

Vodafone is developing its core ideology amplifying the concept 'in touch with the people important to you'. The 'how are you?' advertising line is empathetic as it is the first thing one says as a greeting (when you care about someone), in any language, 'ça va?' The logo springs from this brand essence. It is a speechmark symbolizing the connecting point of any relationship and the richness of lively human discourse.

Mental ownership of these CEqs™ is crucial, and this takes time. Legal ownership is also critical. Sometimes there are barriers to ownership and it is therefore important to use good advisers and lawyers.

From the inside out

The reasons why metaphors should not just have a meaning for customers and consumers is because any brand that is genuine starts from within and therefore a metaphor should have its greatest meaning for those people within the organization itself. In the introduction to my last book *Warriors on the High Wire*, I discuss at some length the notion that the core proposition of any business and its values need to be assimilated into every aspect of the business, in order to deliver the true brand promise.

In the last year I have taken up yoga, and in studying its benefits, I have understood that, in a funny kind of way, one can draw an analogy between the benefits of yoga and the benefits of a brand that starts from within. *Qi* is the Chinese word for positive energy. Yoga consists of techniques for dealing with human energy flow. In applying these techniques, one employs the use of the human body's chakras and meridians, which are the body's focal points and channels through which the *Qi* flows. While visiting Tong Ren Tang, I accepted an invitation to meet one of the most distinguished women doctors in China. She explained the philosophy to me and also diagnosed my various ailments, prescribing medicine to help alleviate some of the irritations. In the view of Chinese medicine, many illnesses are caused by blockages in these channels. By learning to recognize, utilize, circulate and direct the internal energy of the human body, an individual can also connect with the energy of the universe and of the earth, and learn to interact with all of nature as a whole. Through use of certain energies and techniques, yoga can relieve pain, strengthen the body's constitution, improve intelligence and prolong life. Yoga is concerned with discipline and building positive energy from within. Runners in the West who do not practise yoga or an equivalent discipline are not necessarily training their body from within; they may not be learning how to breathe properly and create inner equilibrium and positive energy. Similarly, a brand that is only flexing its muscles and training through outward-reaching activities is not likely to build an inner strength. The interconnection between mind, body and spirit is something that is engaging more and more people in the world. A holistic approach to one's own personal well-being is a parallel to successful brand building.

For a brand to be fit it needs to be fit from the inside out. The rational, sensory, emotional and spiritual responses to a brand are connected. Of course, the notion of a brand having a spiritual connection may sound weird to some people, and it is not a subject that naturally arises in the boardrooms of many Western companies. Yet, in China, reference to the spiritual needs of the staff and the concomitant spiritual needs of customers is not unusual. The senior management for brands as diverse as Broad and Erdos recognize that their obligation includes being sensitive to the spiritual needs, as well as the more practical demands, of their employees and customers.

Battle-weary, hardened business executives regard any discussion relating to spiritual matters as fluffy irrelevance. However, global disenchantment with many aspects of business practices (or 'enronitis', a new term of affection for the individual neurosis that one's own company may be charged with fraudulent behaviour) has led to fundamental questions about the traditional definitions of business goals and modus operandi.

There has been a tendency for many companies in the West to assume that, so long as they have a great product, memorable advertising and promotions, they will be a sure-fire success. Today, not only are people waking up to the fact that every one of their employees is their greatest ambassador for their brand – their most inspirational evangelist – but also that it is through people that one transforms new ideas into reality.

Perhaps one of the most surprising findings from our research in China has been the importance that people place on making sure that they communicate well with one another. Haier, for example, has created its own book full of anecdotes, cartoons and poems written by employees illustrating what their brand means to them – what specifically the values signify in their day-to-day working life. This kind of thing is done in the West but it is still quite new, whereas one gets the impression that organizations such as Haier must have done this for a long time. They recognize that it is very much their own people who are living and representing the brand. It is their own personal stories that bring corporate values to life. Also there are examples of employees themselves choosing to initiate a particular new way of doing something based on one of the values. For example, the employees at AsiaInfo decided that it would be a good thing for the company to support the Hope charity initiative and they volunteered to donate money to this charity. The idea was not introduced by senior management.

International brands and the banana skin slip-ups

The mistakes made by countless international companies entering the China market are well documented. Foreigners falling for the attraction of the

1.3 billion market and believing that the advent of the middle-class with certain disposable income would arrive sooner than it actually did are reported in many books and articles. Of particular note is the recent publication of Joe Studwell's *China Dream*[5] which paints a very detailed picture of the huge range of companies that have slipped on many a banana skin, including pharmaceutical companies such as Pfizer, Novartis and Glaxo-Wellcome which were left with $30 million, $50 million and even $100 million factories operating at as little as 10–20 per cent of capacity. Car companies, such as GM, also invested in China having made the assumption in 1993, when total car sales were only about 300,000, that the number would jump to 1 million in 1995. With the exception of the car industry, the other market sectors who hurt themselves in China in the 1990s were repeating history. In the 1930s drug companies, along with others, made overoptimistic estimations of opportunities based on little more than intuitive reckoning.

Fast-moving consumer brands have been severely challenged by local competition and fake brands. For example, brands such as Panadol have been undermined by generics. One company that has developed a thoughtful strategy on sustainable brand capital is Nestlé. Armed with a strong, confident corporate brand emblazoned across all its products, it has chosen to use aspirational product brands such as Nescafé to act as a flagship for its overall portfolio. Nestlé is reinforcing its central proposition 'Good food, good life' to the Chinese community in both product offer and a coherent, visionary communications programme.

We have chosen Wall's as an example of a company which did not initially get it right, and which had to learn through painful experience what would be a successful strategy for China. The Wall's case study reads a little bit like a parable and provides some useful guidelines for those companies wanting to succeed. There are also other companies that have fared well in China, such as AIG. But even for this insurance company there were years of investment and disappointments. Further market opening for insurance companies will in fact only take place three to five years after accession to the WTO.

China's B&Q stores are flourishing. The average transaction value in Britain is £25, whereas in China the figure is closer to £50, a reflection of the fact that Shanghai residents, who were given permission to buy their own homes a decade ago, tend to buy empty shells. The decision on paint, decoration and kitchen fittings is made afterwards. Ian Strickland, B&Q's managing director in China, is bullish about the future and reckons that the company will be profitable in China from 2003. Strickland passionately believes in the role of good consumer research.

Supermarket retailers, including Carrefour, have also invested a great deal in China. They have put emphasis on training and developing local staff. Today, of its 60,000 employees in China, only 80 are expatriates and they now have the human resources to open seven to 12 hypermarkets a year for the foreseeable future. Finding the right local partners has been one of the critical factors in building successful businesses in China. One of the risks is dominant partner myopia, where one believes that, because it works somewhere else, it will work in China. Taking the best from each of the partners' practices and combining these strengths is the safest way forward. There has been an arrogance amongst many international companies which believe that they are more sophisticated than their Chinese counterparts and therefore bound to be successful. Those companies that have come with a certain humility, have listened harder, have taken the time to choose their partners wisely and have developed a tailored local strategy with local management for each of the regions have tended to do better.

Ultimately, for many international companies it is a question of being true to oneself whilst paying attention to local nuances, local sensitivities, local passions, local insights, local needs, local sense of humour, local values, local tastes and local competition.

Nation and region branding

This is the time to create greater synergies between the emerging brands and the China brand as a whole, and reciprocally the impact of the enhanced profile of China on the individual Chinese brands. This symbiotic relationship has been described in *Warriors on the High Wire*. Here it is worth focusing on the particular opportunities for China. We have chosen to use Shanghai as a case study, not only because it is the best-known Chinese regional brand, but also because Shanghai is employing some very imaginative techniques to strengthen its reputation.

Shanghai is attracting many high achievers to settle there through its attractive tax schemes, for example, anyone purchasing a property today is given significant tax incentives on the understanding that the individual provides all the information required on their earnings and savings. For a city that is looking to tighten up on its tax systems and the information provided by its citizens, this scheme is ingenious, because it is a way of collecting this information while giving a huge financial incentive to people to come to live and invest in the success of Shanghai, at least in the foreseeable future. The incentive scheme is due to come to an end during 2003.

We talk about customer and employer loyalty. Citizen loyalty is a bigger problem for all countries today. With the formation of transnational organizations such as the EU, NAFTA and other similar bodies, there will be fewer barriers to the movement of people. Talent has to be protected, whether we are talking about intellectuals, sports people, artists or whoever. These people are the future lifeblood of a region and their needs have to be valued. It is vital that a country is able to retain the loyalty of its citizens and attract new talent. Shanghai is welcoming back many 'returnees' from the West. A country's brand can be used as the anchor upon which to build loyalty with its people. This is essential in order to ensure that each of the country's citizens, one way or another, becomes the living embodiment of the brand.

There are countless examples of how the symbiotic relationship between country and product and service brands has delivered benefits for each. German cars immediately evoke the positive characteristics of German precision engineering and efficiency. Japan and Korea are well-known today for their hi-tech brands such as Sony and Samsung. In the future China can equally benefit from this kind of mutually beneficial relationship. In the foreword we refer to craftsmanship, creativity and care as some of the characteristics that may spring from Chinese heritage. A wide range of products and services may become direct supporters of the China brand. These may include traditional Chinese medicine, silk, paintings, ceramics, tea, kites, bicycles and foods such as dumplings (dim-sum). The hi-tech brands will also play a part in strengthening the Chinese brand – indeed, most of the examples in this book are focused on these sectors. A country or regional brand is, by definition, complex and multifaceted. The risk is that a country overemphasizes a single facet to the detriment of the whole. Japan, for example, has historically been so outstanding in the field of technology that people in the rest of the world have forgotten its more traditional strengths such as its art, literature and architecture.

Mr Zhou Hanmin has articulated, in Chapter 2 about Shanghai, a deep understanding of the complexity inherent within any regional or country brand. Given the size of China, there will inevitably be well over ten regional brands emerging over the next ten years. This will help reinforce the point that China is composed of many different peoples, cultures and histories. The protection of these local nuances and cultures can only enrich the overall China brand. Homogenization and standardization across all aspects of life can improve convenience and service aspects but can also represent a certain kind of deprivation and loss of richness and colour. In the West we are used to going to Chinese restaurants, but some of us are not yet accustomed to discriminating and being selective between Szechuan cuisine and Cantonese, for example.

The spirit of the people and the place are deeply connected. The values that lie at the heart of a country or region have implications for all aspects of life, impacting on the environment, culture, economy, leisure and work life.

Although identifying and articulating this spirit is difficult, it is very real and palpable. It is really important that the people of that region participate in the thinking about the brand, particularly young people whose hopes are fresh and who still regard their dreams as precious. It is often through these aspirations and dreams that one understands the particular characteristics that differentiate a particular region or country. The diverse characters of these people and places together make up China. People in each of these regions are in the process of redefining their goals and their aspirations. They are exploring their traditions, historical experiences, their skill base, their natural resources, the gaps, and defining new futures where past equity is not thrown away. It may be hard for people outside China to comprehend the pace of change, but for people within China today it is equally challenging to know exactly what China stands for. The different stages of the evolutionary journey will require new definitions, but the core values should remain timeless and spring from the spirit of the people and the place.

The new calibre of entrepreneurs

The new breed of entrepreneurs emerging in China are ambitious and aggressive. They are also very charismatic and charming characters with an understanding of business which is on a par with that of entrepreneurs in any other country; in fact, many of them have been Harvard-trained or have attended some equivalent business school in the US or Europe. One of the astonishing common features of these entrepreneurs is their relatively young age. The opportunity to be entrepreneurial once again in China has only emerged in the last 15 years and therefore the average age of the entrepreneurs heading up privately owned companies appears to be the late 30s or early 40s. Many of these people started their own business in their late 20s.

Nevertheless, the innovative spirit is not a new character trait in China. In 1979 Rong Yiren pioneered a whole new sector when he founded China International Trust and Investment Corporation (CITIC) and provided a new financial support for China's economy in transition.

The young entrepreneurs are not the first but they are open-minded, have a good sense of humour and are trying to share some of China's newfound wealth creation with a broad base of management people and other employees. Many of them talk about the fact that they want to do something to improve the quality of life in China, and that personal gain is only one factor driving them forward. Whilst such sentiments are commonly expressed, we actually believe these entrepreneurs are speaking sincerely. There is evidence of their social concern in the way they behave and in their actions. Entrepreneurs see themselves as the chief brand warriors, and are constant ambassadors for their brands. They are involved in managing the business, knowing and understanding the quirks, the issues of the day and the faults of their brands. They do not appear to use bullying tactics, but rather seek to create teams with clear responsibilities and accountability. They delegate and show trust in their people.

Entrepreneurs in China respect Western best practices, particularly with regard to legal, accounting and regulatory systems. They also ascribe great value to the traditional Chinese respect for emotional commitment and loyalty to their own people. They talk openly about making mistakes and recognize that, because everything is so new in China, they will be learning on the job, and solving problems and correcting errors as they go along. For these people a 'blame' culture is not acceptable; they prefer to give encouragement and freedom for people to act on their own instincts as well as being guided by good analysis. Although there is a shortage of experienced, highly skilled brand builders in China today, these entrepreneurs who are leading their own ventures have instinctively acquired both the science and art of brand building. They are already using qualitative as well as quantitative research to understand stakeholders' attitudes to their brands and the competition. They are exploring customers' underlying motivations. They are constantly reviewing their communication and promotional programmes to improve effectiveness. They put great emphasis on instilling cultural understanding amongst all employees and are using imaginative techniques to help bring the brand to life. Most importantly, they are living their brand every day.

Many of these entrepreneurs have an intuitive understanding of how to use the competitive advantage derived from a well thought-through brand architecture strategy. In *Warriors on the High Wire*, brand architecture is discussed in terms of the strategic relationship between the corporate brands and the business or product brands. Many of these new brands have adopted focused architectures in which their core brand ideology is central to the thinking on what products and services should be provided. The benefits of more focused architectures are described in some detail in *Warriors on the High Wire*.

This focused portfolio management style contrasts sharply with the conglomerate or chaebol,[6] where a single corporate brand encompasses a vast, but often diverse, range of services and products. The state-owned enterprises are diversifying quite aggressively, whilst the private company entrepreneurs tend to stick more to the core business and to what their vision dictates. Earlier in this chapter Sony and Samsung were mentioned. The Sony portfolio is narrower than Samsung's and therefore Sony can tap into the individual's creative urge. Saddled with a more diverse portfolio of products, Samsung's message is broader and less specific to the interactive media context. There are clear trade-offs for each of them. Sony can be 'edgier' and Samsung can be of more general, but universal, appeal. Portfolio management (or architecture) strategies need to be selected and designed in parallel with the primary tasks of deciding what business one wishes to be in (purpose) and how to stand out from the competition (brand positioning).

China's innate creativity

We have discussed in this introduction the importance of breaking patterns and thinking differently. There are various kinds of creativity:

- **Practical creativity**. The Chinese have been innovators throughout the ages. There need to be new ways of encouraging innovative thinking, such as award systems, rewards and secondments to join dedicated innovation project teams.
- **Conceptual creativity**. This is where the education system should encourage lateral thinking, metaphor development and visual/verbal idea generation.
- **Aesthetics**. Chinese views on aesthetics are to be valued. The Western view is only one perspective. The Chinese need to build their own self-confidence and belief in their sense of what is good, bad and ugly. In Shanghai, for example, the town planners are thinking of demolishing some of the unattractive modern high-rise buildings because they judge them to be a blot on the landscape.

There is always the risk that some people will try to follow Western tastes and fashions exclusively and lose their connection with their own rich cultural heritage. Protecting and encouraging Chinese art, music, architecture, performing arts, crafts, design and all of these creative pursuits is not only important for China, but also for the rest of the world.

Conclusion

One of the most famous Chinese poets, Du Fu, over 1,000 years ago said: 'The state is shattered, mountains and rivers remain'.[7] Whatever political reality evolves for China during the next 20 years, a quiet revolution has been occurring and will continue to do so. China's economic transformation, giving consumers the opportunity to have goods and services that enhance the quality of their life at affordable prices, is now an absolute reality for at least 120 million middle-class Chinese. Within five years, this figure is predicted to rise to 240 million.

Many people have got carried away over the years, thinking about the 1.3 billion consumer market, imagining that it will only be a question of a few years before the majority will benefit from these goods and services. Previously overoptimistic investors have now become more attuned to the gradual transformation and the slower pace of change than that anticipated ten years ago. On the other hand, to most people the pace of change is quite extraordinary. One of the principal contributory factors to the future pace of change will be the development of successful local and national brands.

It is possible, but difficult, to turn the clock back. With these new awakened desires, Chinese people will be keen to earn more money to improve their lives as part of their raison d'être. A permanent change has therefore occurred. It may not be as permanent as the certainty of mountains and rivers. On the other hand, there is a strength of will here and, like the biggest rivers, the waters run deep.

When Deng Xiaoping made his famous journey to the South in 1992 and symbolically chose the southern towns closest to Hong Kong, rather than Shanghai, to deliver his message, he was opening the door to many of these new opportunities. Tiananmen Square is most famous for the 1989 riots, and we can now look with a certain historical perspective at those events. People's lives are being transformed today. There is greater freedom of speech, freedom of movement, freedom of true commercial enterprise. 'There is a tide in the affairs of man':[8] nothing can stop this tide and its very positive momentum. We saw this most dramatically when we stayed on campus in Changsha at Broad Town. Situated in the midst of paddy fields, the factories stand proudly alongside an imitation palace of Versailles and imitation Egyptian pyramid. When we strolled around the campus, we kept coming across statues of Deng Xiaoping, and when we later met Mr Zhang Yue he made it clear that eighteenth-century French philosophers had heavily influenced his thinking. 'La liberté, la fraternité, l'egalité', he said. 'I have not studied this at any university, but I read it for myself. I am a painter, a creative person who enjoys the aesthetics and the thinking of great artists.' That night we slept on campus after eating delicious Szechuan food. The restaurant was situated across the river Xiang where Mao Zedong took his famous dip. Here in the locality where Chairman Mao started to develop his Marxist philosophy, Mr Zhang Yue is developing his hugely successful and attractive Broad philosophy.

Although China's brand warriors will benefit from international expertise, at the same time they rightly have the confidence to create new ways of doing things, building on Chinese culture, creativity and their own wisdom.

1. B. Joseph Pine and James H. Gilmore, *The Experience Economy*, Harvard Business School Press, April 1999.

2. Gail Sheehy, the author of eleven books, is best known for her landmark work *Passages* and the book that broke the silence about menopause *The Silent Passage*.

3. Maslow's Hierarchy of Needs: P = Physiological S = Safety L = Belongingness and Love E = Esteem SA = Self-Actualization. Maslow believed that an individual must substantially satisfy the needs at the lowest level before he or she could begin to satisfy the needs at the next higher level. Only when the needs of all lower levels were satisfied could self-actualization needs begin to be satisfied. Self-actualization is the fulfilment of one's human potential, and is often the point at which an individual becomes truly creative.

4. Douglas Adams was born in Cambridge in March 1952, educated at Brentwood School, Essex, and St John's College, Cambridge, where, in 1974 he gained a BA (and later an MA) in English literature. He was creator of all the various manifestations of *The Hitchhiker's Guide to the Galaxy* which started life as a BBC Radio 4 series. *The Hitchhiker's Guide to the Galaxy*'s phenomenal success sent the book straight to number one in the UK Bestseller List and in 1984 Douglas Adams became the youngest author to be awarded a Golden Pen.

    He followed this success with *The Restaurant at the End of the Universe* (1980); *Life, the Universe and Everything* (1982); *So Long and Thanks for all the Fish* (1984); and *Mostly Harmless* (1992). Other publications include *Dirk Gently's Holistic Detective Agency* (1987) and *Long Dark Tea-time of the Soul* (1988). In 1984 Douglas teamed up with John Lloyd and wrote *The Meaning of Liff* and, after a huge success, *The Deeper Meaning of Liff* followed this in 1990. One of Douglas's all-time personal favourites was written in 1990 when he teamed up with zoologist Mark Carwardine and wrote *Last Chance to See* – an account of a worldwide search for rare and endangered species of animals. He sold over 15 million books in the UK, the US and Australia and was also a best seller in German, Swedish and many other languages.

    Douglas was a founding director of h2g2, formerly The Digital Village, a digital media and Internet company with which he created the 1998 CD-ROM *Starship Titanic*, a Codie Award-winning (1999) and BAFTA-nominated (1998) adventure game.

    He died unexpectedly in May 2001 of a heart attack at the age of 49. He had been living in Santa Barbara, California, with his wife Jane and daughter, and at the time of his death he was working on the screenplay for a feature film version of *Hitchhiker*.

5. Joe Studwell, *China Dream*, Profile Books, 2002.

6. Chaebol – Korean translation of the Japanese word *zaibatsu* or business conglomerate: a group of specialized companies with interrelated management servicing each other.

7. Extract from 'Spring View' by Du Fu (712–770), Chinese poet, *Selected Poems of Du Fu*, Columbia University Press, 2003, translated by Du Fu and Watson Burton.

8. William Shakespeare, *Julius Caesar*, Act IV, Scene 3.

1 | China Mobile: Preparing to Capitalize on its Customer Base

Introduction

Imagine a profitable telecommunications company with the world's biggest subscriber base in a home market where mobile phone penetration is a modest 15 per cent. That company is China Mobile, China's leading cell-phone operator. State owned, it is the largest mobile phone carrier in mainland China with a coverage of 98 per cent of the counties and cities in mainland China. The company also offers its mobile phone roaming services in co-operation with 63 countries and areas and 95 joint venture companies. With 123 million subscribers mostly in China, China Mobile ranks ahead of even Vodafone which has about 100 million subscribers spread over a few markets. This is equivalent to controlling 70 per cent of the Chinese mobile customer market.

If the growth trend in mobile phone usage continues, China's mobile phone users will rise to 270 million and outnumber landline phone users by the beginning of the year 2003. Nevertheless, China Mobile's work will be cut out if it wants to maintain its dominant position because competition is rapidly intensifying in the mobile communications industry. Mr Lu Xiang Dong, Deputy General Manager of China Mobile, explains the part that branding has to play in China Mobile's development strategy.

Da Ge Da – the Big Brother Mobile Handset

To be frank, when we started out in the mobile business in China, branding was not an issue that concerned us. And I can say this because I was there – I was one of the early participants in the building and the launch of China's first commercial mobile telecommunications system in 1987 in Guangzhou. That was the TACS system, developed by the Guangdong Postal and Telecommunications Bureau. In 1994, to meet development needs, we were established as a subsidiary under the China Postal and Telecommunications Ministry with nationwide responsibility for developing China's mobile telecommunications network. As a government agency owned by this ministry, you could say that the name of the ministry was our 'brand'! We felt no need for anything like a corporate brand or product brands.

To give an example of just how removed we were from branding, when we first provided mobile phone services, we didn't even have a name for our service. All there was, was the mobile phone itself. It was our customers who came up with the first product name for the mobile phone – 'Da Ge Da' meaning literally 'big brother big'. Most of the mobile phones in those days were used by wealthy Hong Kong businessmen. They would come up to China for business, arrive at meetings and put their huge handsets (made by Motorola) on the table for all to see. They were such symbols of success that people started to call them 'Da Ge Da' – indicating that the owner was the big brother – the number one in the crowd.

The Chinese government then began introducing an element of competition into the telecommunications industry, especially into the mobile communications sector. This had a huge impact on us because, as a monopoly, we were used to operating without competition from within China or from abroad. Suddenly companies like China Netcom and China Unicom came into the picture. There was a market and we needed a strong brand to compete. Market forces were driving us to start building our brands.

In 1995 when we switched to the GSM system, we created 'Go-Tone', a service where customers subscribe to a mobile phone contract with us. It started off only as a name but, with time, we developed and optimized it as a brand by working on its design, packaging and other brand-related details. It has now become our most famous product brand. We did the same thing with Shenzhouxing, a prepaid mobile service, which was created in 1999. In 2000, Monternet, our mobile data and Internet service, was created. The name is actually derived from a combination of the word 'mobile' and the word 'Internet'.

Around the same time, China Telecom, our predecessor, underwent restructuring and mobile services were finally separated from other telecommunication services. On 20 April 2000, the China Mobile Group was officially formed. This was a 'brand' milestone for us because it marked the beginning of our corporate brand with the creation of an entity intended to be an independent, professional mobile communications company for China.

Our success

In the beginning, the level of economic development and the market demand for mobile services in China were very low. In 1990 we had a mere 20,000 subscribers. This increased to 3.65 million in 1995. By 1997 the number was 10 million. We shifted to express development mode and, in 2002, achieved a customer base of 100 million – effectively the largest mobile customer base in the world.

Some of the reasons why we have developed in leaps and bounds are external. Deepening economic reform in China, rising standards of living, increasing disposable incomes and increasing communication needs, both internationally and domestically, have all turned mobile phone services into a daily necessity in China. Furthermore, the Chinese government is emphasizing the importance of information to the economy and using information to drive the development of industry. This means that there is tremendous support given to the telecommunications industry, which has given all telecommunications businesses in China a huge boost.

But other reasons are internal. For instance, our decision to use the GSM standard after extensive internal debates in 1994 turned out to be the right decision. We had the right development strategy and were able to adapt to the changing and intensely competitive environment. We emphasized innovation and a thorough understanding of consumer needs, providing our customers differentiated and customized services. Our listing overseas meant that we had sufficient development capital and we adopted internationally accepted management principles that improved the way in which we managed our operations and systems. Last but not least, we had a highly effective and productive team of employees who were very cohesive.

The 'Monternet stadium' business model

During our period of growth, we have seen the business scope of the mobile communications industry change in line with the advancement of time, technology and the development of consumer trends and needs. We started off providing only voice services to the consumer but, with the rapid development of the Internet and the changing environment of the home and the office, customers are no longer satisfied with just having a voice channel. They now seek information solutions – services for voice, for data, for high-speed video and so on. They also have special requirements regarding the content of the data that they receive. The mobile communications market is changing and customers' requirements are also changing. We have to constantly ask ourselves how we are going to adapt and adjust to best meet these changes.

A good example is Monternet, our mobile Internet product. Monternet is frequently misunderstood. People see it as just a product but it is also a new kind of business model for us. I have an analogy that I often use to explain Monternet more clearly to friends and customers. Imagine Monternet as a large stadium or concert hall that has been set up by China Mobile. This stadium is a hub where all our present and potential customers gather as an audience. China Mobile has provided within this stadium all the best facilities – air conditioning, a fantastic stage, great lighting, comfortable chairs. Then we invite our suppliers to showcase what they have to offer as programmes on this stage. If these programmes are received well by the audience, we will ask them to return. But if the reception is bad, they will not be asked to give another show. China Mobile will sell tickets to this stadium and the profit generated will be shared between the suppliers and us. This is the Monternet business model analogy. We hope that it is going to be highly successful.

'What's in a name?'

Having a name like China Mobile places us in a rather contradictory position. When a country's name is used in front of the type of business that the company is conducting, this is likely to give the impression that the organization in question is traditional, old, state-owned, bureaucratic and conservative, probably with a monopoly hold on the market. Just consider, for instance, how, in other countries, brands like British Telecom or Deutsche Telekom or even China Telecom in China itself are perceived. Yet, if you consider how long we have actually been around, China Mobile is fairly young and can be considered a modern organization with the potential to be very open and progressive. Nevertheless, at the same time, the truth is that most of our shares are held by the state and we are not a private company.

The reality we have to accept is that we don't have much of a choice with our name. 'China Mobile' was not chosen by us, but was given to us by the Chinese government, much like a grandson named by his grandfather. In a country like China where the government has tremendous power, having such a name can be looked upon as an honour and a tool to facilitate the smoothness with which we can do business. However, if we look into the future, imagining a fuller range of businesses that we could potentially enter, then the name 'China Mobile' is not to our advantage. Furthermore, Chinese customers are becoming increasingly market-savvy and, to them, a name like 'China Mobile' is a minus.

But we do remind ourselves that a name is but a name. The important work that needs to be done lies in enriching the content and meaning of the brand behind the name 'China Mobile' and in improving the quality of our service to support this name.

Communications that start from the heart

The China Mobile brand is the embodiment of the corporate philosophy that governs how our company operates. Our corporate philosophy has five components: the corporate mission, corporate values, operational aim, enterprise spirit and service spirit.

China Mobile's corporate mission is 'to create a borderless telecommunications world and to be a pillar for the information society'. When we devised this mission, we examined our understanding of the past and present, as well as our judgement of what the future was likely to be. This mission is the basic principle that underpins our growth and also the basic force that drives our development.

China Mobile's corporate values are 'to continuously create more value for the society and the group'. We aim, with our excellent service, technological and operational innovations, to create both individual and shared value for all the different segments of society and its interest groups. Through continuously creating value for society, we also increase the value of our company.

China Mobile's operational aim is to 'pursue customer satisfaction in services'. This reflects our focus on using customer satisfaction as our permanent goal and using customers' needs as a guide in our operations.

China Mobile's enterprise spirit is a spirit of 'reform, innovation, seizing the day and high team spirit'. In developing the enterprise spirit, we drew from the richness and depth of Chinese culture, preserving many of its superior traditional foundations. This enterprise spirit expresses the healthy attitude that our employees have of always trying to improve standards and is also an expression of the trust, pride and honour that they feel towards the company. It is a force that drives the company's development and the maturity of the employees.

China Mobile's service spirit is 'communications start from the heart'. This line highlights the emphasis that we place on excellent customer service and is used as the main message of our China Mobile corporate brand. When we were a monopoly, senior management often spoke about improving service to our customers, but this was just lip service because we never faced the pressure nor felt the motivation to actually implement the concept. This has changed now that we are brand building to compete more effectively. We know that we need to communicate with customers from the bottom of our hearts – sincerely doing what we promise as a brand. The whole company, every employee, should be providing a service to our customers in a way that shows it comes from our hearts.

'Communications start from the heart' also explains our corporate brand positioning. We have never viewed ourselves merely as a provider of telecommunication services. What we are doing is using our 'heart and soul' to provide services that facilitate communication and, in that process, we hope to become an enterprise that creates 'communication value' for people.

I believe that, unlike an American or a European company, you cannot get a job done well in a Chinese company simply by setting up a system or a process for it. Other factors need to be considered – factors such as corporate culture and spirit which are particularly important in a Chinese company. This company spirit will have developed according to the business sector in which the company is operating, and the company's history as well as the personal viewpoint and management philosophy of its leaders. For China Mobile, the vision, mission, internal culture and philosophy that you read above are not things that were simply copied from a Western company model. Our corporate philosophy evolved as a result of our needs and alongside our growth. It is something that has become richer and more complete with time. It reflects, in my view, not only China Mobile's uniqueness as a company, but also expresses our development direction, our beliefs, our spirit and dreams and is a force and core strength that motivates us to continuously attain and exceed our corporate goals.

The importance of branding to China Mobile

At China Mobile we know that having a well-known brand will give us significant competitive advantages. Because consumers have a high level of awareness of our brand and are loyal to it, we as a company are able to enjoy large savings on our sales channel spending. Because consumers are interested in purchasing our services, it puts us in a stronger bargaining position when we negotiate with dealers and distributors. Because of the amount of trust that resides in our brand, we can also easily extend it into new areas. Because of what our brand promises and delivers, we are able to set higher prices than our competition. This last advantage is critical because it means that our brand is both a shield that protects us as well as an effective weapon that we can use in price wars.

Price wars are a big headache for us. As the first player in the mobile communications market – the 'Lao Da' as we call it in the industry – we still occupy 70 per cent of this market. However, new entrants into this market are always trying to rapidly expand market share and they use price wars as the simplest method to achieve this. When the six mobile operators of China and Hong Kong enter into a price war, the fight goes so far and so low that no one is able to make any profits.

China Mobile is put into a difficult position because, if we do not match the competitors' pricing, our customers start to complain. If we do cut our prices, our products become valueless. The solution therefore is to increase the quality of our service and products as rapidly as possible so that we can raise the profile of our brand. This will allow us to explain to our customers how our brand is different from, and better than, that of the competition and why they should pay us higher prices.

Many foreign companies and domestic companies place much emphasis on nurturing their brands. With China's entry into the WTO, the first losers are going to be the companies that do not have strong, competitive brands and products. Building a brand has therefore become a number one priority for us. Our brand strategy, explained below, is all about how to create a superior brand.

Our brand strategy

Our brand strategy is focused on doing the following:

1 Establishing a strict quality control system as a first step to building the brand. This is because the core of the brand lies in having a product that satisfies customers' needs and has a high quality of service. The telecommunications industry is a service industry. One unique characteristic of this industry is that the 'manufacture' of the product coincides with its consumption. Therefore the service quality has a special significance in terms of building the brand. To provide this high service quality, we have to ensure that we have completely reliable technology, comprehensive network coverage, good service and a swift and effective customer complaint response system. And it is only when each employee recognizes the significance of high-quality service to the survival of the company, and the part that he or she plays in it, that the level of service can be guaranteed consistently by this company.

2 Placing a heavy emphasis on public relations work. The company's public relations mission is to win the attention, co-operation, support and trust of the public through advertising, promotions, communications and so on. This will provide a conducive context for the development of the company.

3 Abolishing any corporate thinking that is price-focused. As explained above, there are no winners in a price war. Currently, consumers are demanding a level of service that costs one to two times the current pricing. If we do not actively seek to build a service brand, but only concentrate on price reduction strategies, then we will be facing our own exit from this industry.

4 Actively innovating to develop new services to meet the needs of society. In some ways, a brand is the relationship that forms between the customer and the product/service that the company provides him or her with. This relationship takes time to build. It requires constant revitalization to ensure the longevity and vitality of the brand. Innovation is of particular importance to the telecommunications industry because of

constant advances in information technology. Our company needs to keep keenly abreast of these developments and the changes in society's needs that relate to it, in order to develop services, technology and brands that will enrich and expand our present portfolio.

Through this strategy of enhancing our service and business capabilities, we will build a superior brand and brand image. The brand advantage that we get can then create market advantages for us, narrowing the gap that exists between world-class telecommunications companies and us. In this way, we hope to build a world-class, leading telecommunications company in two to three years.

Brand building tools

To help us build our brand we use certain tools. For instance, we have conducted surveys among our customers to get their feedback. We write them letters enclosing questionnaires that ask for their opinions on our service and products, as well as their expectations of China Mobile the enterprise. We have used professional call centres that collate huge amounts of information from and about our customers. Currently we also employ performance indicators that measure customer satisfaction by product category and by region. We examine our churn rates. Towards the end of the 1990s we implemented a system of regularly inviting our customers to act as service supervisors for us for a fee. These tools help us quantify what sort of results we are achieving in the market, such as the level of customer satisfaction or whether our pricing is reasonable. They also track and check on the performance of our service and our brand.

The collection and analysis of information on our customer base has helped us realize that there are two important attributes governing how customers decide what mobile phone service suits them:

- The customer's need for mobile usage (linked to the need for convenience, work requirements, need to save time, emergency use and so on).
- The customer's level of mobile phone expenses (linked to their financial situation).

So using these two attributes, we have segmented our customers into nine target groups. By further analysing these groups to understand their different characteristics, usage patterns, interest levels and levels of satisfaction with China Mobile's services, we have been able to define the brand positioning that we need.

So, for example, the targeted segment for Go-Tone is the high- to mid-end customer whose needs centre on work requirements, saving time, improving effectiveness and ease of use. Therefore the Go-Tone brand promises an extensive and reliable network coverage (especially in the commercial and office districts) and comprehensive business services and capabilities. Its characteristics are: specialized, spirited, refined, strong. Go-Tone promotions say things like: 'Trust Go-Tone, Professional Spirit', 'Trust Go-Tone, Roam the World' and 'Trust Go-Tone, Superior Network'.

The Shenzhouxing brand, on the other hand, is targeted at low-end customers whose needs are focused on emergency use and ease of communication. With less volume of telecommunication traffic involved, the brand is about cost effectiveness, promises that the customer has control over his or her expenses, that it does not require a monthly fee and enables easy top-up with a pre-paid card. For this brand, we emphasize characteristics such as economy, speed, convenience, control and, in our advertising, use slogans like: 'Your Own Choice' or 'Control Your Own Phone Costs'.

Finally, the Monternet brand is targeted at three groups:

– young and trendy customers who are driven by entertainment;
– business customers who are driven by convenience and speed;
– corporate customers who are driven by productivity.

Monternet is about being modern, stylish, highly effective and innovative. Under our main Monternet brand we have sub-brands that are targeted at the three different consumer groups. Each sub-brand has a different profile and different suppliers. For example, for the young audience, the sub-brand M-Zone provides more fashionable and fun content such as games and picture downloads. For business audiences, our sub-brand M-Office provides broadband access to the Internet, mobile banking and mobile securities trading.

With the introduction of these brands, we make great efforts to ensure that they each have their own standard visual image (including logo) which is then promoted aggressively nationwide through a variety of channels such as TV, newspapers, journals, magazines, shop design, direct mailing, product packaging and so on. The goal is to create a very strong visual impact on consumers, achieving high brand awareness in a short time. We also try to emphasize the proposition behind each brand and stress the benefits that it will bring to the consumer. According to our last study, Go-Tone has 97 per cent brand awareness.

With promotions, we employ an integrated sales and marketing communication plan that includes sales promotions, advertising, SMS, door-to-door sales, exhibitions, sponsorship of charitable events and so on. We pay special attention to each brand's positioning and differentiation. We have a 'brand firewall' that ensures that promotions such as discounts and rebates on certain brands do not 'cannibalize' the sales of other brands.

Using our knowledge of the customers' usage patterns, time spent on the network and other characteristics, we find ways to lock them into our service. For instance, for Go-Tone we have a points system for rebates. Go-Tone Diamond Card holders can accumulate points for airport VIP services and other rewards. These are all differentiated services that target various spending levels. The governing principle with all advertising and promotions is to use the brand to increase customers' understanding of the business and to use the brand to drive the business.

When I think of our customer base today, it is one that covers high-, mid- and low-end customers in the market. This is very different from the early days when mobile phones were a sought-after luxury item and most of our customers were at the high-end of the market – commercial or professional users, government officials and white-collar workers. With the rise in people's purchasing power and the reduction in the price of mobile services, barriers to owning a mobile phone have lowered considerably.

Mobile phones are now proliferating among the masses. Today there seems to be an unending surge of low-end customers subscribing to a number of our brands. Chinese consumers are increasingly attracted to well-known brands and show greater loyalty to them. They are beginning to understand what a reputable brand, such as ours, can promise and deliver in terms of high product quality and high service satisfaction.

Distribution

Our distribution channel is another very important tool for building our brand. Distribution channels can help to build awareness and recognition of the brand among consumers. For instance, for our physical sales channel which includes dealers, self-operated outlets, joint venture outlets and appointed specialized shops, we have created a standard interior design image so that we can increase customers' understanding of the China Mobile brand. We have a channel management plan with a clear reward and punishment system to ensure that a good corporate image is maintained at all times and proper procedures are complied with. We look to the interests of our channel partners, making sure that they achieve sustainable growth so that we can create a long-term, mutually profitable partnership. In this way we increase their loyalty to us, which in turn influences the image that they portray of our brand.

In the future, we intend to focus on customer relations as a way of pursuing increased customer satisfaction. We see a growing market need for customer service that goes beyond selling a SIM card and therefore intend to transform our current model of physical sales channels into one that more effectively integrates sales and service provision. We are also considering whether to build specialized brand shops within which customers can experience the true richness and flavour of our brand and how advanced our products and services are. For instance, Monternet has very special brand characteristics which offer a great deal of potential for a Monternet concept shop. This would be a venue where customers cannot only experience the Monternet concept and culture but also interact with one another within a unique environment.

Building core competitiveness

Given that we will constantly be faced with more pressure and more competition, maintaining steady growth and development of our business is vitally important. In order to maintain this steady growth, we need to have what I call 'core competitiveness'. Without this, our business will not survive. Right now, China Mobile is facing good market conditions and an expanding Chinese economy so our company is growing too. But many things can change in the external environment – the government may stop giving out concessions, markets may fluctuate, competitors may become that little bit stronger. We have to think about future challenges and the strategy to meet those challenges. If brand building is one prong of China Mobile's strategy, then building core competitiveness is the other prong.

Business management experts around the world have analysed the concept of core competitiveness and have all reached different conclusions about it. I have my own understanding. Core competitiveness of a given company should comprise the following three capabilities:

1 The ability to foresee and predict the future.
2 The ability to have insight, that is, the ability to understand its positioning in the market and in the wider context of the environment in which it exists – it should know what to do and what not to do.
3 The competence to manage the organization's behaviour – in other words, once the company has an accurate projection about the future, can it implement its strategy, transforming thought into action in a fast and successful manner?

If a company has the above-mentioned three abilities then I think it will have an extremely good chance of surviving and developing successfully into the future. Right now, China Mobile has a lot of hard work to do in these three areas.

Although we may have one of the largest customer bases in the world, we recognize that we are a relatively young company and that many things within our company, like culture and philosophy, still need to mature. To aid this maturation, we hope to become what is fashionably known these days as a 'learning organization'. As a learning organization, we hope to absorb and incorporate into our organization good corporate practices irrespective of whether they come from Western countries, Western organizations or other more traditional Chinese companies. Our approach to competition reflects this attitude.

Competition and co-operation

In terms of domestic competition, China Unicom is currently our main competitor. In the next two to three years, China Telecom and other domestic operators will be granted licences to operate mobile networks and may become strong competitors as well.

What is threatening is the fact that most companies in China lack know-how in terms of branding. Some of them are focused on the short term, using price wars to gain market share, for example, which has the effect of reducing profits throughout the industry and increasing customers' sensitivity to price. This will make our task of brand building even more difficult. We may understand the importance of branding but, because we are constantly barraged by the illogical competitive actions of others, our efforts yield only sub-optimal results.

With China joining the WTO and the opening up of the telecommunications market, many foreign companies with capital, technological expertise, management and marketing experience are going to wage an intensive war against us. Competition is going to be taken to a global level. How are we or other Chinese companies going to respond? Many Chinese companies are undergoing restructuring and do not have time to pay attention to branding issues. Because we are a developing country, we have an abundance of cheap labour and have become a manufacturing base for many international companies. If we stay as a manufacturing base, however, we will always be 'controlled' by international companies and will eventually lose the battle in terms of branding.

To combat these difficulties I believe we must seize the present opportunities to establish partnerships with foreign companies. At China Mobile, we intend to embrace the principle of competitive co-operation in order to adapt quickly to the new competitive landscape. In this way, we can import into China, and into our own company, international management techniques, technological know-how, capital, experience, high-quality talent – all the things that will help us attain, as soon as possible, the goal of becoming a world-class player ourselves.

I think Vodafone certainly had an eye for beauty when they selected us as their partners for China in 2001. This relationship is not just one of Vodafone simply investing in us and being a shareholder. We are looking towards a future where we are going to be true partners. We are co-operating in terms of market promotions, customer relationship management and improving network quality. We are also discussing setting up a technological platform together, as well as possibilities in roaming and in joint development of new business. Our targets of providing unified services and product standards to our mutual customers are going to benefit both parties.

The scale of our network and the size of the market here in China, coupled with the synergies we will achieve in technology and marketing will, I believe, have a big impact on our development. Of course, our competitors are not sitting still. Unicom is tying up with Japan's NTT Docomo, and it remains to be seen what sort of competitive challenge they are going to pose.

The administrative policies in the telecommunications industry are bound to undergo major change as well. The regulatory environment in China's telecommunications industry is going to have to meet the standards set by international agreements. The serious challenge for us will be to improve our operations and our management standards during those few transitional years before market deregulation takes place completely.

The next five years will also be an epic period in terms of change in information and telecommunications technology. For example, the main bulk of telecommunications will change from voice to data and multimedia. Wireless networks will make the transition to third-generation networks (3G). These advancements in technology will require congruent changes in companies. We will not only need more capital but will also need to build production facilities that are suitable for the new technology. Data communications and voice communications businesses will have different value creation processes and different commercial models.

Ultimately, whether we can transform all of these future challenges into development opportunities will, I believe, depend on our ability to wield our competitive advantages in a more open market and compensate for our short comings as quickly as possible. Our competitive advantages are obvious – the largest GSM network in the world, the largest customer base in the world and advanced technological facilities. Our short comings include backward operational management systems, not being agile enough, not having sufficiently strong innovation capabilities and a lack of world-class management talent. We will have to prepare ourselves for the policy changes and learn how to abide by international rules. We will have to employ a smart competitive strategy in this new environment. We will have to continue building superior brands and creating core competitiveness.

The information backbone of the country

Any company that exists within the context of a country and a society needs to be aware of its social responsibilities. We at China Mobile see our company as being the backbone or the pillar of the information society in China. The Chinese government is trying to actively promote the 'informatization' of our society in the hope that this will lead to the growth of the entire national economy and future development of relevant industries.

We want to be major players in this process. We want to help move China towards becoming a society that is information-based. We want to have, as our biggest contribution, an extensive network covering China. Some of the areas that we service at present do not make any sense in economic terms, but we continue to service them because of the social and economic benefits to the local communities there. If you ask consumers or companies about China Mobile's network, they will tell you that we offer the best network coverage you can find.

Economic development in China at the moment is quite uneven. The western regions are developing more slowly than the eastern regions and, in response, the Chinese government has put 'Go West' policies in place. China Mobile has invested heavily in the western regions to boost local development of the mobile sector.

For example, Xinjiang – one of the largest autonomous regions in China – once organized an international convention to attract foreign investors, but it was a complete failure because the foreigners could not use their mobile phones there. Now if you go to Xinjiang, you will find that it has complete mobile network coverage, even out in the oilfields. The situation has completely changed – you will not perceive any difference in terms of mobile communications between Xinjiang and, say, North America or Europe. I would like to think that we played a considerable role in advancing the state of the region's telecommunications, giving it a basis for further economic development.

We also make donations to certain poor areas in China, helping to set up schools. In addition, we are sponsoring a foundation that is dealing with the problem of the encroaching sand from Inner Mongolia. These activities have given us a very positive corporate image among the general Chinese public. Because we have not ignored our social responsibilities, we have not put our brand image in danger.

Our corporate values of promoting sustainability of society and thereby creating more value for the company reflect the fact that China Mobile is integrating both long-term and short-term interests, unlike other corporations. Our corporate mission and our values are reflected at all times in our day-to-day business operations. We hope to become a communications partner that everyone in society can rely on and trust, co-existing and growing with society.

COMMENTARY

What does a company do when it has the largest subscriber base in the world? Find out as much information about each and every subscriber in that base, use this information to segment the subscribers into target groups and then attempt to market and sell to those target groups as many useful and interesting services and products as possible. China Mobile is in the enviable position of being able to do this in the future.

When successful, we call this Brand Shifting™. As a brand gains popularity because it is offering the right functional benefits and the right emotional benefits to its customers, these customers also begin to form a stronger loyalty to the brand. They start to look to it to provide more value to their lives in different areas. So, for instance, a customer in the UK who likes flying with EasyJet might consider renting a car from Easy Rent-A-Car because he has enjoyed the experience and benefits of one type of service under the brand and believes that he will have a similarly enjoyable experience with another service under the same brand. The values and core proposition of that brand translate with credibility across two different forms of transport. In the same way, if China Mobile is currently providing mobile services to its 123 million subscribers, what other access/content services will it be able to provide these subscribers in the future?

China Mobile has already displayed rigorous marketing skills in the way in which it has aggressively profiled its current subscribers and created sub-brands within mobile services with different characteristics and values in its quest to offer tailormade solutions to its customers. And it is not resting there. The company is continuing to micro-segment even as this subscriber base increases and Chinese consumers' tastes change. As the rate of this change is phenomenal, China Mobile will have a challenging task of understanding current needs and projecting future ones in order to offer relevant branded products.

Today's increasingly technology-savvy customers identify with emotive brands like Orange and O2 rather than France Telecom or BT. Similarly, the name 'China Mobile' may hold limited appeal in the future. But, as Mr Lu Xiang Dong rightly points out, a name is but a name and China Mobile has wisely invested efforts into its vision and the values behind its corporate brand. The result, 'Communications Start from the Heart', we feel, is a very strong core proposition that holds a tremendous amount of potential for Brand Shifting™ in the future. This is a core proposition that can drive China Mobile into new markets and services.

2 | Shanghai City: Spectacular Shanghai

Introduction

In the battlefield of economic development, it is widely believed that branding by cities and countries has become a necessary competitive advantage. Cities constantly compete against each other for investment dollars, foreign trade, tourists and even intellectual capital in the form of scholars, artists and business entrepreneurs. In addition, they compete with each other to hold these resources within their borders.

Shanghai city is no exception. As the traditional gateway into China for the rest of the world, it has been, and will continue to be, a focus for foreign companies attempting to enter the Chinese market. But where does it stand in comparison to places like Hong Kong, Singapore or even other cities within China?

Winning the World Expo 2010 presents an opportunity for Shanghai not only to showcase its social, cultural and economic accomplishments to the rest of the world but also represents an opportunity for it to exhibit its prospects for the future. Success begets success, and winning this bid will accelerate the development of Shanghai's infrastructure, improve living standards and enhance its international reputation.

In this chapter, Mr Zhou Hanmin, vice-chairman of the Shanghai World Expo 2010 Bidding Office and deputy chief commissioner of Pudong New Area People's Government speaks about why having a brand for Shanghai has been critical to winning this bid and describes what makes Shanghai special and different from other cities in the world.

A city can be a brand

I believe a city can definitely be a brand. This is a fact. Take, for example, the current competition between cities like Shanghai, Moscow and Seoul, who each vied to be the selected host city for the 2010 World Exposition. To win such a competition, the city needs to be a 'well-known' place. And it is not about being well-known in terms of the size of its geographical area or the size of its population but being well-known in terms of its unique characteristics and values. That is what makes the city a brand. That is what differentiates one city from another.

Whenever you mention any city – London, for instance – you immediately have a certain sense of the place. A very quick thought goes through your head on the history behind London, the elegance of its architecture and also the very innovative endeavours that the city is known for, especially in the field of finance. There is something about London that defines it. When you refer to Paris, a totally different picture comes to mind; even though the cities are only three hours apart by Eurostar, to Londoners Paris is a completely different concept as a place. Paris is a city defined by charm and romance. It is a city full of culture that welcomes expressions of culture.

How is Shanghai city a brand? Shanghai is a part of China, a country with a civilized history of 5,000 years. The history of China has a huge influence on what Shanghai is about. Yet when I think of Shanghai, I think of a city open to the West as well as to the East. It is a place where the West meets the East in the past and for the future. The uniqueness of the place, and therefore the purity of the brand, lies in the fact that Shanghai simultaneously belongs to both China and the world. It is a city that possesses a sense of responsibility towards the world. It has an influence in the global arena, not just within the Yangtze River Delta.

Second I think of the spirit of the Shanghai people. There is a definite sense of entrepreneurship in Shanghai. It is a city that plays in accordance with the rules, but with a creative flair. People themselves are brands, and the people of Shanghai, with their enterprising and creative inner resources, contribute to the flavour of the city. Shanghainese people are used to reinventing themselves, absorbing all that is good from the foreign influences that have come into the city.

Shanghai in fact is not a new brand: it has been one of the best-known brands in China for many decades. There are two reasons for this. First, internally, Shanghai has always served as the driving force for China's economic and social development, especially in terms of culture. Second, externally, it is one of the most popular places in China. People can pronounce the name 'Shanghai' easily in different languages. Shanghai has had an open policy towards the outside world since 1842, right after the Second Opium War. Because of this period of openness, much has entered China via Shanghai, making Shanghai the bridge – the window to and from the outside world. Today if you want to see the latest fashions in China, you go to Shanghai first. If you want to establish your corporate image in the Chinese market, the testing ground is Shanghai and, once you make it there, you are a brand for ever.

Quite clearly, cities can be brands and, in fact, I believe that both cities and the countries they belong to need to be brands.

People are natural ambassadors

As a brand, a city carries with it different complexities to the ones associated with company brands. To a certain extent, you can control a company's activities but you can't control all the people of a city to make them ambassadors of the brand. It is a dilemma but I like to think about it in the following way: wherever you go and whatever you do, you are a unique individual representing the place where you were born or where you have lived for a long time. In that way, you are always transmitting certain ideas and thoughts, particularly to the city that you belong to. You automatically constitute an ambassador for your city and will be one for the rest of your life.

But there is a natural limit to what you convey. No matter what kind of person you are, you can only reflect certain characteristics of the place that you come from and the rest is left to the imagination, expectation and anticipation of the people with whom you interact. For instance, if we send a troupe of dancers from Shanghai to a foreign city, they will perform Shanghai culture and display aspects of Shanghai in a language of their own. The audience will get a small taste of Shanghai, a glimpse of the genius of these dancers, but nothing more than that. Yet their performance will have provided a direction for people to consider their impressions of Shanghai and will have channelled their thoughts about the real place.

It is difficult for people to behave in a consistent and representative fashion all the time. Nevertheless, outsiders can form a judgement, however basic, from meeting such people and from there, reach a certain understanding or conclusion about the city that they come from. That, in my opinion, is enough because people by nature see things from different angles. It is difficult for them to behave alike. Neither is it necessary.

The image of a country needs to be substantiated

Learning and perfecting should never end. We need to constantly enlighten ourselves about how to better our city's brand. That may mean launching a movement in Shanghai focused on improving the city's image, especially in the eyes of outsiders.

The White House, for example, has recently established a special office just to improve the image of the US. This is a country that supposedly shoulders the heaviest responsibility in the world for peace and development and is usually considered one of the most attractive places in the world for visitors, students and immigrants. Yet why does it perceive a need to work on its image? I think this is a very interesting point.

Countries, and the people who lead them, should try to learn something from history. I give you this example. If you conduct a survey in China today

asking the question 'Which country do you hate most?', most Chinese people
– even those below the age of 24 – will answer you in a very surprising way. As
many as 97 per cent will say that they hate Japan. And this will be the answer
even from youngsters who, although they have not personally experienced
any suffering at the hands of the Japanese, will be familiar with those stories
of pain.

Compare the two events that have affected China, the Opium Wars that
were started by the English and the Japanese invasion of China in the Second
World War. The question we need to answer here is why the results of these
two wars are so different. Why do most youngsters in China still hate the
Japanese even though they are removed from the event and many years have
passed? Although many young Chinese people go to Japan for training and to
earn money, ultimately very few will remain in Japan for life. Whenever I visit
Japan and I meet my fellow countrymen or women, my question to them is
always 'Do you like this place?', and the answer is often a story of both love
and hate.

The essence of the Shanghai brand

What is the essence of the Shanghai brand? I believe it has several elements.

First, there is a clear sense of our roots – that is, a recognition that we are
Chinese. Second, there is a strong sense of entrepreneurship. By 'entrepreneurship', I do not mean that every Shanghainese person is set to become an
entrepreneur; I am referring to the creative drive that exists in the Shanghainese mindset. Shanghainese people are never satisfied with what they have
achieved. They constantly think about how they can do something more economically, more effectively. Entrepreneurship is all about the spirit of
freedom. What everyone understands in Shanghai is that we need to think
freely in order to become successful. In other words, if you enjoy that opportunity to think freely, you will be able to stretch yourself and discover your
own boundaries. This is central to the spirit of Shanghai.

Third, the way in which Shanghai has developed from an obscure fishing
village 700 years ago into an international metropolis where businesses from
around the world gather forms an intrinsic part of the brand. The word
'Shanghai' means 'a place on the sea'. This has nurtured a belief that our
success depends on an ability to readily absorb foreign advancements, no
matter where they come from.

For example, if there is an important art show from London on display in
Shanghai, people will attend it. They will do the same if it comes from
Mozambique. The reason for this? The need to absorb, much like plants
absorb nutrients from the sun and the air. The sun to the people of Shanghai

is a kind of spirit – necessary to excel in this world. And the air is all the good things that we can assimilate from abroad.

This is the reason why all kinds of food find their way to Shanghai city. Europeans will do well if they come to Shanghai to do business. People in Shanghai do not want to just experience McDonald's and Kentucky Fried Chicken. All European food and drink would be very welcome in Shanghai because the people there are so cosmopolitan.

This is also why we have always believed Shanghai to be the right city to host the World Expo 2010. The magic of the World Expo lies in its ability to bring together the nations of the world – people from all the countries of Africa, Asia, and Europe converging in one place to display their diverse cultures. It is a unique opportunity for the people of one country to explore and understand the people of another country. Our chosen theme of 'Better City, Better Life' is also one that will allow all countries, whatever their stage of development or culture, to participate. Look at one of our bid posters entitled 'Aspiration'. It shows a Chinese child standing under a rising sun symbolized by our logo. This child is reaching out with his hands, showing his expectations for Expo 2010 in Shanghai. The poster truly reflects how our city wholeheartedly supports the Expo and all the good things that it will bring from and give to the whole world.

Shanghai on the world stage

Let's compare Shanghai with the three major cities of the world: London, New York and Tokyo. London is the oldest city, New York is the second oldest and Tokyo is the youngest of the three. As the city with the youngest history, what has happened in Tokyo is an absolute miracle. In a space of 38 years, after losing everything at the end of the Second World War, Japan has managed to create the second strongest economic power in the world with Tokyo as its capital and driving force. And even though, for the last ten years, Japan has had thirteen different prime ministers and its economic growth is really sluggish, it is still an incredibly strong world economy.

Shanghai needs to work the miracle that Tokyo has done and I certainly do not underestimate how difficult this is going to be. Rome was not built overnight. We do, however, recognize two needs. The first is that we have to 'get on and do it'. We do not have the time for extensive study and research. We are going to have to learn on the job. This very much mirrors how the entrepreneurs of Shanghai operate – mistakes will be made on the job and we will have to learn even as we build this city.

The second need concerns the quality of our people. The Chinese education system needs to change. At the moment it is based on learning by rote, by memorizing, by listening to instructions. That has led to industry that is good at imitation and copying, making us the manufacturing capital of the world. But what we need to do is to extend ourselves beyond this capability. And for that we need an education system where teachers no longer restrict creativity in our young people. The teachers themselves have to start thinking and teaching differently. Let me give you an analogy of what I mean. The people of Shanghai are all stuck at the neck of the bottle. There is so much potential there that is waiting to be released. What we have to do is to break the neck of this bottle that is holding us back. The first and foremost step is mental preparation. So education is crucially important.

The people in Shanghai sometimes think that Shanghai is one of the best cities in the world already. Let's not make that mistake. It is far from that. There are many things that the people of Shanghai can learn from others. There are cities in the outside world that are much more splendid in comparison. Consider these two points.

First, if Shanghai is going to be a very prestigious brand in itself, we should have many famous corporate or product brands originating from the city. Are there any at the moment? None that are established on a worldwide basis. At present, there are possibly only one or two Chinese brands that are known outside of China – Tsingtao beer, for example. Everywhere you go in Shanghai city today you will see all kinds of stores, but they are carrying foreign brands. We need our own Shanghainese brands to come into prominence to help the city brand itself.

Second, we need more talented people to emerge from within Shanghai and to bring prestige to the city. For instance, I would like Shanghai to be the city from which the first Chinese person will win the Nobel Prize. This must unquestionably be the case, otherwise it will be a big failure for the city. I do not see why our vibrant city cannot produce famous brands or nurture famous people.

In terms of potential, I would consider Shanghai to be a booming city because it is thriving not just economically but socially as well. It has always been a city that respects achievements in the social arena, in arts, in sports, in the creation of what I term 'human spiritual products and endeavours' – music, novels, art. In this respect, Shanghai does attract a lot of people. However, after a while, people do leave to explore their personal development in other places.

For instance, we have world-class opera singers like Madame Wang Ying who has played the role of Madame Butterfly in Europe but no longer lives in Shanghai today. However, that is not really a worry because she still originated from Shanghai. We have young ballerinas in Shanghai who have won world-class competitions. Our youngsters excel in acrobatics as well as in the

Olympiad competitions in the fields of physics, mathematics and chemistry. These promising young Shanghainese people are the roots for the modernization of our city. They will migrate from the city to other places, but they will still represent Shanghai.

A branded city needs its branded elements – people and business brands. No matter how splendid the overall image of a city is, it still needs all the separate and basic elements of its construction to be splendid, from design to raw materials, to manpower and craftsmanship. That is what I am trying to achieve here with Shanghai.

Some issues of immigration and urbanization

Rapid urbanization is a phenomenon that is occurring everywhere in China. How do we integrate all the immigrants who come to Shanghai into the life of the city, into mainstream Shanghainese society? This is a very big challenge. The greatest hurdle is limited resources. Let me give you one example – education. I believe that when people are well educated, they will behave and carry themselves better, leading to an improved society. But in Shanghai it would be difficult for us to offer the same education system and benefits to all the newcomers who arrive in Shanghai – the workers, the farmers and the young people – not because we want to discriminate against certain groups of people but because the resources allocated to education in Shanghai are too limited to allow this.

Second, Shanghainese people have a unique way of doing things, of living and even of eating. Even if the people who come to Shanghai to live are well educated and well-to-do – meaning that they would be assets to the city – how do we ensure that they become and behave 'Shanghainese'? The movement of people into Shanghai needs to be managed well or else there may be resulting damage to our brand.

A large proportion of overseas Chinese, especially students, have Shanghai and Pudong as their first choice when they return to China. I would say that Shanghai is a good brand in their eyes. These overseas Chinese need the kind of atmosphere that we have in Shanghai – the freedom, creativity and sense of entrepreneurship. The Shanghai brand has been useful in terms of attracting these people. But people still make comparisons between Shanghai and other cities where they could live and work. And Shanghai does have a problem with the way in which it is perceived by the people of neighbouring regions.

On the one hand, people respect Shanghai's achievements but, on the other hand, they consider the Shanghainese to be very arrogant. The two defining characteristics of Shanghainese people are aggressiveness and ambition. Frankly speaking, it is sometimes difficult to introduce oneself as

Shanghainese. Shanghainese in China are just like New Yorkers in the US. We walk faster. We work more effectively. We dress better. We eat well. But we are also resented more. How we strike a good balance between our achievements and how these achievements are perceived is an issue for all Shanghainese to think about.

The same can perhaps be said for the physical construction of Shanghai city. On the one hand, people who visit Shanghai admire how quickly we are progressing and the energy that flows in the city. But we have all the problems associated with a rapidly expanding metropolis – the inevitable overcrowding and the pressure on limited city resources, an ageing population which must be cared for and poor living conditions that still exist in some parts. But that is why we chose 'Better City, Better Life' as our theme for hosting the World Expo. It is a personal goal for us. We believe that such a theme is going to improve our own understanding and concept of urban development. Expo 2010 will be an opportunity for us to exchange ideas with other countries on the subject.

We have set aside a downtown area in Shanghai composed of factories and residential quarters for the World Expo. This area sits astride the Huangpu River, the watercourse that has nurtured Shanghai's growth, and is awaiting renewal. But, again, we recognize that there is a balance that needs to be struck. We must make sure that buildings of historical and cultural value are kept intact while the area is undergoing redevelopment. We are also planning to restructure the city's industries to get rid of industrial pollutants, to make it more eco-friendly and to promote sustainable development. By the year 2010, we hope that Shanghai will be established as an international economic, financial, trading and shipping centre in the Pacific Rim. In our vision, it will be an ecological paradise in the East, with 'blue sky, clean water, green land and comfortable residences'.

The competition faced by Shanghai

As far as competition is concerned, there are different levels to it. At the national level, we face competition from two areas – one in the north and one in the south. In the south, it is the city of Shenzhen. Even though it in no way compares with Shanghai in terms of size and population, Shenzhen is still a very modern city. In the north we compete with Dalian – a beautiful, charming and attractive city of considerable prosperity. Internally within China, I would say, however, that neither of these cities can compete fully against Shanghai.

In the past, Shanghai has always been, in a sense, regarded as the eldest son of the family – the one expected to carry all the family responsibilities – or as a goalkeeper in a football game, playing an important but defensive role. In fact, that was a problem for us then, because we felt that our real role was a pioneering one. When Deng Xiaoping made his symbolic trip to the south of China in 1992, he chose to go to the Guang Dong area rather than Shanghai. Deng wanted to make the statement that the economic miracle that was Hong Kong could in fact be replicated just across the border.

It was so unfortunate for Shanghai that he didn't stop at our city. At that time, everyone viewed the cities of the south as China's pioneering cities. But if you look back with hindsight, it can be seen that Shanghai decided at that point to work really hard to re-establish itself. And as the date of Hong Kong's return to China approached, more and more international businesses moved their headquarters to Shanghai. The spotlight was on us and from then we grew from strength to strength. Today this pioneering spirit of freedom is right at the heart of the Shanghai brand.

We continue to face competition from cities like Hong Kong and Singapore. The functions of these cities vis à vis the world are quite similar to Shanghai's. But Shanghai has its own merits. First, we have a very strong industrial and manufacturing base. Second, we have a very strong training base for human resources in terms of universities and research institutions. On these two bases, I believe that Hong Kong and Singapore cannot match Shanghai. Nor can Singapore with its 3 million people and Hong Kong with its 6 million be compared to the 17 million people who live in Shanghai. However, if we measure ourselves against the cities of Tokyo, New York and London, we face a totally different level of competition. It is much harder for us to reach the standards set by those three cities.

Promotion of the Shanghai brand may be our weakest point. Internationally speaking, our embassies and other government organizations seem to have their own concepts of promotion. My personal suggestion to the government is that we need to build specific 'windows' into Shanghai from around the world. That means creating cultural centres representing Shanghai in the cities of London, Paris and New York. This, I believe, will have much more of an impact and be far more effective than just sending out troupes of dancers and singers. The question is: how do we achieve 'zero distance' between ourselves and the people of those countries. For instance, how do we effectively use the public relations companies in those countries to establish a securely rooted relationship between Shanghai and the people of those countries?

The world does not stand still for Shanghai

Ten years ago it was extremely difficult even to find a public telephone in

Shanghai. Nowadays, China is the third largest market in the world for telecommunications. The Internet has changed the world, and Shanghai is no exception. So many people in China and Shanghai surf the Internet today – they are searching the world. I maintain that Shanghai is the city where people can find their dreams. Or at least this is the place where people can always find a way to express their dreams, their hopes and their thoughts.

As far as Shanghai's future is concerned, more and more opportunities and challenges will come our way, just like the World Exposition in 2010. This particular opportunity represents a chance to further develop Shanghai's infrastructure. The challenge will be how to make Shanghai a permanent location for similar international events. We are toying with so many ideas at present. For example, each of the pavilions used in the Exhibition can be turned into a permanent cultural centre after the Expo is over. The British pavilion will become a British cultural centre. This could have so much potential. At the moment it is difficult to conceptualize the reality that these ideas can bring, but they represent some of my most current thinking.

To improve Shanghai is such a very urgent task for us because this is not a world that stands still, even for a moment. There is so much competition rising up around us. At the current rate of change and development, the future very quickly means tomorrow. And, as I said earlier, larger does not necessarily mean better. Only those of us with ready minds and hearts can win the battle of tomorrow – can fulfil the promise that is Shanghai.

I would like to end with a quote taken from an article written by William Keller, Honorary Citizen of Shanghai, for one of our Expo 2010 newsletters. As a Swiss businessperson who has lived in Shanghai for ten years and has witnessed its changes, he says:

> More than 30 years ago, when I was still young, I had a friend who lived in Shanghai during the 1950s. Every year, his family received parcels of Chinese tea from his Chinese friend. I asked him: 'How long will your Chinese friend send you tea for?' He replied, 'Forever, William, forever.' Once you have a Chinese friend, he will be your friend for life. This is what the word promise means in China. Ten years ago, our Chinese partners and the Shanghai Municipal Government assured me that the long term potential of Shanghai was bright and, at that time, I knew I could fully trust them. They have fulfilled their promise. Today, Shanghai once again assures the world that Shanghai will develop into an even better city offering an even better quality of life. We can give our full trust to this promise.

COMMENTARY

Mr Zhou Hanmin's understanding of the complexity involved in branding a city comes across very clearly in this chapter. Although many leaders in both regional and national governments recognize the critical need to improve the image of their home-lands, they struggle with the immensity of the task. How can you distil the richness and diversity present in any conglomeration of individuals who live and work together on a piece of land adequately into a single brand?

The first step, as Mr Zhou points out, is to recognize that it is the spirit of the people that defines the land. It may be the spirit of entrepreneurship that the Shang-hainese display in business in combination with the spirit of openness with which they assimilate influences from all over the world that helps capture what Shanghai is about and therefore the Shanghai brand. Defining this spirit is difficult because it involves looking both at the past – what Shanghai has been – and the future – what Shanghai aspires to be; the dreams of the young and also those of the old.

This spirit exists, however intangible it might be, and it needs to be articulated so that the city's people can add their voice to it. As Mr Zhou himself says, people are automatic ambassadors of the city's brand, whether knowingly or unknowingly. It is their interaction with other people around the world that builds the perception of the brand, so it is important that they themselves know what the spirit of being Shang-hainese is.

Practical steps have to follow. Mr Zhou says that Shanghai needs to do two things, both of which we regard to be highly important to building a city's brand. The first is helping Shanghainese brands make their mark on the international markets. The second is nurturing talent within the city, especially through education that encour-ages creativity. Both these elements will feed-back into the success of Shanghai.

Look at the way in which Spain has managed to rebrand itself. Twenty-five years ago, Spain was suffering from the effects of having been under the grip of the Franco regime. It was isolated and poverty-stricken. Today it is a modern democracy with a thriving economy and the destination of choice for holidaymakers. How did this happen? Its repositioning involved a national promotional programme that used Joan Miro's sun symbol to represent the modernization of the country.

But the result was also achieved through the privatization and rapid global expan-sion of Spanish multinationals such as Telefonica, the hosting of international events such as the Barcelona Olympics, the rebuilding of great cities like Bilbao with the Guggenheim museum, the work of talented film makers and actresses such as Pedro Almodovar and Penelope Cruz, and the artistry of architects like Santiago Calatrava all pooled together. How much more can Shanghai achieve along these same lines?

China is booming at the moment, and Shanghai's potential is at an all-time high. Shanghai is a spectacular city in so many ways, from its beguiling, seductive past as the 'Paris of the East' to its monumental building projects represented by that iconic skyline. International companies are moving their headquarters to Shanghai so that they can be part of its dynamic commercial environment. The task of branding and maintaining the brand of the city has to be an ongoing one. Shanghai's breathtaking rate of progress will be both a blessing and a challenge for the successful development of its brand.

3 | Haier: Dancing and Competing with the Wolves

Introduction

Haier, the home appliance brand, started from scratch just 17 years ago. Today it is the number one home appliance brand in China with the largest market share. In 2001 the Haier brand was valued at 43.6 billion yuan. Its growth rate of 78 per cent over the past 17 years has attracted the interest and attention of the world business community: in August 2001 Forbes *magazine ranked Haier sixth among the world's top ten manufacturers of white appliances.*

With such a record of growth, it is hard to believe that Haier's predecessor, Qingdao Refrigerator Plant, was almost bankrupt at one time. In 1984 this plant was severely in debt to the tune of 1,470,000 yuan. Despite changing plant directors three times in quick succession, the company's deterioration could not be halted. It was at the end of that year that Zhang Ruimin (its present CEO) was assigned the position of plant director. We are told that it was the time of the Spring Festival and the plant did not have the money to pay its employees for the Spring Festival holidays. Zhang himself went to the nearby countryside in the freezing winter weather to borrow money to pay the employees. Those were Haier's difficult beginnings.

In this chapter, Zhou Yunjie and Su Fangwen from Haier recount how, since those wintry days, the company's fortunes have changed dramatically under the leadership of Zhang Ruimin.

Early recognition of the importance of branding

Companies in China's present market economy face the challenge of 'sustainable development'. The average life span of US enterprises is 40 years, about half of the life span of a man. Chinese statistics show that, since the reform and opening of the market, the life span of Chinese appliance plants has been less than five years. What is the reason for this big gap? We at Haier feel that one of the main reasons is the lack of attention to branding by Chinese companies.

Back in 1984, Chinese people had no concept of branding. Everyone was in the business of just 'selling'. That is why we hardly have any famous Chinese brands today. What the Chinese market has to realize is that a brand is the lifeline of an enterprise. Once a brand becomes well-known and established, it will drive profitable growth of the company. Whether a brand is or is not well-known cannot be judged by votes or tests. Ultimate approval lies with the market. We have a saying at Haier that 'no well-known brand exists within the walls of an enterprise'.

Adopting a brand strategy has therefore played a critical role in Haier's turnaround. During those difficult times, we analyzed the refrigerator market and the competition. One point became very clear – there was no refrigerator of a 'well-known brand' in the market. As we understood it, a 'well-known brand' was one with the highest quality amongst competition and was the leader of market and consumption trends. With this insight, we decided to begin branding Haier and its products not only to influence, but also to head, the overall development of the industry. It was because our CEO, Zhang, prioritized branding that today Haier has become the most well-known and reputable brand in China.

Haier's three phases of brand building

Our brand building efforts have comprised three phases, each constituting a successful strategic transformation of the company. The first period from 1984 to 1991 involved creating the brand name of Haier. The second period from 1991 to 1998 involved a diversification strategy – extending production from refrigerators to all lines of home appliances. The third period since 1998 has involved the internationalization strategy – to turn Haier into an international brand name.

Phase 1 – building Haier into a well-known brand

Smashing refrigerators to create a quality-conscious mindset

In 1984 demand for refrigerators was much higher than supply. A quota coupon for a refrigerator could be sold for 1,000 yuan, let alone the refrigerator itself. Anything that came off the production line could sell, so there was no incentive for manufacturers to ensure quality control. Quantity was more important than quality. Because of this high demand, it was very common to sell refrigerators that were graded A, B, C or even off-grade.

At Haier we decided to adopt a different approach. For the first seven years we concentrated on creating a team of employees who would be skilled in making high-quality refrigerators. We adopted the principle that 'a defective product is a waste product.' For the first time, we re-tested refrigerators that had already been designated ready for sale and found 76 appliances with defects. Most employees wanted to buy these defective appliances at a discount but chief executive Zhang had a different idea. He believed that destroying the machines would make a deep impact on employees. So, even though the 76 refrigerators could be graded B or C and sold, they were put together and the people who were responsible for the defects were told to smash them!

At that time, refrigerators were very expensive, costing about two years of an employee's total salary. Zhang announced: 'Since we've had no idea of quality control here in this plant before, this is not your fault, but my fault. This time, management's monthly pay will be deducted for the errors. And I will not take a penny of my pay. But, from today, you will be responsible for defects. In the future whoever allows defects will be punished by pay deduction.'

The creation of this quality-conscious mindset has been very important for the building of the Haier brand. A lack of quality control could have led to Haier failing to be competitive in overseas markets. A *Far East Economic Review* reporter once remarked that the sledgehammer that was first used to destroy those defective refrigerators is actually the hero behind Haier's development. This hero is now on display in the Haier showroom.

Being market-oriented

Besides quality, a market-oriented mindset within the company also helps to build the brand. We have trained our salespeople to believe that the only low season is the low season that exists in their minds, not in the market. This prevents complacency from setting in. For example, summer is the low season for washing machine sales, and salespeople of most other manufacturers return to their plants to wait until the next peak season. Our salespeople and technicians, on the other hand, decided to develop a new model called the Haier Little Genius. With a capacity of only 1.5kg, it is the smallest model in the world and differentiates itself from other 5kg capacity washing machines that consume too much water and electricity in the summer. We first launched Little Genius in Shanghai because people in Shanghai have higher consumption levels and are very particular about cleanliness and tidiness. This model was then promoted widely across China. Over 1 million appliances were sold in two years.

To develop a market-oriented mindset, we practise another principle as well – that of saying 'no' to yourself before someone else says 'no' to you. For example, we found imitations of our Little Genius generation 1 model only six months after its launch. We sued the imitators and, at the same time, moved on to Little Genius generation 2 and 3 models to keep our leading position in the market. Since then, we have had 12 generations of Little Genius.

In another example, chief executive Zhang once found the local farmers in Sichuan using Haier washing machines to wash their sweet potatoes. Our technicians wanted to teach the farmers how to use the washing machines properly. But Zhang told them, 'Develop a washing machine to meet this market need.' The development of our sweet potato washing machine has given Haier an additional market share. We think it is important to be able to make the cake (that is, the market) by ourselves. So long as we can enjoy the cake, it does not have to be big.

Meeting the flying needs of customers

Market needs change very fast. Let's take shooting as an analogy. If the problems that our customers have with their home appliances are considered targets, then trying to solve them is like trying to shoot down not a fixed target, nor a floating target, but a flying target. How do we do this effectively? Our R&D technicians are not paid a salary. Their earnings depend on how many problems they discover for customers and what they do with the problems – that is, transform them into R&D subjects, commercialize the results and increase our market share. When we research consumers' needs, we have two governing principles: (1) to humanize designs; (2) to simplify designs. Consumers want easy and fast application, not complicated technology. We reserve the complicated job of research and development for ourselves in order to simplify the operation for our customers.

We once acquired a refrigerator plant that was strong in technology. The head of the factory asked chief executive Zhang: 'We are much stronger than you in technology, so why are our refrigerators not selling as well as yours?' Zhang answered, 'Your strong point is that you have good technology. Your weak point is that your technology is too good! Your technical people are confined to their labs and are not focused on the market. They are working, but not on the needs of customers.'

Phase 2 – diversification of the Haier brand

Keeping a third eye on opportunities

In the transformation from a planned economy to a market economy, enterprises in China need to have three eyes open:

– one eye focused internally on the employees to build their loyalty

- one eye focused on the customers to maximize their satisfaction
- a third eye focused on policy.

We began to consider diversifying in 1992. But the time wasn't right. When Deng Xiaoping made his speech in the south of China later in the year, we used this opportunity to start construction of the Haier Industrial Park. Then in 1997 when government policy encouraged mergers and acquisitions (M & As), we grasped the opportunity and entered into M & As with 18 different enterprises thereby allowing expansion at a very low cost. Some were actually free deals offered by local governments.

For instance, Haier entered the TV industry and the PC industry via M & As. The same goes for our overseas operations. During the period of financial crisis in Southeast Asia, we stepped up our advertising efforts in Southeast Asian markets. Our analysis showed it was not that consumers did not want household appliances but that they were holding back their money for future purchases. So we grasped the opportunity. We advertised and promoted when most global enterprises cancelled their advertising and at a time when advertising costs were only one-third of what they were before the financial crisis hit. When the economy started to recover, our sales increased dramatically as did our brand awareness.

Extending the Haier brand

Without extending the brand, Haier's market share and profitability cannot increase. However, extension cannot be sustained without a strong brand. By 1991 we had been making refrigerators for seven years. We had built up a quality team and a proven management system. The Haier legend had started with our refrigerator brand and this brand fame now laid the foundation for our diversification.

Sales of our refrigerators in 1991 amounted to 830 million RMB (100 million USD) with a net profit of 40 million RMB (4.6 million USD). From 1992 to 1995 we introduced the Haier brand name into new categories such as large coolers and air conditioners. By 1994 Haier's total sales revenue was 2.56 billion RMB (320 million USD) with a net profit of 200 million RMB (23 million USD). In 1997 Haier entered the black household electrical appliance market. In 1999 the Haier PC appeared on the market.

At present, Haier products cover all fields of household appliances – white, black and brown, from 69 different categories with 10,800 different models. Haier's image as a household appliance empire has become firmly rooted in the Chinese consumer's mind, along with the following key image characteristics: 'innovation, perfection, sincerity, responsibility and dignity'.

In extending the Haier brand name, we have followed three principles:

- The extension should be based on Haier's brand advantage.
- The new product category should be closely related to existing categories in terms of technology, sales and category classification.
- The new product should have good market prospects – that is, it will allow Haier to become one of the top three in the market in the shortest time.

With these principles, Haier has been able to extend into related categories without much difficulty. New products are able to use Haier's existing brand attractiveness to lever themselves substantial market space at lower cost, faster speeds and with a greater chance of success than competitors. The success of our new products also has a positive feedback effect on our existing products.

To Haier there is no difference between core and non-core business. Different categories have different advantages. Therefore in 2002 Haier also decided to branch out into the area of finance in co-operation with New York Life Insurance and other internationally well-known institutes. Overall, our brand advantage has played a very critical role in our business extensions.

Phase 3 – internationalization of the Haier brand

Our internationalization phase has three stages: the seeding stage, the rooting stage and the harvesting stage.

The seeding stage is about Haier, the brand, and gaining approval in the international market. Our strategy is not just to earn more foreign currency but, more importantly, to earn brand reputation. To us this means starting off in the most challenging, demanding territories and establishing the brand name there before expanding to developing countries. For example, in order to enter the German market in 1990, we spent one and a half years on the certification of our products. When we brought our products to Germany after certification, the German dealers thought it was impossible that products from a Chinese company that had just learned how to make refrigerators could enter their market. So we removed the trademarks from four of our refrigerators and did the same to four of the German refrigerators, and let our dealers test them.

Without the trademarks, the dealers couldn't tell the difference. They started to order from Haier. Soon after we began exporting to Germany, testing organizations in Germany conducted an overall quality test on all local and imported refrigerators. The test results ranked Haier top in quality. What was amazing was that we did not have to use a price war strategy to enter the international market. Instead, we relied on the quality of our products and on how the local consumers identify with Haier, the brand. We have done the same thing with the US market.

The second stage is our rooting stage. We call it 'three at one' – that is, localization of design, production and marketing. We have achieved this in both the US and Europe. Currently Haier accounts for 35 per cent of the US market for small refrigerators. We have set up a plant in South Carolina which is our biggest US investment in terms of capital and land area. We have also set up a design centre in Los Angeles to localize designs and a marketing centre in New York that is growing very rapidly.

The third stage is the harvesting stage. We call it 'three integration and one innovation', which means making use of local human resources and capital to integrate Haier's culture with the local culture and promoting the localized brand.

At Haier we have always valued the culture and customs of each country and region we enter. Whether it is Haier in China, the US, Europe or the Middle East, each operation has a consistent, yet unique, style of its own.

Haier's courage to explore – strategies and markets

If you examine our three phases of brand building, you will see that our strategies have always matched the leading management concepts on the international market. When quality-driven management was dominant worldwide during the 1980s, we attached great significance to quality control at that time. In the 1990s strategic emphasis moved on to enterprise restructuring at which point we seized the opportunity to build the overall structure and scale of our enterprise. The year 2000 was the year of speed, and we placed emphasis on internationalization.

We believe that unless an enterprise defines its strategy or positioning, it will find it difficult to grow. We also believe that strategies cannot be defined without an innovative way of thinking. Many of our strategies have not been understood by others and have been attacked. For instance, some critics say that there is enough 'meat to eat' in the domestic market and ask why Haier needs to get a share of the international market.

We think that if you don't have enough courage to explore, you won't have enough 'meat to eat'. What differentiates us from others is that we always expect our enterprise to grow to a higher level through continuous effort. There are two questions to be answered. First, what is our goal? Our goal is to become a world-famous brand. Only by striving to reach that goal can we stay ahead of others. And it is only when we can rapidly implement our defined strategy that we can step beyond it, that we can devote time to futuristic innovations. So the second question is how can we execute more rapidly? That is mainly achieved through our corporate culture which encourages employees to engage in continuous improvement.

Success to an enterprise is like an oasis in the desert, very possibly overlooked unless you expand your horizons and explore. Only with constant development, constant discovery of new oases and constant exploration in the desert can the enterprise survive.

Haier's core values

Quality and service – the two bases of competitiveness of the Haier brand

Quality and service are two values on which our brand is based. We believe that these two values form the basis for our competitiveness.

Running through our entire system of quality management is one simple principle of 'Clear Everyday and Improve Everyday'. Finish the tasks of today with better quality than yesterday. Aim at a higher goal tomorrow than today. Every employee has a '3 E' card: 'EVERY ONE, EVERY DAY, EVERYTHING'. This card specifies and personalizes the company's general goal for each person. For instance, the refrigerator production process has 156 steps and 545 working areas. Each step and area is someone's responsibility, so that total quality is guaranteed. The employee's monthly pay is directly related to this card.

In the early days, to ensure quality we also linked the expansion of our production with improving the skill of our employees. In the beginning, when our employees were not sufficiently skilled, we kept production small, starting with only 10,000 appliances per year, then 30,000, then 50,000. Although the market demand for refrigerators was huge at that time, we sacrificed profit to guarantee quality. In 1989, when many refrigerator manufacturers struggled to survive and cut prices, Haier did the opposite, raising prices by 10 per cent. Business boomed. It was totally unexpected. It proved the success of our brand strategy of valuing quality.

Our other brand value is service. When market demand surpasses supply, quality has to be the core value of any well-known brand. When the demand–supply relationship shifts, it is service that makes the difference. Our idea of service is different to that of other enterprises. First, when we say service, it is not only after-sales service, but also pre-sale and during-sale service. Second, we believe that offering good service is not just about repairing, installing and troubleshooting, but also about understanding consumer needs and generating ideas for product development and improvement. Consumer problems are seen as further opportunities to create brand-new markets.

Let me give you an example of our service. When Haier staff install an air-conditioning unit for customers, they will put on shoe covers before entering the customer's house. They will cover the furniture with large cloths to keep it clean during installation. Then they will vacuum the floor after installation. Before they leave, customers will be asked to fill in a questionnaire on whether they are completely satisfied. Although these are small things, they serve to distinguish Haier's service from the competition. We have heard that customers sometimes use Haier as an example when they are complaining to other companies. They say, 'Why are you not serving us as Haier does?'

Right now, we also have an after-sales service hotline '9999' in all the big cities in China. All a customer has to do is make a phone call and Haier will do the rest. It serves as a 'bridge of heart' between Haier and the consumer. By doing all of this, we have won customers' respect and approval and also gained a brand reputation. This is an intangible wealth that Haier has built. It is also a source of power for us.

Brand loyalty – the resulting competitiveness of the Haier brand

The company's strategy of valuing quality and service has led to the building of consumer loyalty to the Haier brand. How does this loyalty manifest itself? Some consumers are proud to own Haier products. Some even regard their ownership of Haier products as a symbol of their social identity, status and taste. In recent years many appliance brands have tried promotions based on free gifts or price cuts. However, even when signs like '50% off (except Haier)' can be seen everywhere, Haier still manages to keep its top ranking in sales volume. This is evidence of the power of consumer loyalty to the Haier brand.

Loyal customers are also a market resource. With this resource, Haier is able work on expanding its market share continuously because loyal customers are a stable source of earnings. New customers are attracted by word-of-mouth and these existing customers' experiences of using our products.

Winning brand loyalty from our customers means that we, as an enterprise, first have to be loyal to our customers. We do a great deal to keep and cultivate consumer loyalty. For example, we carefully segment the market to differentiate market needs and we meet those needs with new products. On average, Haier launches one new product and two patent declarations every day. Since 1998 our new products have accounted for 75 per cent of the total sales revenue for the entire Haier Group.

Haier's charisma

In the beginning Haier was no more than a trademark that identified it as the maker of quality refrigerators. Today Haier has become a brand of rich substance. How did we get there?

Most companies know that advertising can increase brand awareness. But it doesn't follow that the more money is spent on advertising, the more powerful the brand becomes. We believe that a powerful brand image has three levels: brand awareness, brand trust and brand merit. Awareness alone is unsustainable unless it is backed up with brand trust and brand merit.

One of the things we did to enhance our brand image was to create 'The Brothers Haier' – a cartoon series of a mystical adventure based around the Haier brothers and their friends. The Haier brothers are two boys – one Chinese and one German, symbolizing the fact that Haier started business with technological investment from a German company called Liberhaier. They hold an ice cream between them, again symbolizing the fact that Haier started business manufacturing refrigerators. Starting from the Silk Road in China, they tour the world to save humans from disaster and to solve endless riddles about nature. With a theme of bravery and wisdom, the cartoon has become very popular amongst Chinese audiences and is soon going to debut on US TV.

Now when we export air-conditioning units to the European Union, French female consumers who have seen our cartoon actually ask us to add the sticker of the two brothers to the fan frame of the outdoor unit because it identifies the product as Haier.

More importantly, we also have a corporate slogan 'Sincerity For Ever' which encapsulates the inner meaning of the Haier brand. This slogan is about each Haier employee, each Haier member of staff who has contact with outsiders and each Haier product being regarded by customers and users as honest and real. 'Sincerity' is a characteristic that we want to be shared by the company, the employees and all Haier products, and we want to show this sincerity to consumers. No matter how the market changes, we make a promise to be sincere for ever. 'Sincerity For Ever', as a concept, has opened up a channel of communication – a way of creating an emotional relationship between ourselves and our customers – because sincerity is such a desirable quality and attitude between friends.

As a concept, however, sincerity is much more difficult to carry out than, say, product design or company image planning. In fact, the most difficult part of it is making each Haier employee protect the company's image of sincerity spontaneously. An employee's behaviour and the company's image are such interdependent things.

Haier's corporate culture

Haier's brand culture in China

The Haier brand culture originated with chief executive Zhang. Zhang has always regarded the building of corporate culture as one the most important duties of senior management and a greatly needed business qualification. In the early days of Haier's growth, he studied the writings of Mao, Lao Tze, Confucius and Sun Tze to provide himself with spiritual support. In the 1990s, he learnt the Western management wisdom of chief executives such as Jack Welch of GE.

As a result, Haier's corporate culture combines the best of Chinese traditional culture and Western modern management thinking. The liberty of the individual and the race to innovate characteristic of US enterprises are combined with the team spirit and diligent mindset of Japanese enterprises. This corporate culture and Zhang's resulting management team are one huge reason why Haier has managed to realize its dreams.

As Zhang himself says:

> Every successful enterprise has to have a very strong corporate culture to unite everybody together. Every enterprise of over a hundred years must have changed greatly except for its corporate spirit. It is a very powerful message. What is corporate culture? It is the corporate spirit, the corporate soul. If it never changes, if it is always living, the corporation will exist for ever.

Zhang also considers human talent as the strategic capital of the enterprise – the force that sustains the enterprise's development and its competitive advantage. People are the origin of corporate energy. People determine the development and success of an enterprise. Any corporate reform is actually the 'reform of the people'.

This is why, at Haier, we are committed to our people. We believe that 'everybody is talent' and everybody can self-surpass and self-improve. One practical implication of this is that we select candidates through open competition, after strict performance evaluations, paper tests and interview tests. Because of this system, front-line workers who are hardworking and have accumulated the appropriate experience can move to management positions. Young graduates after being trained in fieldwork can take up leadership responsibilities. A cycle of transition from old leadership to new is enabled. In this way, we break the traditional boundaries between professional qualifications and work experience as well as those between leadership positions and worker positions. The fairness and openness in our HR policies activate people's energies and distinguish talent.

It was Zhang who initiated the philosophy that 'quality products can only be produced by quality people'. As such, Haier conducts regular training for management and employees. The development of a home appliance company based on just improving quantity and speed of production is not sustainable. Employees' qualifications need to be 'pushed' upwards, so that not only will the job be done better, but business growth will also be maintained at an optimum speed. If talent is not cultivated to keep up with the scaling up of the business, any apparent success achieved can quickly become an illusion.

Haier's brand culture overseas

Walking into the bright workshops of our US plant, you will find the pervasive atmosphere of the Haier culture most impressive. Slogans such as 'EXCELLENT PEOPLE PRODUCE EXCELLENT PRODUCTS' and 'THE CUSTOMER IS ALWAYS RIGHT' shout at you from the walls. These slogans demonstrate vividly how the American Haier employees understand the Haier culture in their own language.

The fashion among Chinese Haier employees to use cartoons to express Haier philosophies has also spread to their counterparts in North Carolina. American employees at Haier use artworks and poems to display their experience of being part of the Haier Family. For example, one employee, Kelvin Bradley, drew a car broken in half to express his understanding of Haier's quality philosophy: that a 1 per cent defect in the factory is a 100 per cent disaster at home for the customer. Another employee, Gloria Hood, drew two luxuriant trees side-by-side to express the belief that both China Haier and US Haier are members of the same Haier Family. This drawing was later printed in *Haier People*, the corporate newsletter, and it was selected by the Chinese Haier employees for a Special Award.

Our American employees have also managed to agree with their Chinese counterparts on Haier management standards. For Americans, wearing a uniform, turning down music during working hours, and not smoking in the working area is hardly 'normal' practice. However, after realizing that such strict management policies are what made Haier a world-famous enterprise in such a short time, our US employees now agree that Haier needs to have a particular culture and management style.

More and more Americans are proud and honoured to work with Haier. In fact, because of the contribution that Haier has made to the regional economy, the government of South Carolina named a road 'Haier Road' in our honour. It is the only road in the US named after a Chinese enterprise.

Being the wolf rather than the sheep

In the past there was a saying very popular among Chinese enterprises: 'We are heading toward the world.' But with China's entry into the WTO, the world is heading towards us, whether we like it or not. If we handle it well, by 2010 there should be many world-famous Chinese brands on the international market. By then, China will not only be, as the media is fond of saying, 'the manufacturing plant for the world', but will also possess a group of strong, international and highly competitive enterprises.

In meeting this world, many enterprises can't decide which is bigger – the opportunity or the challenge. At Haier we believe that opportunity and challenge are two sides of the same coin. There is challenge in opportunity and opportunity in challenge. In fact, opportunities can only be found when challenges are being confronted. Conversely, it is only when opportunities are grasped to speed up development that the organization gets to confront even bigger challenges.

Our chief executive Zhang once gave a speech in which he introduced the concept of 'dancing with wolves and competing with wolves' which generated strong reactions from the media: 'We have to become a wolf to dance with the wolves. If we position ourselves as sheep, we will be left with only one possibility – to be swallowed by the wolves.' When international companies expand to developing countries, their philosophy is always to be the ultimate winner, exterminating all competition. Chinese enterprises have to recognize this fact and take on the mantle of a 'wolf' to survive.

How can this be done? By fully understanding the international rules of competition and learning how to compete within that framework. If you do not do this, you will not understand how global enterprises compete and you will have no chance of surviving the battle.

Haier in the future – breaking down walls

The battle that Haier has to face in the future is going to become more intense. Accession to the WTO will impact on Chinese household appliance manufacturers in two ways. First, foreign companies will increase their investment in the Chinese market. Some companies that already have plants in China will move their headquarters here. They will transform from enterprises that only invest in Chinese production to localized Chinese-style enterprises. Once they are able to take root in China, they will begin to have the same advantages of low cost as Chinese companies in addition to their existing superior technology. Moreover, they can also start building sales, distribution and service networks in order to match the familiarity that Chinese companies claim to have with the local market. Second, foreign markets will start to raise the barriers to entry for Chinese enterprises. For example, if Chinese products cannot meet certain technical standards, these foreign markets will say to them, 'It's not that we don't permit your entry but that you do not qualify.'

To prepare for these challenges, we will need to knock down two walls, otherwise we will not be able to enter the age of transformation, let alone be transformed. These two walls are: (1) the wall between enterprises (not just that between Chinese enterprises, but that between Chinese and foreign enterprises); and (2) the wall within enterprises.

With the rise of the Internet economy, the most valued resources can be found online – for instance, outsourcing partners. Many products are not necessarily profitable if you make them yourself, but you can find a profitable solution through outsourcing. Take Haier's partnership with Sanyo of Japan as an example. We cross-sell products using each other's marketing networks. Haier also partners with European companies in the same manner. Although we are still competitors in the market, we have become 'competitive co-operators' as well. Unless Chinese companies break down inter-enterprise walls, they will be isolated. The most critical challenge after entry into the WTO is for Chinese enterprises to become more open systems.

The second wall to break down is that between the enterprise's internal functional departments. Western companies have experienced a history of industrial revolution and corporate evolution of over 100 years. They have had extraordinary experience with internal management practices. Our development has to happen almost overnight. At present, our internal structures are quite weak; they are developed from old management thinking where authority and instructions flow vertically downwards, pyramid-fashion.

Instant reaction to market changes is not possible with such a structure. We have to restructure the workflow. Market information should not go from the bottom to the top of the pyramid for decision-making. Everyone should be able to interface with the market directly. In other words, the organization should not be defined in terms of relationships between superiors and inferiors or that between colleagues. It should, instead, be defined in terms of relationships with the market. Everybody needs to face this market. Everybody needs to be responsible for his market goal.

Currently we have 30,000 employees. In the past we had one form of financial reporting only – the sort that combined one for assets and liabilities, one for profit and loss and one for cash flow. Now we have over 30,000 reporting sheets. Each employee regards himself or herself almost as a company. He or she is not facing his or her manager or colleague; he or she is facing the market.

Chinese enterprises may not be able to compete with globally famous companies in terms of human resource, capital or technology, but there is one advantage that we can build – speed. With these two walls knocked down, externally we will have the best outsourced resources at hand and internally we will have the ability to react very quickly to the market. We will be able to satisfy customer needs ahead of others. We will be the wolves.

COMMENTARY

Haier represents to us the evolution that most Chinese enterprises are experiencing or will experience – the transformation from being a high-volume, low-cost original equipment manufacturer to becoming a differentiated brand owner. This demands a shift from 'pushing' as many products off the production line as possible and 'pushing' them out on the market to 'pulling' in consumers with the attraction and promise of one's brand.

The watershed point for Haier was no doubt when chief executive Zhang Ruimin physically smashed refrigerators that were defective in front of his employees, even though the industry practice was to grade them slightly lower and sell them nevertheless, sometimes back to the employees themselves. It was a zero tolerance message that he was sending out, and it worked. Quality levels improved dramatically, giving the brand the necessary foundation that it needed to build its image.

In developed markets, branding is the battleground because it is assumed that products offer the same level of quality. It is mostly in terms of their different values and emotional proposition that consumers see a difference, say, between a Bang & Olufsen and a Sony television. In China, quality is not always assured and companies will need to follow what Haier has managed to achieve in order to prevent their brands from appearing to make empty promises. This means, first, setting a quality benchmark, and then transforming the company into a more market-oriented, customer-focused enterprise before finally looking for opportunities to extend the brand into new businesses and new markets.

Haier has tackled each stage systematically, proving itself in terms of quality against German refrigerators, innovating within China with the Little Genius washing machine and finally building its own plant in the US which it runs just like its other plants in China.

These transition stages are necessary steps for Chinese companies hoping to make their mark on the global markets. And international customers will also need time to accept that improvement is taking place and that 'Made in China' is no longer a suggestion of cheap, low-quality manufacturing. Perhaps this explains why Haier is so confident about taking on the challenge of the US market. It knows it has laid its foundations well. It can compete on the international battleground of branding. Now it really needs to work on the personality and charisma of its brand offer to ensure lasting impact and success.

4 | SINA: Brand Shifting™ for a Connected World

Introduction

SINA is a leading Chinese Internet media and services company offering Internet media and entertainment services, an enterprise solutions platform and telecom access and fee-based services through its three major business lines: Sina.com, Sina.net and Sina Online.

The company was founded in Silicon Valley, California, in 1995 and merged with Beijing-based Stone Rich Sight in 1999, having previously absorbed a news aggregator called Sinanet. Today, SINA boasts more than 60 million registered users worldwide and over 3 million active paid users for SINA's fee-based services. To the world's population of Chinese, the brand is the most recognized Internet brand name.

SINA's portal, Sina.com, currently offers online news, entertainment, e-commerce and other services, and has a Chinese language network of 15 localized web sites targeting Greater China and overseas Chinese in four countries: China, Taiwan, Hong Kong and North America. Each country has its own local content.

Internet use in China is set to grow rapidly with estimates that China will have over 37 million Internet users by 2005. But, like many Internet portals in China, Sina.com faces challenges as it strives to achieve growth. The first challenge lies in China's general shortage of PCs in areas outside the major cities. In 2000, registered users made up less than 1 per cent of the population although that figure had almost trebled by 2002. Other obstacles include the high cost of accessing the Internet. It is estimated that, in China, the cost to get on-line is about 30 times higher than in the US. Another issue is the tight control that the government has over the sector: China content is often supervised for political reasons, although the government has recently been showing signs of shifting from controlling information to using it to China's advantage, as well as granting approval for users to access some Western news sites.

Internet businesses in China also face increasing challenges as the sector converges and new forms of competition enter the market such as telecoms operators. With these developments come the pressing need to form new partnerships and joint ventures. Technologies are advancing and user demographics are continually shifting. All these features create a market that is difficult to track and even harder to predict.

SINA's chief executive, Daniel Mao, now tells us about the company's efforts to survive in a sector that is undergoing evolutionary and radical shifts in all areas. The key according to Mao is to ensure that the company's culture is driven by an entrepreneurial spirit and a willingness to investigate new ways of doing things, such as introducing approaches to consumer understanding based on researching user experience.

Being a web-based brand ultimately means being a brand in flux, and injecting any degree of stability into the brand demands the spirit of a true entrepreneur.

The eye of the storm

With the merger of the two companies, we wanted to have a name that was meaningful in English and Chinese. We chose SINA because the services we provide are targeted to the world's largest population group, the Chinese, and SINA is the Latin root for 'Chinese'. The second reason for the name is its proximity to the word *Xinlang*, meaning 'new wave'.

The way SINA looks today is very different from how it looked when we set out three years ago, having undergone a series of rapid and evolutionary changes.

The story begins with SINA as a simple portal, Sina.com. The first change saw us reposition the portal to a community so that our audience would think of Sina.com as a place you could join and stay, rather than as a gateway to somewhere else. We created a new tag-line 'destination site for Chinese world-wide' to support the move.

Today, that single website, Sina.com, has become the corporate SINA, an all-encompassing umbrella under which sit Sina.com, Sina.net and Sina Online, with cross-media and fee-based services now making up the core business.

To understand the evolution of the services that we provide, we can think about SINA in this analogy: imagine SINA is a kitchen. In the early days when we were a simple portal, with on-line content that could be accessed for free, it was like SINA, the kitchen, was preparing and distributing food for free. We then thought 'instead of dishing out free content, why don't we partner with magazines and book publishers and get them to publish some of our content so it can be sold.' This was like SINA the kitchen, instead of giving out its food for free, freezing that food and giving it to frozen food processors to reformulate and reproduce. That is how we diversified into content processing.

The move demanded a new kind of expertise. We partnered with the cable TV operator Sun Television Cybernetworks Holdings (Sun TV), to boost our broadband R&D capabilities. We also joined up with China Telecom and

China Mobile to share with them our processing capabilities, and to access their distribution channels.

Next we opened the seated restaurant which is the fee-based, customized service. We then went into licensed-based banqueting services targeting corporate clients as well as various governments.

For the end user, the difference between the seated restaurant and the free meal is this: in the seated restaurant you create your own menu to suit your own taste – maybe Chinese cuisine or Cantonese cuisine – and, of course, the service is good so it's an appealing offer. But if you want the free meal instead, you sit at your PC and type Sina.com. Of course the free meal includes advertising and other information which may not be so relevant to you.

How the sector is changing

This pattern of evolution is a familiar one in the Internet sector as more and more companies move into fee-based services to supplement advertising revenue. In fact, I can say from experience that the cardinal sin in the Internet age is for a company to blindly offer free services. It is because of this that competitors in the market are having to swallow losses, although there are signs of change. In the US, for example, out of the three original market leaders, Yahoo!, Excite and Infoseek, only Yahoo! remains. Excite went bankrupt and Infoseek was bought by Disney, which dissolved it. Why did Yahoo! survive? Partly because the company began charging people for e-mails and other services.

Differentiation through specialization

Another shift is in the focus of the content we provide. In China, for instance, where SINA is market leader, followed by Sohu and then East, although Sohu continues to believe in the free meal model, East now occupies a niche market position as an online gaming provider. This is symbolic of things to come; in future, there will be no pure portal companies in the marketplace and each service provider will differentiate through the offer of specialist services.

For SINA, positioned as a comprehensive media company, we have to be both a horizontal media company and specialists in particular areas, such as finance, entertainment, sports and technology.

Shifting the focus on to the quality of information creates certain challenges. For example, in terms of competition, our media site will be up against media giants like CNN or the Wall Street Journal, and our technology site will be facing AOL which has recently partnered with technology leader Legend. So you can either form a partnership with an established online content provider or develop your own site. But whichever you decide to do, the diversification has to be sustainable: you have to acquire or partner with people who are the best in that particular field. You cannot do it yourself. This means that the structure and substance of the brand has to change in line with the offer.

The pattern of convergence

I tend to look at the evolution of the Internet sector from what I call the TMT perspective. The first T stands for Technology, the M for Media and the second T for Telecoms. In terms of the whole consolidation process in the last two to three years, AOL Taiwan is one of the best examples of the model. Starting with an offer of technology, moving into media and then into telecoms, Microsoft has also joined the growing ranks of TMT companies. Microsoft also invests in satellite telecommunications. The key point about the TMT model is that, to be sustainable, the structures that support it must radically change as each new sector is entered into.

For example, using the kitchen analogy, the banquet service, Sina.net, is a totally different ball game to the free meal service. Its proposition is not about the volume of food processing, it is about the ambience, the music and the stage design. SINA is not in a position to provide these services; we don't have that competency. So we have to recruit people to do that.

Anchoring the brand

You have also to consider the brand. Can it sustain a propositional shift? Does it have sufficient depth? If you are a free meal provider and you plan to move into areas like banqueting services, does the brand have adequate meaning in terms of an emotional connection with its audience to survive with its credibility intact? Would you trust a free meal provider to serve your wedding banquet?

That is why it is important to monitor the brand's positioning and rework the substance behind it so that the move does not appear contrived. For SINA, it is our vision and values that drive our connection with the customer. They remain constant, yet have sufficient depth of meaning to transfer across the business, so that our connection with the customer is maintained and reinforced as we expand.

As mentioned earlier, one of the reasons behind the choice of the name SINA was its proximity to the Chinese word *Xinlang* meaning 'new wave', because SINA's vision is to be like a new wave – a new wave that flows forever. In other words, we want to become an integral part of everyday life for all Chinese throughout the world – a necessity like air or, indeed, like water.

'Xinlang Benteng Buxi' – 'the wave that flows forever'. That is SINA's defining vision that carries us through the changes.

The values which drive our behaviour are also fixed. The first is trustworthiness, and that is something that is earned through the provision of consistent quality. It's a similar story with Yahoo! and its English-speaking audience: Yahoo! is where you check out a price quote or use e-mail. The trust is there, even to submit your credit card details, for example, to buy flowers. Trustworthiness is very important and that does not change.

Another of our core values is about expecting change – real, qualitative change. This, too, is critical for if our audience stereotyped us as being providers of a certain set of services, sustainable expansion would be difficult. We therefore work hard to create an image of SINA as being synonymous with energy and change – as a symbol of the future. The strapline 'Xinlang Benteng Buxi' reinforces that value.

There are other values – for instance, to try to reach consensus in decision-making. That is an Eastern style of management. We also encourage teamwork and individual accountability. But perhaps the most important feature of SINA's internal culture is the way in which we try to maintain and nurture the entrepreneurial spirit. That spirit has been one of the defining characteristics throughout our development, helping us not only to recognize and plot the changes in the environment, but also to devise innovative solutions that fit the needs of our audience.

In fact, if you really think about the whole history of media, and about the success stories such as Murdoch, Redstone or Universal, that success can be traced back to an entrepreneurial spirit rather than to the company chief executive's claim of good management skills. In fact, the media industry is a very different industry, especially when it marries with technologies such as satellite and cable TV. This is because although a true entrepreneurial spirit is not about jumping on a bandwagon, in the media sector it appears that if one jumps, everybody jumps. Entrepreneurialism in the media sector has to be about having the flexibility and the energy to change quickly in response to changing technologies and, indeed, changes in demand.

Customer understanding as a source of competitive advantage

We have defined the evolution of the brand SINA, how it can be sustained, what must be preserved and what has to change. Now we must look at the underlying causes driving that change. Diversification and attaining the status of TMT was not something we planned when we set out three years ago. For a young industry like this one, the future is impossible to map out.

Not surprisingly, it is the understanding of the customer and his or her needs that is the energy driving the changes. For this reason, SINA is not going to create an ocean – just new waves. When you consider the people who use the Internet and the suppliers of Internet services, the speed of shifts in demand is much faster than the speed at which the supply side changes. In terms of users, the Internet revolution is moving very quickly, from 15–18-year-olds to 20–50-year-olds. Changes in demand are not about quantity; they are about demography.

The development of the Internet is like the development of the TV – but compressed to just three years. Suddenly your grandmother is using the remote control to watch MTV. And things are changing so fast that it is very hard to anticipate with 100 per cent certainty the nature of the changes. What is more, that development is not continuous; it is piecemeal. That is why we describe our development as being like waves – it is not a steady current. And it is also rather like rock climbing: when you reach for the next foothold, you might fall. That makes us very cautious.

The speed of change also makes sustainability critical. If you look ahead five to ten years in the future, the waves we, or anybody else, create, compared with the whole ocean, are nothing. Who cares about the waves last year in Hawaii?

How did we become sustainable? In the media domain, it is possible to get into content creation, content processing and content distribution. We will not be moving into content creation because I don't consider myself to be a creative person; I am an engineer by training, so we have focused on content processing – the kitchen. Content processing is easy for an engineer because it is mass production – you just get a few computers and a few chefs and they go away and process. But you can only process so much free of charge, so we entered into partnership with people who allowed us to get into content distribution.

If SINA was a spider, the move into distribution was like giving us the legs. It is very interesting that the Internet is called the web because, if you look at a spider, it has a huge body but that huge body without a few thin legs can do nothing. In the early days, our kitchen was like the huge body but without the distribution it had no legs. We couldn't sustain it.

The distribution of content has enabled us to build an understanding of our users' needs giving us the competitive advantage. That understanding, as I have said, is possible because we have a corporate culture that nurtures the entrepreneur. A fighting spirit and energy has to predominate over a general desire to run the mundane day-to-day business.

Insights into the customer are derived from a number of sources. First, we have millions of users providing us with a lot of data to research. That gives us the scientific insights. Our human insights come from observing other technologies – for example, mobile phones or cable TV. Our own personal beliefs also play a part. For example, I do not use a Palm Pilot – a fact which people may find surprising given that I am a Stanford alumnus and I have been in Silicon Valley for 15 years. But I don't have one simply because I want to experience what people who don't have one experience – the late adopters. I make do with pieces of paper to record phone numbers which, of course, I sometimes lose, so appointments get missed. Once you understand the attitudes and experiences of 80 per cent of the population, it is easier to produce something relevant to that population.

I am not representative of the mass population, so I have to force myself into that category. By doing that, I have learnt, for instance, that if something is too complex, people won't adopt it. But if they do get into it, that creates a huge driving force for the marketplace. Consider the growth of SMS. Most of my friends – just ordinary people – use their cell-phone to send text messages in Chinese and they are much more adept at it than me. You might also find an 18-year-old girl, a college fresher, punching a few keys to send a text. Yet she does not even use a computer. She hates computers. The popularity of SMS is proven.

In the beginning, we recruited people who were brave enough to jump into this revolution – the young Stanford BAs and the Beijing top school graduates. Because of the changing needs of the business we began recruiting people with 20 years' experience in the top four advertising agencies. Now we are looking for people who have investment banking experience or telecoms experience – people with grey hair.

We are also trying to recruit more female executives because we want to create a management team that reflects the talent pool needed for market growth. A few years ago, Internet users in China were typically 80 per cent male, aged 16. Now that figure is more like 60 per cent male, aged 25–26 years. This means that women represent 40 per cent of total users. And I can predict that, three years from now, the audience might be aged 30–32 and 50 per cent male as it is in the US right now. So, although I may understand the experience from a non-Palm Pilot user's view point, for insights into the psychology and Internet requirements of women, I have to rely on inputs from my colleagues.

All this is necessary for getting closer to our audience and creating more personalized products. Between the ages of 30 and 32, individual differences between males and females are far greater than between, for example, a group of 18-year-olds at college. There is greater diversity. At 18, if you buy a pair of Gucci sunglasses, everybody else will buy the same pair. Even for a 25-year-old there is a lot of peer pressure to conform. By the age of 30, however, the personality begins to become more defined, more distinct. So my thinking is this: three years from now the typical profile will be 30–32 or even 35 years. These people's preferences will then become the driving force for service providers and our management team will have to decide which products and services would best suit their needs. To adequately meet such a diverse set of needs will be a challenge.

Nevertheless, the Internet is by far the most suitable medium for personalizing a service. On the one hand, you have privacy, but you also receive personal attention. The alternatives – newspapers, terrestrial, cable and satellite TV, radio, books and magazines – have a fixed content. They may offer a wide choice but have limitations in terms of relevance. For this reason, I believe the Internet is the future.

But, just as with the popularity of SMS, the future is impossible to predict. We thrive because we are versatile, and that, as I say, is because we have a very strong entrepreneurial spirit. We are not smarter than anybody else, just practical. In this business, if you stay still, you are doomed, yet if you move too fast, you overexpand with a similar end result. The sensible position is to stay in the centre and be ready to change in response to technological developments and changes in demand.

The future for SINA and its stakeholders

In the future I see SINA as becoming part of the everyday life experience of Chinese people throughout the world: from user experience to life experience; from SINA to SINA Everywhere. SINA is a comprehensive media information provider so whenever a Chinese person accesses any type of information, SINA will be there. In fact, 35 years from now I envisage that we will be all-media. An antique collector will pick up a newspaper and there will be a SINA column in it; a jogger using earphones will be experiencing some part of SINA. When that day arrives, SINA will indeed be like air or like water.

But SINA's vision isn't only for itself. SINA has been instrumental in pushing forward the development of an infant Chinese Internet industry on both sides of the Pacific. From day one we have tried to bridge the information gap that existed. We started as a free portal so everybody who could afford to get online could access SINA. We are dedicated to bridging the efforts of all communities of Chinese, in North America, in Tibet, in Beijing, Chang Hai, Taipei and those in Hong Kong.

Second, we are deeply committed to presenting China to the rest of the world in a way that can be trusted. I cannot do everything but if I can do just one thing right, that would be to let people know more about China in an honest and trustworthy way. Misunderstandings are always there, preconceptions are always there, but it is important to strive for objectivity and let other people make the analysis and the judgement. That is the main reason why we are not joining the content creation set: we want to let people's creativity and imagination fly. We do edit a little bit, so our own subjective judgements do creep in but we really try to preserve the original flavour as much as we can.

This stance is taken to support a belief in the importance of diversity, particularly in a world where everything is becoming globalized and homogenized. On the other hand, no single brand can do everything, so you consequently either have to limit yourself to certain areas of specialization or you create a family of brands.

In the media world, for example, there are about five or six conglomerates controlling 70 per cent of the market share. Do they do a good job in terms of music distribution, record publishing or book publishing? I don't think so. If, in two to three years' time, the Internet could be seen to bridge the gap between the needs of a globalized world and the needs of the individual, that would be very powerful. My personal view is that we are all very lucky to experience this phase of history. But, whilst we have to respect history, we also have to look into the future in order to really understand people. And so the content business is like the restaurant business, which is perhaps why the French, Italian and, indeed, the Chinese create the best gourmet food: they understand people's taste.

COMMENTARY

Brand Shifting™ is a familiar phenomenon in fast-moving sectors of industry such as web service providers. It is a term we use at Springpoint to describe the behaviour of brands in high-velocity markets where boundaries between businesses are breaking down and where sources of growth and wealth are unpredictable. The brand shifts its positioning in response to changes in the environment so that new opportunities can be seized. The emotional contract with the customer is set by the vision and values which must remain fixed.

Competitive brand shifting demands that managers adopt strategies that are loosely defined and flexible. 'We live on the edge', as Yahoo! founder Jerry Yang said, and survival demands that the company culture fosters and supports the entrepreneurial spirit and people's willingness to change. In these uncertain environments, the only source of lasting competitive advantage is an understanding of the customer.

In fact, the Internet offers unprecedented opportunities for getting to know the customer, and SINA is making the most of those opportunities by tracking its customers' online behaviours, purchase histories and preferences. By tapping into the actual user experience, the approach yields a rich bank of data that is invaluable for the development of a bespoke user experience. The challenge for SINA in the future will be to get its users to attach value to such a service and to pay for it.

From research such as this, SINA has understood, for example, that it can further its e-commerce objectives by building user communities around its websites. Consumers who use online community spaces such as chatrooms and bulletin boards are responsible for around two-thirds of online sales, despite accounting for only one-third of actual users. Empowering people to feel part of a community leads to sales.

Despite the recent bursting of the technology bubble and the demise of a number of e-businesses in China and around the world, analysts are optimistic about the future of China's Internet businesses, and China is poised to become the global leader in terms of online population as well as a world leader in e-commerce.

5 | TCL: Going Deeper with the Brand

Introduction

*The TCL Group is a multi-electronics group engaged in the research and develop-
ment, manufacture, sales and distribution of consumer electronic products, audio-
visual products (VCDs and TVs), domestic appliances, telephone equipment (fixed
and mobile), electronic accessories, batteries and IT products. The group is controlled
by TCL Holdings Corporation Ltd, a state-owned enterprise, and it has a Hong Kong
listed arm, TCL International Holdings Ltd, as well as a Shenzhen listed arm, TCL
Communications Equipment Share Co. Ltd.*

*Established in the 1980s, TCL started off by manufacturing and selling fixed-line
telephones. From 1990 to 1996 the company expanded into the field of electronic components and audio-visual products with colour televisions, building a strong brand
name and distribution network. From 1997 it entered the field of telecommunications, consumer electronics and information technology, and from 1998 to 2000 it
moved into information-oriented electronics and the Internet field. According to the
Chinese Ministry of Information Industry, the TCL Group today ranks fifth in the
list of China's top 100 electronics manufacturers based on sales revenues for the year
2001. It is China's number one television and mobile phone handset manufacturer.*

*TCL's rapid emergence in the Chinese market has been almost like a fairy tale. Mr
Li Dong Sheng, its chairman and president, attributes this to the fact that it has
behaved quite differently to a typical state-owned enterprise. Ranging from traditional household appliances to modern communication products, Mr Li talks about
how his management thinking and views on brand strategy have played their part in
TCL's growth.*

TCL's beginnings

My involvement with TCL started at the time of its founding. I joined the
company as a fresh graduate from Huanan Technological University. The
expansion and diversification of TCL's business since then are totally beyond
my expectations. Nor did I expect that I would become the president of the
company!

The name TCL was derived from 'Telephone Communication Limited', a joint venture company that was set up to manufacture fixed-line telephone equipment in the 1980s. It was one of the first Sino-foreign joint venture companies to be set up in China, and it was the success of TCL's telephone equipment business that first established TCL as a good brand name. At that time, TCL had three divisions, the Electronic Products Group, the Property Group and the Communications Group. In fact, the Electronic Products Group lagged behind the others in terms of sales because we had no market-leading products – at least until we spotted the opportunity in the market to make and sell big-screen colour television sets.

Initially we encountered many difficulties. The Chinese government, for instance, had stopped issuing manufacturing permits. Moreover, we lacked sufficient capital to build the necessary manufacturing facilities. But we managed to overcome these difficulties through the clever use of partnerships and resources. First, TCL entered into a joint venture with Great Wall Electronics to form TCL Electronics Sales Company to distribute our colour televisions throughout China. Then we subsequently established another joint venture company to acquire an existing manufacturing plant that already owned a permit to produce televisions.

The colour television market at that time was also dominated by foreign brands. Foreign brands held a 90 per cent share of the market because domestic companies simply did not have the capacity to manufacture enough units to meet demand. But by comparing the premium prices charged by the foreign companies against the spending power of the local consumer, we realized that there was a gap in the market for a lower-priced quality product. Into this gap we introduced our branded television set, priced at half the price of the foreign brands and offering a much larger screen. In this way, we were differentiated both in price and benefit. Our advertising campaign featured Liu Xiaoqing, the famous Chinese actress, as our spokesperson. In the process of doing all this, we stimulated market demand for big-screen colour television sets, knowing that the demand for big-screen televisions would be far greater than that for ordinary televisions. Since our colour televisions hit the market in 1992, our profits from that business have grown from 5 million RMB in 1993 to 70 million RMB in 1995 to 350 million RMB in 2001. We are now number one in terms of national sales.

In 1993, TCL was the first Chinese telecommunications company to be publicly listed. Since the year 2000 we have become the leader in the Chinese colour television market. In the mobile phone sector, our sales of mobile phones increased by 478 per cent from 2000–2001. In just three years, we beat all the foreign brands in China to become the number one player in mobile phones.

You could say that our leadership position in the television market provided the foundation and the initial impetus that we needed to flourish and expand into the company that we are. On a more personal level, it has also provided me with the wide experience (covering all areas of marketing, branding, sales, finance and management) that enables me to lead TCL today.

The beginning of brand strategy at TCL

TCL is a very young enterprise but it still needs to reinvent itself. In a sense, the company's development over the past 20 years mirrors, in miniature, the development of China. We are still exploring the best way forward to achieve our goal of becoming an internationally competitive enterprise.

If you were to ask when TCL started to develop a brand strategy, I would need to set this in the context of three stages that TCL experienced in its growth.

The first stage was when TCL was still a very small local enterprise. Our goals at that time were more basic: how to generate enough money, how to survive and how to build a foundation for growth as an enterprise. Our product categories were very narrow at that time. Frankly speaking, there was no strategy for branding at that stage of our development.

Then, during the period 1992–1998/99, the latter part of which was marked by the Asian financial crisis, we started to think more seriously about our strategy for branding. This was our second stage. At this point, we recognized that we had an opportunity to build our competitive advantage at a time when the Chinese economy was still financially stable and growing amidst the turmoil that was affecting the rest of Asia. Branding was an essential part of building our competitive advantage. In fact, it was during this stage that we became one of the first companies to engage an advertising consultancy in China to advise us on branding concepts, to give training courses to management on branding and to redesign our logo. At that time, branding concepts were still a very novel idea to most Chinese companies.

The third stage began in 2000 after I took part in the Shanghai Fortune Forum, an event attended by CEOs from all over the world. It was then that TCL started to operate with more of a long-term vision for the future because it was at this forum that I recognized the great need for a group of Chinese enterprises to play a more significant role on the international business platform. And the only way to achieve this was to have a long-term global vision rather than just a domestic vision.

Comparing Chinese companies to international companies is like comparing different classes of boxers. The Chinese company is the lightweight boxer, simple but agile and responsive. However, it is unable to withstand the heavy blows of a heavyweight boxer. In order to compete more effectively against the heavyweight boxer, the Chinese company needs to be nurtured and strengthened to grow into the heavyweight class and become globally competitive.

In the future, Chinese companies have a choice of three routes. The first is where the Chinese company is obliterated by the growing competition. The second route is where the Chinese company is subsumed into a world-class company. The third route is where the Chinese company becomes a world-class company itself. Most Chinese companies will go down the second route, but I would like TCL to be amongst the small percentage that goes down the coveted third route. In order to do that, we have to ensure that we play a dominant role on the international marketplace.

An atypical state-owned enterprise

I think one of the critical elements that led us to start seriously planning our brand strategy was that TCL was an atypical state-controlled enterprise. There was no state capital invested in our company, nor did we have state-assigned projects for our market. Lacking such state assistance, we had to conduct our own exploration of, and research into, the space that we occupied in the market and we also had to plan how to promote and sell our products on our own. During this process of planning and implementing our own product promotion and product distribution strategies, we discovered what a driving force a brand could be.

In the early days of the Chinese economy, supply was much smaller than demand, so a company could make sales very easily. This was the planned economy in which consumers had to obtain a coupon to even purchase a television set. In those days, manufacturing enterprises did not have to worry about marketing their products effectively to the consumer. They could sell as many as they made as the state would dictate which organizations would buy or sell which products. But, even during those times, because TCL was an atypical state-owned company, we always had to work hard at our own marketing and sales.

Since the late 1980s, however, supply has become at least equal to demand and sometimes even exceeds it. In such circumstances, when there is a need to influence your target customers to make a purchase, the brand becomes an extremely important factor. It becomes a reason why your product is chosen over another company's product.

The TCL brand core values

As I understand it, a brand consists of different elements, including quality, customer service and corporate culture. Each of these factors – quality, customer service and corporate culture – contributes to how the brand develops and is perceived. And ultimately, as a result, every brand is different and will leave different impressions on customers.

From the very early days of TCL's operations, we have combined branding with our corporate culture and have tried to ensure commitment to our core values. These core values are to provide good value to customers, to offer excellent opportunities to employees, and to create benefits to the society through dedication, teamwork and innovation.

Why did we choose these as our core values? As a producer of consumer household appliances, it is very clear to us that we rely on our customers to support our business. It is customers who have made TCL a successful business today. That is why we prioritize consistent and excellent customer service and why we try to be as market-focused as possible. Moreover, we do not treat this core value as just a saying or slogan within our organization; providing good service to our customers is a long-term relationship building effort that we are engaged in. It is only through long-term effort that your customers and your dealers will learn to trust you. Even though quality and product innovation are two things that form a product's lifeline, it is not uncommon for companies that have very good quality products and product innovation to fail, simply because they have not put enough effort into their marketing, their branding and their relationship with their customers. Nowadays, in particular, when most companies have the capability to produce high-quality products, the quality factor alone is no longer something that differentiates one company from another.

Let me put it in these terms. Companies with poor-quality products will be the first to be kicked out of the market. Those that offer poor customer service will be eliminated in the second round of competition.

Where does corporate culture fit in, then? Corporate culture is closely related to the brand because brand awareness is built by the interaction that takes place between the company's employees and its customers. It is also a result of the interaction that occurs between the company's leadership and the general public through the media. And because corporate culture influences how both employees and the company's leaders behave, corporate culture is definitely closely related to brand awareness and branding.

I think that a good brand can only be built by having a dedicated, committed and excellent team of people within an organization. So, in some sense, I could say a brand is the essence of the corporate culture of the enterprise but, circularly, the corporate culture of the enterprise has a feedback effect on the development of this brand.

My management philosophy

TCL's mission is to create a premier Chinese brand and build a first-class business. By first-class business I mean that TCL should aim to occupy a leading position where each of its products or businesses is operating. How are we going to attain this goal?

I believe that an organization's goal must be the common goal and shared vision of all its employees, especially those at management level. The traditional practice of using authority in a top-down hierarchical fashion no longer results in long-term sustained optimal company performance. Instead, I believe that each employee at every level of the organization needs to feel a sense of responsibility towards the company. This sense of responsibility will foster commitment from the employee towards the company's goals. This is particularly important in the context of Chinese organizations which, typically, will not have the advantage of a professional management team or, as in the case of TCL, will have to operate in a complex and highly competitive environment. In the latter case, it is crucial that management is able to rally the employees' support, loyalty and commitment towards doing what will be in the best interest of the organization.

In creating this sense of responsibility amongst our employees, I believe that clear communication of shared goals and corporate strategy is paramount. Recently, we organized a corporate event that invited employees to participate in the setting of goals and strategies for TCL. This event not only tapped the creativity of our employees but also increased the level of their buy-in to corporate goals and gave everyone a motivational high.

I also believe in nurturing my employees, making sure that we give them maximum opportunities to fulfil their career ambitions, increase their responsibilities and maintain their morale. Compared to other Chinese companies, I would say that TCL has a much higher level of focus, motivation and morale amongst its employees, and this is the result of management efforts at nurturing people.

At TCL we believe that there is a need to constantly outdo ourselves and exceed the standards of our own work. TCL is in a race – not a sprint but a marathon. Therefore, like a marathon runner, we have to cultivate endurance, stamina and perseverance in order to ensure that we will continue growing and developing, inching past our competition slowly but steadily.

Competitive advantages in the electronic products industry

In terms of competition, Sony and Samsung are definitely two brands that we will face in the international arena. But, if we are honest, TCL's capabilities or skills have not reached as high a level and are not as extensive as those of Sony or Samsung, especially in the field of branding. Maybe in a few years we will be a serious competitor to Sony, but not now. At present, I take the approach that I have much to learn from these companies. Right now, the path I want to take for TCL is to broaden our profile and our portfolio of products.

In my view, companies in the electronic products industry can be positioned on a competitive landscape in terms of four types of competitive advantage:

1 Manufacturing and production efficiencies and expertise;
2 Intellectual capital or the capability for technological innovation;
3 Size or power of the brand;
4 Vision of the enterprise.

Using these four dimensions, you will see that companies like IBM and Intel score very high in terms of manufacturing expertise because they have a great deal of intellectual capital. For Sony, the power of its brand is immense, but its efficiency in terms of supply chain management cannot compare to some Taiwanese OEM companies like Hong Hai or Da Ba. Chinese companies such as Legend, Haier and TCL have some brand equity, but tend to have local recognition rather than global recognition, although, at TCL, we are trying to build more global brand equity. We are now also trying hard to build up our intellectual capital as a lack of core technologies is a common weakness amongst Chinese companies. Nevertheless, our brands, although not that strong, are still better than, say, some of those technology-focused OEM Taiwanese companies.

At the moment, most Chinese companies have an advantage in terms of efficiency in supply chain management and the ability to react quickly to market conditions. Scaling up our operations will allow us to compete against bigger international companies, but it will be a long-term challenge for us to maintain the same efficiencies whilst we expand. This is especially the case for TCL because we are not an OEM enterprise. OEM enterprises can continue to enhance their efficiencies even as they expand because their focus is entirely on supply chain management. We at TCL, however, also have to allocate efforts to marketing, sales and operations. We have to manage our brand as well.

Becoming more consumer-focused

How do we combat the competition that we face from these international electronic giants like Sony and Samsung? I think one way is to try to develop into a more consumer-focused organization. The challenge currently facing

Chinese companies like TCL in the mass products market is that the profit margins are very narrow and the cost of providing good customer service is very high. That is why some large international companies can provide or offer good service to high-end customers but cannot support the provision of service to low- or middle-end customers. Maybe that is where our challenge and also our opportunity to perform better than our competition lie.

Understanding consumers and having insights into their needs and motivations are critical to developing a more consumer-focused organization. Our products department is therefore responsible for carrying out regular monthly research on our products and customers. They provide deep and very detailed monthly reports on TCL's strong points and weak points, and also report on the competitive situation. Our market report on the TV market for May 2002, for example, runs into 60 pages. Ultimately, this research and understanding of our customers and of the market becomes part of the intellectual capital that we are trying to build as a competitive advantage for TCL. Intellectual capital is not only about the capability for technological innovation.

Keeping and evolving the character of the brand

Because TCL does have quite a broad product profile, ranging from refrigerators to phones to electronic products, one of our other current challenges is how to maintain the character and the clarity of the TCL brand. However, our target market is quite a focused one, consisting of a certain type of home user and individual user. Consequently, we try to orientate everything about our brand to this target market. We also try to find a common ground between the different products for our customers and, at the same time, encourage differentiation for each individual product to bring out its uniqueness. That's why we have different spokespeople for different products.

Our thinking on our brand has evolved substantially on one point, however. We have realized, for instance, that at one stage of our development we were too focused on the product itself. But nowadays we are more people-oriented and that is also why we recently organized a corporate culture innovation event at TCL intended to encourage employees to help the company reposition the company's brand image. In addition to involving our own employees, we have invited experts and professionals to help us create a more people-focused, human-related brand image.

Our approach to branding is similar to that of Samsung which now uses the concept of 'Everyone's invited' as an overall brand proposition for all its products. This is a brand based on an attitude of mind rather than what the products can do. Alternatively, look at Sony's brand proposition of 'Go create'. It is very visionary. We are currently working on a brand concept for TCL that is to do with innovative technology and how it leads to people sharing and enjoying life together.

The effort of a generation

China has already become a brand that stands for good manufacturing and that is why more and more Japanese, Korean and European products appear with the label 'Made in China'. I hope that this label 'Made in China' will come to mean good quality and good value for money. However, most consumers in the world can accept the label 'Made in China' only as a manufacturing label on products that are already supported by internationally famous and popular brands. To these consumers, a 'Made in China' label on a Chinese branded product only says 'cheap but not good'. For example, a designer brand product that has 'Made in China' on the inside is fine, but if it were a TCL product and 'Made in China', its quality would be open to question.

It will require the efforts of a generation to help change this perception of 'Made in China' and of Chinese brands. Brand reputation in the eyes of global consumers will not be won through the work of one single Chinese enterprise, but through the collective hard work of many excellent Chinese enterprises. We need more than a handful of globally successful Chinese enterprises to achieve international market attention and recognition.

Up to this point, the Chinese economy has created both challenges and opportunities for Chinese enterprises. Right now, the Chinese economy is becoming freer and more globalized. This means that Chinese enterprises like TCL have more of an opportunity than ever before to take advantage of these trends and make an impact on the world. Another advantage is that, because of increased interaction and competition with international companies, we are forced to 'grow up' as an organization much faster than before. In comparison with the past five or ten years, our current growth is taking place at an accelerated pace. And this growth is not confined to just the company; it is also taking place on a personal level. I think I am improving faster as a manager and a leader.

The disadvantage or challenge is that, with entry into the WTO, the Chinese market or industry will be open to the outside world. For the past 20 years the growth of Chinese enterprises has owed much to protectionist and other governmental policies. When these policies disappear in the next three to five years, it will be telling which Chinese enterprises will also disappear from the marketplace. Hopefully the ones that remain will be strengthened as a result.

Strategic partnerships

Going international for TCL in the future will definitely involve us harnessing foreign power. With China's entry into the WTO, it is obvious to me that
Chinese companies cannot operate in isolation. We need to attract strategic
investors from overseas to help us make the leap, and this is not an easy task.

What I try to ensure, first, is that these investor companies are leading
players in their industries. Second, they should have a similar corporate
culture to ours at TCL so as to minimize culture clashes and other problems
that will arise from working together. And, third, I try to ensure that these
partners can somehow add value to TCL, whether in terms of products, technology or markets. Multinational companies are always attracted to the
market opportunity in China, and TCL will be the gateway through which
they fulfil their dreams for the Chinese market. Co-operating with multinational firms will bring synergies and integrate our resources. It will be
win–win for both parties.

At present, we are working on strategic partnerships with many candidates
and we hope that, in one or two years' time, there will be more and more news
about TCL and its strategic alliances with different multinational companies.
For instance, Philips has a 4 per cent share in TCL, and it chose TCL as its
Chinese business partner over TCL's strongest competitors after an in-depth
market study. We are also considering broadening the function of our distribution channels so that, in future, they not only distribute our own products
but also those of our international partners. This will be something that we
can trade for technological and international market support from our partners.

TCL and its stakeholders

Because a corporation is part of the social fabric of a country's economy, I
believe that a company has a responsibility towards that country's social
progress. China has a very special political history and context, and it might
therefore be said that companies in China are expected to have even greater
social responsibilities. Furthermore, I do not think that the obligation for
companies to fulfil their social responsibilities should be considered in isolation. We also have to think about fulfilling our responsibilities to our shareholders and also to our employees.

Strictly speaking, of course, giving benefits to shareholders is not in conflict with giving benefits to employees. All of these stakeholders are related. If
you cannot gain the trust and commitment of your employees by ensuring
their well-being and satisfaction, then the profit or the benefit to shareholders will not be guaranteed. In the same way, I think that benefiting society will

have similar good effects on generating sustained commitment from employees. Society, customers, employees and shareholders – all these stakeholders are important to TCL.

COMMENTARY

The description of TCL's realization of the importance of branding paints a very realistic picture of the development of many Chinese companies. Stage one is often about pure survival and the generation of sufficient funds to continue operating. Many companies like TCL are honest and admit that branding was not a priority at that stage. Stage two is the recognition that branding can be a tool that will propel the company to become leader of the pack within China. Whoever manages to wield this tool most effectively is going to race ahead of the others.

The third stage is reached when the company realizes that global competitiveness means having a brand that can stand up to other international brands. TCL has reached that stage. Mr Li Dong Sheng certainly does not want TCL to be subsumed by an international corporation in the future; he wants TCL to be a world-class player in its own right. Here TCL joins the ranks of Legend and Haier in wanting to place Chinese companies on the international business platform. The 'Made in China' label has to progress to 'Brands of China'. But this task, as he observes, is going to take considerable time and the collective efforts of many excellent Chinese companies.

How will TCL develop itself into this new breed of Chinese brands? As a manufacturer of electronic products, it needs to compete against the likes of Sony and Samsung if it wants to go international. These brands sell themselves with emotional propositions like 'Go create' and 'Everyone's invited'. Looking far into the future, they have decided to dispense with functional brand propositions that lack depth and breadth and therefore sustainability.

TCL has responded quickly by deciding to become more people-focused and less product-focused itself. It has realized that technology per se is no longer desirable; it is how technology enhances life and living that appeals. TCL is taking the development of its brand very seriously. It is not only working on giving its brand a more human face but also ensuring that its internal culture reflects this people-focus. Getting employees to participate in the crafting of TCL's future brand proposition is certainly a very effective way of harnessing internal creativity and obtaining buy-in and understanding at an early stage. We look forward to seeing what emotional space TCL, the brand, will stake out in the market in future.

6 | Tong Ren Tang: A National Treasure, Not Just a Brand

Introduction

Few brands in the world can boast a history like that of Tong Ren Tang – one that spans a few hundred years. The brand of Tong Ren Tang in China first came to prominence in 1723 when the company acted as medicinal suppliers to the Chinese imperial court. The company survived the rise and fall of the Qing Dynasty and China's Cultural Revolution to become one of the leading manufacturers and exporters of traditional Chinese medicine products in China today.

Tong Ren Tang Group Company is now owned by the Beijing government and has subsidiaries listed in Shanghai and Hong Kong. It is one of the most recognized consumer brands on the mainland, with famous products such as Angong Niuhuang Pill, Niuhuang Qingxin Pill, Ganmao Qingre Granule, Liuwei Dihuang Pill, Niuhuang Jiedu Tablet and Ganmao Soft Capsule. These are all household product brands in China and enjoy a very high prestige in Southeast Asia.

The future for this company looks bright. Although annual per capita spending on pharmaceutical products in China stands at only one-fifth of what the average US citizen spends, the rise of China's consumer class, urbanization and an ageing population are all factors that are going to increase pharmaceutical spending in the future. But the company also faces the challenge of modernizing and internationalizing its Chinese herbal medicine business and products to keep up with competition without losing its uniqueness and its traditions. Mr Jin Yongnian, head of the propaganda department, traces for us the development of this ancient and famous brand.

A 333-year history

In the eighth year of Emperor Kangxi's reign in the Qing Dynasty, 333 years ago, a doctor by the name of Yue Xianyang founded a Chinese medicine business. He called it Tong Ren Tang – a name that describes a society where fairness and openness, benevolence and kind-heartedness are valued, where peace and greater mutual understanding are sought among human beings.

Yue was from the town of Qishui in the city of Ningpo in Zhejiang province. Belonging to a famous family of doctors, he was the administrator of the royal hospital during the Qing Dynasty. But he was not interested in fame or in spending the rest of his life as a royal officer. He believed that, as a doctor, he had a duty to improve the lives of the common people. It was this sense of duty that drove him to retire from his appointment and to set up Tong Ren Tang in 1669. Yue was determined to use his family's medicines and the Tong Ren Tang name and business to benefit the common people.

In 1688 Yue Xianyang died and his third son Yue Fengming inherited the business. Yue Fengming played an extremely important role in the development of Tong Ren Tang. In 1702 he produced a book entitled *The Formula Recipes for Pills, Powders, Pastes and Pellets*. Handed down from Yue's Ancestors, the book sets out, in careful detail, a total of 362 different prescriptions, together with instructions for the manufacture of the pills, powders, pastes and pellets. This book strictly stipulated the kinds of material that had to be used and the rules that had to be obeyed in the manufacturing process. It also compiled ancient and secret recipes handed down from different families and past dynasties.

Because of the book, certain standards were set in the production of the medicines, and the craftsmanship required to carry this production out was also taken to very high levels. The quality of the medicine produced and the reputation that it enjoyed among the people was so high that, in 1723, Tong Ren Tang was officially recognized as the royal medical supplier to the Qing Imperial Family by Emperor Yong Zhen. But this was perhaps a difficult honour to accept because it also meant that the Tong Ren Tang pharmacists had to pay a great deal of attention to the accuracy with which they made the medicines. One small mistake was punishable by decapitation!

Today, these prescriptions and their manufacturing methods are like the 'core technology' of Tong Ren Tang. Due to the hard work of the Yue family through the generations, these recipes and prescriptions continue to form the secret of our commercial success. And because of our ancient origins, Tong Ren Tang can also claim to be the oldest pharmaceutical company in China. The fact that we were once medicinal suppliers to the imperial court puts us in a very unique position. We feel that we are unlike any other Chinese medicine company.

In the 1850s the business was handed down to the tenth generation of Yue's family – Yue Hongda. He was another important figure in the development of Tong Ren Tang because he was personally responsible for 'research and development'. According to our records, he was involved in the production of more than 100 new kinds of medicine for Tong Ren Tang. After Yue Hongda's death, his wife, a very skilled businesswoman, took over and the company enjoyed steady progress under her management for about 27 years. In 1907 this lady passed away and China entered a time of chaos with the leaders of different geographical regions warring against each other. In many ways, the development of Tong Ren Tang had mirrored the evolution of the Qing

Dynasty. When this dynasty came to an end and the political and economic situation in China deteriorated, Tong Ren Tang's operations were forced to come almost to a standstill. The Tong Ren Tang brand, however, lay deep in the hearts of the Chinese people. This situation persisted until 1949.

1949 and nationalization

In 1949 the People's Republic of China was founded. Tong Ren Tang was inherited by Yue Songsheng from the thirteenth generation of the Yue family. Yue Songsheng was responsible for the modernization of Tong Ren Tang's medicines. He believed there was a need to reinvent the way in which traditional Chinese medicines were taken. Traditionally, the pills and granules had to be boiled for a long time before being consumed, making it very inconvenient for patients. Together with Mr Peng Zhen, the then mayor of Beijing, the two men decided in 1952 to co-establish the National Herbal Medicine Research Institute under the guidance of a professor of medicine from Beijing University. This research institute worked for one year to invent a new format for Chinese medicines – a tablet. They were able to produce four kinds of traditional Chinese herbal medicine in the form of tablets, making consumption of Chinese herbal medicines much easier than ever before.

Yue Songsheng was also a very good socialist. In 1952, in response to a national movement for businesses to be jointly operated by their private owners with the Chinese government, he became one of the first business owners to take the brave step of sharing his family business with the government. From that time on, Yue Songsheng himself began to gain prominence in the Chinese political arena. He became a representative of the National People's Congress and vice-chairman of the National and Industrial Commercial Union. In 1955 he was appointed as deputy mayor of the Beijing municipality. Because of what he has done for the company and also for his country, Yue Songsheng is considered a very important economic and political figure in the northern part of China.

When China entered the period of the planned economy, businesses that were co-owned with the government in 1954 became nationalized in 1966. And that is how Tong Ren Tang became a state-owned company. The founding Yue family are now advisers to, and minority shareholders in, the company. In the period between 1966 and the eventual economic rejuvenation of China, there was almost no development of Tong Ren Tang's business because of the Cultural Revolution. Many old brand names were forgotten and many traditional and valuable things were destroyed. It was the same for Tong Ren Tang. In 1992, Deng Xiaoping initiated the opening up of China. Businesses were able to be dynamic again. Tong Ren Tang was revived with the formal establishment of China Beijing Tong Ren Tang Group Company. Since then, in the last ten years, we have enjoyed rapid and strong growth.

The Tong Ren Tang ideology

That Tong Ren Tang the company has several hundred years of history and China itself has several thousand years of history may seem amazing to people in the West. We believe that the success of Tong Ren Tang is based on the fact that we have such a close link to the great culture and history of our country. China has a very long tradition of herbal medicines, and Tong Ren Tang has successfully absorbed, and now represents, the essence of this tradition. Our cultural ideology is also a strong factor in our success – when we do business as Tong Ren Tang, we are learning, at the same time, how to be good people, how to be benevolent. We are teaching our employees how to practise the Tong Ren Tang ideology encompassed in the three words 'virtue, honesty and credit'. We believe that our employees should be driven by a common vision – a common objective – and that is to 'cultivate kindness and virtue together, to help people and preserve health'. Those are the words that describe our enterprise spirit.

Our ideology also influences our management philosophy. For more than 300 years Tong Ren Tang has followed the principle of 'Making the best medicine irrespective of the cost of materials and the time it may take'. For example, although the cost of our medicines is very high, we will not avoid critical stages in the manufacturing process and, although the materials we use are very complicated, we will not eliminate any component of these materials however small it might be. Our self-discipline is built on the creed 'Your efforts will not be noticed by the people, but your intention will be known in heaven.'

To ensure raw material quality we have contracts with farms in Henan and Zhejiang to grow our herbs exclusively and we intend to set up our own agricultural bases to guarantee an uncompromising supply of raw materials. Our products are a combination of 'distinctive recipes, superior materials, excellent techniques and high therapeutic effectiveness'. I believe that this is the primary factor responsible for our success. The second principal factor is that, through all these years and through all these different developmental stages of Tong Ren Tang, we have always managed to successfully understand market demand and market needs and have adapted our products accordingly. That is why, up until now, Tong Ren Tang has survived and is still a very dynamic player in the market. We continue to gain market share and our reputation grows stronger by the day.

'Moral significance' is our most important operational guide. If there is a conflict between doing what is morally correct and doing what would bring the company increased economic profit, we will surely choose to do what is morally significant to us. There is no doubt about this. We believe that, as a pharmaceutical company, the social benefit of what we can achieve as a business is more important to us than maximizing economic gain. From the first day of Tong Ren Tang's establishment, our objective has never been to seek fame or fortune but to produce the best medicines to heal people's illnesses. This goal has not changed. Some Chinese enterprises believe that their ultimate goal is the seeking of maximum profit, but not Tong Ren Tang. This is also the reason why, we think, Tong Ren Tang has lasted several hundred years.

We feel that there is a particular challenge to placing 'moral significance' ahead of 'economic significance' – especially nowadays. China is now going through the early stages of the market-oriented economy where the rules of competition are not yet fixed and companies are doing everything they can to out-compete one another. If, at this critical stage, our company's business can be carried out honestly and the company can fulfil its stated commitments to society, how much more will we be able to achieve when the economy matures? We believe that, ultimately, we will profit much more than those who do not manage to conduct themselves according to these principles. In our eyes, there is in fact no conflict between 'moral significance' and bottom-line profits.

For example, some of the services and products offered by Tong Ren Tang at the present are not profitable. Special medicines for children – influenza granules – really produce no profit at all but we provide them because we believe our society needs such medicines. We also offer some additional services such as delivery of the medicine to the customer on request or further processing of the medicine if needed by the customer without further charge. Although there is a lot of additional labour cost incurred in providing these services, we believe it benefits the patients, so we do it. On the other hand, such products and services do attract more customers to Tong Ren Tang, so providing them brings economic benefits as well as building a very good social reputation for the company.

The Tong Ren Tang business

We have great faith in our strong brand name and the high quality of our products. Currently we have over 800 registered proprietary medicinal products, as well as 3,000 kinds of medicinal material. Among these, 47 have been named 'excellent products' by the state, ministry and municipality. So, despite China's entry into the WTO, we feel that we face no direct market threats.

We are a very strong company. One of our strong points is that people equate the name 'Tong Ren Tang' with 'traditional Chinese medicine'. Tong Ren Tang, the brand, stands for Chinese herbal medicines produced the traditional way with really good craftsmanship and authentic materials. Unfortunately, the perception is also that Tong Ren Tang's medicines can be old-fashioned and inconvenient, unlike modern medicines that are easily consumed and easily portable. To combat this perception, we are investing in improving these aspects of our medicines. For example, in the area of new product development, we are constantly working to create new formats for our medicines. Currently, we already have 24 different dosage forms available on the market.

China is such a large country that we have found that our customers often encounter different regional climates and conditions and suffer different health problems. We try to adapt our product portfolio to meet the demands of these different regional markets. For example, we have a product called Guogong Liquor which is sold mainly in the southern part of China in three provinces – Jiangxi province, Hunan province and Hubei province. In these provinces humidity is very high, winters can be very cold and the farmers need to work in a lot of water in the fields. This means that the possibility of being affected by rheumatism is much higher. To meet this consumer need, we developed a special 'liquor' which, when drunk, helps the body to successfully fight rheumatism. We launched special product promotions targeting those specific provinces and, today, this drink has become a household item for the people who live there. They drink it daily to strengthen their bodies. While we target Guogong Liquor at the southern parts of China, we target our Liu Wei Di Huang Pill at the northeasterly parts of China.

To market our products, we do use some television commercials, but not very many. Tong Ren Tang has a very special reputation of its own, and most of our marketing and advertising happens by word-of-mouth. And because we are very active participants in social welfare programmes, many newspapers and publications, like the Xinhua News Agency, report on Tong Ren Tang, generating good publicity for us. Lastly, we have sales representatives who travel throughout China providing services to our customers and patients, as well as visiting hospitals to advertise our products. We even send well-known physicians from Beijing to our overseas drugstores to see patients and prescribe medicines. All these people spread the good name of Tong Ren Tang.

Within Beijing, we sell our medicines through 56 Tong Ren Tang branded sales outlets. Outside Beijing but within China, we have 20 more sales outlets and outside of China, we have around ten outlets. We are continuing to strengthen our distribution network. By 2005 we hope to have a total of 600 medicine stores spread throughout China and overseas. One day, you may even see Tong Ren Tang hospitals which will allow us to train our employees and conduct clinical trials for our products. But this will take at least two to three years, as we are only at the planning phase.

Being such an old brand, we have a very large base of 'old' customers. They tend to be very familiar with our products and know what they want to buy, but we try to recommend that they continue to seek the guidance of Chinese doctors. Our customer research surveys have shown that the older the customer, the better the understanding he or she has of Tong Ren Tang and the greater the belief he or she has in the effectiveness of our medicines. These are customers over the age of 40. This tells us that one of our most important challenges is to promote the Tong Ren Tang brand successfully to the below 40 age group. This may mean that we need to inject some new meaning into our brand that will make it relevant to a younger audience. We may need to examine market trends to update and reformulate some of our old products. The goal will be to ensure that the young people of China today understand Tong Ren Tang and will continue to choose and use our products like their parents have done.

Young people today have a much faster pace of life. When they catch an illness, they want immediate recovery. This makes them choose antibiotics, for example, when they catch a cold. Traditional Chinese medicines work differently. They need a longer period of time to take effect but they are not a quick fix. They act to give the body system a comprehensive tune-up, making it function better. So, although they are slower-acting, they do not have adverse side effects on the body. This is one fundamental point about Chinese medicines that is not well understood by younger people. Only our elderly customers understand this point of difference. Again, this presents a challenge to us. We see it as our responsibility at Tong Ren Tang to inform and educate young people about how Chinese medicines can be good for them. This is a responsibility that extends to the rest of the world – I feel we have a duty to tell global consumers about the benefits offered by Chinese herbal medicines.

Going international

Right now we export some medicines outside China, and we believe that they can really represent the safety, effectiveness and reliability of Chinese herbal medicine to the rest of the world. After all, some of our products have passed 'clinical trials' for hundreds of years! One of our special products, the Angong Niuhuang Pill, is very effective in the treatment of high fever, brain damage and coma and was given the National Gold Award for the best Chinese medicine in China. Its effectiveness was most dramatically demonstrated on a famous television anchor woman by the name of Madam Liu Hairuo who was working for Hong Kong's Phoenix TV station. She was involved in a car accident in the UK and went into a long coma. The British doctors said that there was no hope for her but, after she was given seven Angong Niuhuang Pills, she regained consciousness and could speak. It was nothing short of a miracle. I would like to think that it was Western medicines working in combination with traditional Chinese medicines that produced this result.

Although our main markets are still in Asia, our medicines are being recognized by more and more consumers in the West. In the past, we had a slogan within the company that said 'Where there are Chinese, there is Tong Ren Tang.' Now this slogan reads 'We will go any place where there are foreigners.' Our vision for the future is that Tong Ren Tang products will one day become widely used by consumers all over the world. We hope that the brand of Tong Ren Tang will spread to the four corners of the earth. Internationally speaking of course, Chinese medicine companies do not have a very prominent role in the pharmaceuticals industry at the moment. Last year our sales reached 3 billion RMB. This is nothing when you consider that some international foreign pharmaceuticals have profits that reach several billion US dollars. But we do not intend to compare ourselves to them. Our goal is to reach sales revenues of 20 billion RMB in ten years and to build an internationally well-regarded traditional Chinese herbal medicine enterprise.

One way in which we are trying to achieve this is through strategic alliances. For example we are co-operating with Li Jiacheng, the Hong Kong businessman who owns the famous He Ji Huang Pu (Hutchison Whampoa) brand name, to establish a joint venture which we have co-branded Tong Ren He Ji. We have signed co-operative agreements with firms in Malaysia, Canada, Indonesia and the Republic of Korea to open Tong Ren Tang pharmacies in these countries. We already have joint venture companies to handle local sales as well as several pharmacies in Hong Kong, Britain, the US, Australia and Thailand. In Malaysia, we have agreed with Hai-O Enterprise Berhad to set up a joint venture called Beijing Tong Ren Tang that will manage stores in Malaysia, selling preparations, medicated wines and health foods. Traditional Chinese physicians will be at hand in these stores offering medical services such as diagnosis, acupuncture, massage and traditional Chinese medicine prescriptions. In the US, we have set up a HK$40 million marketing joint venture called Tong Ren Tang Hutchison Pharmaceutical Development with Hutchison Whampoa. This joint venture is aimed at marketing Tong Ren Tang's products as health foods in the US market.

Going international is fraught with challenges. With China's entry into the WTO, trade barriers have been lowered but technical barriers have been strengthened. At present, Europe and the US have strict requirements regarding prohibited ingredients within traditional Chinese medicines.

Without a well-established certification system for traditional Chinese medicines, it is difficult for us to obtain FDA (Food and Drug Authority) certification from the US, which is why we are currently selling our products as health foods in North America. However, our researchers are introducing chromatographic analysis to map out the components of our best-quality medicines. Production of the medicines must follow these maps, and this will help our products reach global standards. Within our farms we are trying to control the use of pesticides, for example, in order to meet import regulations. In addition, we are conducting research into our traditional recipes and developing new products that will cater specifically to the international markets.

A national treasure

The Tong Ren Tang brand means very much to us. We believe it is the instrument that will enable us to reach our vision of becoming a global Chinese medicine company. Our brand is a valuable asset – even more valuable than the enterprise itself. We have always recognized that, without this name, there would be no enterprise and therefore no development of that enterprise to speak of. So protecting, loving and growing the Tong Ren Tang brand is the responsibility of every person within our organization. As a state-owned enterprise, we value working in teams and the importance of team spirit. Even our top executives work as a team. Decisions are made not by one person but through a democratic decision-making process, so it is truly an entire team within Tong Ren Tang that supports and champions our brand.

Tong Ren Tang is currently involved in a joint project with the State Council Development and Research Centre. Many experts from different fields in this research centre are going to appraise the financial value of our brand. Right now, there is no published figure. Frankly speaking, I have mixed feelings about doing such an appraisal. Tong Ren Tang is not just a company and successful brand and business; it is almost a national treasure. Some of China's top political figures also believe this. As a national treasure, perhaps we should not try to ascertain its value. It should be left as an unknown so as to be truly invaluable.

COMMENTARY

One of the most respected and well-known brand names in traditional Chinese medicine, Tong Ren Tang has a unique position among China's consumer brands. Backed by history, prestige and quality, it is a brand that symbolizes the impressiveness and the richness of China's cultural heritage. Whereas most of the other businesses that we have examined in this book started to gain prominence from the 1980s, Tong Ren Tang has survived for centuries, bringing new meaning to the concept of building sustainable brand capital. Perhaps the mark of a truly visionary company in today's business world should be that it can survive market changes for at least 100 years.

Yet Tong Ren Tang's history could stand in the way of its development. A rapidly modernizing Chinese population may prefer Western medicines on the basis that Western medicines represent progress, whereas Chinese herbal remedies represent the ineffectual past. Sales of imported medicines have been growing at 35 per cent compared to the 20 per cent increase for home-grown products, and the market is fragmented without any major domestic medicine manufacturer holding obvious dominance – none of their market shares exceeds 10 per cent.

With a brand that already commands such respect, Tong Ren Tang needs to find a way of taking the lead. Mr Jin Yongnian touches on a key point when he talks about educating the younger generation and the outside world about Chinese medicines. It is only by clearly differentiating Chinese medicines from Western medicines and then by distinguishing Tong Ren Tang's Chinese medicines from other brands that Tong Ren Tang can begin to define its own competitive space on the market. The latter could involve branding its medicines as combining the best of Eastern medical knowledge and tradition with the best of Western production technology, if not Western medical know-how. With simple and strong communication behind it, the brand could find great resonance among Western consumers who are increasingly looking to homoeopathic and other more natural remedies.

We hope to see Tong Ren Tang take its place among the pharmaceutical giants of the future. Like Johnson & Johnson, it already has founding principles that have guided decision-making in the company from day one. Like Merck, it already sells medicines that benefit society even if these medicines generate little revenue. Placing 'moral significance' over economic gain will be an even greater achievement if this company manages to adhere to its principles and become the market leader in the fierce competitive climate of China.

7 | CITIC: In the Front Line of Reform

The rise and fall of the international trust and investment sector in China

One of the most significant outcomes of China's reforms was its opening up to foreign markets in the late 1970s. This created an opportunity for export-led industrialization and with the import of foreign capital, technology and talent, China's economy grew quickly. But opening up a country that had previously been entirely government-controlled created structural problems, and a number of changes had to be made. One of those changes was to the financial sector that supported Chinese businesses.

Prior to China's reforms, the state-owned banks were the sole providers of financing for businesses. But, as the economy became increasingly market-oriented, demand for loans grew. The banks were governed by tight banking regulations and were unable to meet the rising demand. With the economy under threat through lack of financing, the Chinese government began to explore new ways to finance businesses. As a result, a number of experimental institutions emerged in China including non-state-owned banks, credit co-operatives, leasing companies and China International Trust and Investment Corporation (CITIC).

CITIC was the first, and is the largest, of many international trust and investment corporations (ITICs) to be set up in China under the late Deng Xiaoping during the late 1970s and 1980s to help China in its opening up and reforms. The ITICs' principal role was to collect foreign capital for strategic investments under the direction of central and provincial governments and provide a financial resource for local projects. They could also engage in most of the activities traditionally reserved for the banks, but were outside central bank control which meant that they could offer better interest rates and lower service charges. They could also conduct business in foreign exchange, which the state-owned banks could not. They attracted China's uninvested cash and grew their assets quickly.

For the first few years, they enjoyed a relatively unregulated existence, investing in a diverse array of businesses from manufacturing and food production to tourism and real estate. Then in the early 1980s, the Chinese government, keen to push ahead with its financial reforms, began to tighten the regulations governing the non-bank financial sector. The outcome was a series of shake-ups the most dramatic of which came in

1998 with the collapse of the Guangdong International Trust and Investment Corpo-
ration (GITIC), the investment arm of the Guangdong provincial government.

GITIC was the second largest ITIC in China and the first non-bank financial
institution to be made bankrupt since the foundation of the People's Republic in 1949.
It was one of a handful of so-called financial 'window companies' set up to act as inter-
mediaries, borrowing overseas to help China's economy develop. Others included
ITICs in Hainan, Tianjin, Dalian, Shanghai and Fujian as well as CITIC, the
investment arm of the central government.

GITIC collapsed owing more than $2.5 billion in foreign debt. Its closure sent
shock waves through the world's investor community, stirring up fears about the cred-
ibility of such institutions, and prompting a reassessment of their credit risk.

Immediately after GITIC's closure, international investors backed away and the
nation's 240-plus ITICs were left more or less bereft of foreign lenders, rendering
their future suddenly in doubt. The sector was about to come under very close scrutiny,
and a number of weaknesses inherent in the ITICs were to be identified as contribut-
ing to GITIC's defaults.

An economy in transition

Some of the problems that came to light as a result of GITIC's demise existed because
China's internal structures and the intellectual capital that supported them were
developed to assist a state-planned economy, not a market one. Other problems came
about as a result of the economy shifting from one direction to another. The economic
and financial environments were in a constant state of flux, as was the regulatory
structure that governed them. Regulations were almost impossible to implement or
monitor effectively.

To begin with, the style of management that existed in China was qualitatively
different to that necessary to sustain a business that was open to market forces.
Without state intervention, many ITICs would not have survived. In addition to this,
the purpose and role of a trust business, as defined by the Chinese government, did not
correspond to that defined under international trust law. Trust businesses in the US,
for example, are concerned principally with facilitating the transfer and management
of properties where the original owners of the trust assets have a relationship with the
trustee based on trust or faith. Trust asset owners are basically shareholders and, by
law, a trust is characterized as a fully independent agent requiring an independent
authority and examiner whose decision-making must be impartial.

In contrast, China trusts are state-owned, so decision-making is immediately
biased in the state's favour. China trusts originated as a financial resource to supple-
ment the banks and trust assets owners are given debt holders' rights similar to those
of commercial bank depositors. Trust asset owners, while stakeholders, are not consid-
ered to be shareholders of which, in fact, there is only one – the state.

These differences were allowed to exist because there was no effective legal frame-
work for the Chinese ITICs. In fact, they were without proper regulation of any kind.
Regulations were introduced, but they were constantly under revision. This meant
that the ITICs were free to provide services duplicating those provided by other sectors,
principally the banking sector. But without central bank control, chaos reigned. They
could invest in more or less anything, which left many of them with an ill-focused
spread of weak assets, with little synergy between the businesses and no real core to fall
back to if any of the investments failed. Many of the investments were also high risk,
such as condominium building, which is subject to seasonal fluctuations. And they
themselves could move with ease into high-risk business areas such as underwriting
and security trading.

The lack of effective regulations, together with managerial inexperience, allowed
many of the ITICs to fall into unsound business practices such as borrowing inappro-
priately, servicing debt with more borrowed debt, and performing fictitious trans-
actions.[1] This added to their troubles and, throughout the 1990s, many accumulated
massive debts, both from China's four domestic banks and from offshore lenders and
bond investors. This situation was brought to the attention of investors in 1997 when
the World Bank issued a warning about the creditworthiness of some of the ITICs.[2]
But investors, keen for a foothold in China's booming economy, continued to pour
money in.

It is interesting to look at some of the reasons why this happened. First, the ITICs
were run without effective transparency – a character trait of all China's state-owned
enterprises, not just the ITICs. That not only allowed many of the problems to persist
but also made accurate risk assessments impossible. In reality, by the mid-1990s many
of the ITICs, if judged by international standards, would have been technically 'bank-
rupt' in terms of debt-to-equity ratios and operations.[3]

Second, although investors believed that their investments had the full faith and
trust of the government, in fact unconditional support had been withdrawn in 1995.
The state/private ownership structure was not clearly nor legally defined and became
increasingly difficult to track. The outcome of a government decision about whether
or not backing would be provided often depended on the soundness of the defaulting
ITIC's business strategy. What the investors had failed to understand was that, ulti-
mately, the government's commitment lay in seeing the reforms succeed, not in prop-
ping up any one single company, particularly one that might later be accused of
mismanagement.

GITIC's fall was a wake-up call for China and marked a turning point for the
sector. It was in China's interests that the relevant authorities took substantial steps to
bring the ITICs into line with international expectations, such as shutting down the
most debt-ridden and initiating new regulations and laws to limit the activities of
those remaining. Those steps are underway today, although it will be some time before
we see them take effect and the ITICs are once again trusted. But that is because

China's economy is in transition and the problems that this has caused will continue until the transition is fully complete. Despite this, however, many ITICs are optimistic about their future.

CITIC's advantage

There is a general consensus among analysts that CITIC will be one of the ITIC brands to remain strong because it has a number of features that set it apart from other ITICs such as GITIC. For example, CITIC has strived to maintain a certain moral standard and integrity in its operations, following an approach that treats the repayment of debts and interest as a priority, often preparing to do so a year in advance. This has greatly reduced its risk of default and has built up trust in the corporation. Such an approach may be commonplace in the US, but in China, typically, the corporate governance of a business is shielded from view, leaving the management to run the company in a way that may not be in all stakeholders' interests. CITIC has not only chosen to practise with integrity, it is also making adjustments to increase its transparency.

CITIC's management has demonstrated a deep commitment to improving ineffi-ciencies in other areas too, such as risk management, in addition to making necessary structural adjustments to bring greater focus and stability. The restructuring is now in its final stages of completion.

CITIC's chairman, Wang Jun, now takes us through CITIC's story: how CITIC began and the problems arising from supporting the financial needs of an economy in transition. There is a balance, says Wang Jun, between sustainable innovation and 'sailing into the fog, like Columbus'. And it takes experience and good judgement to know when that balance has been reached. He talks candidly of CITIC's most difficult times and the areas in need of improvement today. He also explains the strategic thinking behind the restructuring and how this may impact on the shareholder base, pushing the corporation towards a more privatized form of ownership.

But the message has a wider implication. As perhaps China's model ITIC brand, CITIC's strategies to increase its own sustainability also signal to world investors that the trust and investment sector in China is on the way to economic viability and that the enormous potential China holds for US exporters can be harnessed once more.

CITIC: Deng Xiaoping's window on China's reform

CITIC was founded in 1979 by the former vice-president of the People's Republic of China, Mr Rong Yiren. Prior to that the Rong family had been the wealthiest in Shanghai, based on the textile and flour industries. Mr Rong Yiren decided to stay in China after the Revolution and, in 1956, handed his business over to the government. In the 1970s, the Chinese government began to work out the reform policies for China's economic development. Then a significant incident occurred that laid the foundation stone for CITIC.

The late Deng Xiaoping called a meeting with Rong Yiren, who was, at the time, regarded as one of the Republic's greatest nationalist capitalists. It was January 1979. During this meeting, Mr Xiaoping stated that China should never be closed to the outside world: it should open its doors. He asked Rong Yiren if he could help.

Since stating its 'open-door' policy, the basic goals of the Chinese government have been to encourage the import of foreign capital, technology and market-led management expertise from overseas.

Rong Yiren asked his capitalist friends from Shanghai to come to Beijing to discuss what could be done and, a month later, he submitted to the government a tentative proposal to build a corporation. In June 1979 the State Council approved the establishment of China's first trust and investment group and on 4 October 1979 CITIC was formally founded, with Rong Yiren serving as its chairman and president. Later, in March 1993, Rong Yiren was elected vice-president of the People's Republic of China. The management was reshuffled several times, and I became chairman in April 1995, having been with CITIC since its foundation.

A pioneering spirit

CITIC could not have existed without the support of both Deng Xiaoping and China's central leadership, although I do recall that some State Council members regarded the corporation as very strange – such a monster. We were a novelty to China and, throughout our development, innovation has been our primary goal and methodology according to the spirit of Deng Xiaoping.

Deng Xiaoping reaffirmed this innovative spirit on our fifth anniversary when he wrote the following inscription for CITIC: 'Be bold in your innovations and strive to make more contributions.' Later, on CITIC's twentieth anniversary in 1999, Mr Jiang Zemin, the general secretary of the Communist Party of China and the president of the People's Republic of China, wrote the inscription: 'Be innovative, industrious and self-motivated, and run CITIC well.'

We *were* innovative and we were committed to improving our knowledge in running a business that could survive market forces. For example, we used to send employees overseas to study every year – almost half of them in fact. In this way, we were able to introduce Western styles of management to CITIC and to China.

We led the sector into many business areas, including finance leasing, overseas investing, the issuance of bonds, international economic consulting and the introduction of foreign investments into China. We also pioneered business in foreign exchange, being China's first ITIC.

Our first fully owned bank, CITIC Industrial Bank, was, at one time, the only bank in China to offer Internet banking. Now, we have third-generation computer systems that run imported American software – the same software used by the major banks throughout the world. On introducing the computer system, we were so keen for our big clients to have access to their accounts that we gave them their own computers.

Our computer set-up now enables the corporation's headquarters to control over 300 branches nationwide, and our branch staff can concentrate on developing and managing our clients. Prior to that, every branch had its own books and book-keeping was sometimes dubious. We hired management consultants, McKinsey, to look at how to improve our risk management structures, particularly in our CITIC Industrial Bank, and were advised that much of the risk would be eliminated with the introduction of a linked computer network.

Initially, we had almost 90 per cent resistance from the bank's branch managers. Such technology had never before existed in China, and people were afraid that it would create problems for us. But that is a natural fear when one tries to innovate. I always say that mistakes made for the sake of innovation are forgivable – I make mistakes in my work and everybody forgives me, so long as these mistakes are not moral ones. However, I do agree that we should always innovate with our eyes wide open so that we don't sail into the fog like Columbus. It is quite difficult to predict accurately the future of both of the domestic and the foreign market but, if we feel 60 per cent or 70 per cent sure of where we are sailing, then I think the innovation is worth pursuing.

State support has created many opportunities for us to innovate and lead the way in many different areas, but there was also resistance to some of our proposals in some state departments, particularly in the beginning. For example, when I attended meetings held by the State Council to request approval for the issuance of bonds in overseas markets, almost all the State Council departments opposed the decision, including the Ministry of Treasury, the State Development and Planning Commission, the Economic Commission and the Ministry of Foreign Trade and Economic Co-operation.

CITIC's expansion

On our foundation, the state gave us around 1.3 billion RNB, including three large-scale state-owned enterprises. By the end of 2001 our total assets were worth in the region of 42.4 billion RNB.

In 1982 we facilitated China's first overseas bond issue of 10 billion yen of private bonds in Japan. CITIC has since raised more than US$6 billion from the world capital markets.

CITIC grew quickly, accumulating substantial foreign investments, so we created a number of regional and overseas subsidiaries operating as independent entities – although finance has always been a major business focus. In 2000, assets from that side of the business constituted 81 per cent of the Corporation's total assets. Those assets include two commercial banks, CITIC Industrial Bank which is wholly owned by us, and CITIC Ka Wah Bank in which we have the controlling share.

CITIC Industrial Bank was established in Beijing in 1987 to provide a resource for industrial investments in line with the government's industrial policy. We also acquired the controlling share in the Hong Kong-listed CITIC Ka Wah Bank, and today it is one of the premier financial groups in China.

We also have a number of non-banking financial businesses including a securities firm, an insurance company and a handful of trust and leasing companies. In 1995 we established the holding company CITIC Securities to control all our securities entities – around ten of them. In 2000, CITIC Securities was rated the second most profitable securities firm in China. In the same year, we entered the insurance sector when we signed a joint venture agreement with the UK insurer Prudential Plc to create Guangzhou-based CITIC Prudential Life Insurance Company. And we set up China's first leasing company in 1981 with the purpose of importing advanced technological equipment to hundreds of domestic enterprises.

CITIC invested in industry for many years, supporting projects that covered a range of sectors including energy, raw materials, machinery, infrastructure, telecommunications and real estate, and instigating projects such as Yizheng Fiber Optical Plant in Jiangsu province, Antaibao Coal Mine in Shanxi province, Bohai Aluminium Smelter in Hebei province and Qilu Petrochemical in Shandong province. We have also had stakes in service industries, including tourism and consulting, although current structural adjustments will see us divest many of our non-core assets.

Restructuring for sustainability

When CITIC was founded, the objective was to serve as a window for China's reform and opening up to the world. We did not have the expertise to run financial services, but we still moved into banking, insurance securities and other areas. The result was an organization which had the most comprehensive range of financial services but which was, at the same time, deficient because we lacked the experience to run the business.

After the 1997 Asian crisis, we had a very difficult time: 70–80 per cent of the company's profits had come from overseas and, after the crisis, overseas profits had fallen to 30 per cent. Part of that was due to CITIC Ka Wah Bank experiencing some management problems which have since been resolved. But the crisis brought home to us the point that our financial structure was not optimal at mitigating risks. As a result, we substantially reduced our debt level and began a process of restructuring to improve our asset quality.

It was around the time of GITIC's collapse in 1998 that we initiated the necessary steps towards achieving greater sustainability. First, we began a series of structural adjustments aimed at allowing us to focus on our core financial services business while at the same time developing those non-financial activities that proved to be sustainable. The adjustments were expected to reach completion by the end of 2002.

As part of the restructuring, the corporate brand name is changing from CITIC to CITIC Group, and that will hold all the non-financial businesses. We are setting up a new subsidiary, CITIC Financial Holdings, to house all the financial businesses. The financial holdings company will be the first in China, bringing all our finance entities, such as banking, insurance, securities brokering, futures trading, trust, leasing and real-estate services, together under one roof. This will provide a one-stop financial shop for our customers.

Priority objectives in the restructuring process

Our priority objectives in the restructuring process are threefold. First, we must facilitate the share of information between the various financial businesses. To this end we will build a centralized information database linking the entire network infrastructure to form a CITIC-wide financial network. In future, all businesses will also use a common IT infrastructure.

Our second priority is to introduce a comprehensive risk management system. We will begin by moving all the risk management functions out of the individual businesses and into their respective holding companies in order to standardize and control our risk management function. The principal role of personnel at the holding company level will be to run this function.

The third priority is to develop hybrid financial products that enable cross-selling. The advantage of this kind of product is that it raises our revenues while reducing our capital investments and costs. For example, so that our insurance products can be sold through our banking and securities operations. This will greatly expand our distribution capabilities at little incremental cost.

Although we have a comprehensive range of financial services, the separate businesses do not have economies of scale (except for CITIC's securities businesses). By combining them we can achieve the much-needed synergies and economies of scale, allowing them to complement each other.

CITIC has a distinct advantage compared to, for example, Ping An Insurance and the Bank of China, since our range of businesses are already familiar with each other's operations. This means that our objectives for cross-selling and providing complementary services can be achieved quickly.

The financial holding company challenge

The thinking behind the formation of the financial holding company derives from the full-service banking model that exists in Europe whereby the businesses are structured along customer lines (corporate clients, personal banking) rather than by separate products. This is substantially different from the Chinese model, as defined by Chinese law, which states that we must manage the different financial businesses separately.

The authorities are in the process of establishing the appropriate regulations to support the running of an integrated holding company, but it will be some time before they are formalized. And, as neither CITIC nor the relevant authorities currently have the expertise to make it a success, CITIC will proceed using what experience it has in this arena. We also plan to look at a range of international integrated financial services companies to learn about the various kinds of management technique that could serve CITIC Financial Holdings.

Ultimately, we hope that CITIC will become the first financial services group in China to operate a financial holdings company that manages several different product groups, instead of operating single products and services.

A shift in the shareholder base

CITIC has traditionally operated on a state-owned basis, but the creation of the financial holdings company may see that change. At the moment, CITIC Financial Holdings is a management-holding vehicle, not a profit centre. But we will adopt a wait-and-see attitude as to whether or not that situation alters, based on two factors: the degree to which the People's Bank of China (our regulator) defines and relaxes the regulations; and whether our subsidiaries (for example, CITIC Securities and CITIC Commercial Bank) are successful after their listing on domestic markets. If these two factors are favourable, we may consider listing CITIC Financial Holdings.

The non-financial asset strategy

We cannot afford to sell off non-financial services businesses without reviewing their strategic importance. Although non-financial businesses represent
only about 10 per cent of our total assets, their net assets are about two-thirds
of the total. Some of these businesses also enjoy a considerable reputation
within China (for example, power generation and construction) and are profitable so, for these, we plan consolidation. For example, our six power generation plants total a generation capacity of more than 4 million kilowatts. That
makes us one of the largest power generators in China. Since CITIC Pacific
has built up much competency and expertise in managing power businesses,
we have moved all the plants over to CITIC Pacific, either to be under their
direct control or to operate as separate subsidiaries.

We have acted similarly with construction. Originally we had three contract construction project companies; we closed down one and assimilated the
other two into a new construction holding company. Now we have moved all
the businesses relating to project contracting, such as architecture, into this
holding company. We have already seen the results of this consolidation: over
the last 18 months, we have accumulated contracts worth twice the contrac-
tual volume we have had since the business began.

CITIC began to invest in telecommunications in the 1990s and today we
have more than 10 million clients in 12 provinces and municipalities.
Although we are facing a global recession in the sector with the Internet
bubble bursting, we are optimistic about the future. We have a balanced portfolio of investment holdings which include a backbone fibre optics network
(32,000 km), cable TV and satellite broadcasting which, with the approval of
the State Council, we plan to bring together under one telecoms infrastructure holding company.

As part of our efforts to strengthen our core, we will not continue to invest
as heavily in the non-financial sector as we have in the past. The businesses we
retain will have to be profitable and possess a certain market potential. The
others such as infrastructure resources and raw materials will be sold and we
hope these will raise funds for the development of our headquarters in
Beijing.

The reorganization of the non-financial side of CITIC will be a slower
process than the financial side, although already we are seeing some positive
results in areas such as construction and power generation. The telecoms
business is more difficult since the sector is under reform and Chinese companies are being broken up. We are not yet competitive in this area, but we are
confident that we can develop new products and build a loyal customer base
through cross-selling. For example, we are already planning client-sharing
strategies between our telecoms businesses and our financial entities. And, at

an even larger scale, we are considering co-operation with China Telecom and other players for customer share. We are also contacting various government departments such as customs and taxation to see if we can tap their customer networks.

CITIC Group's structure in the future

Our asset base is continuously changing, but we plan to maintain the status quo while at the same time remaining aware that we may need to dispose of some assets in the future. The future development of CITIC Group will necessarily involve making adjustments in line with developments in both the economy and the market.

Improving the financial strategy

In addition to the structural adjustments, we are working to improve our financial strategy. Currently we have a twofold strategy: cost-cutting and debt restructuring. The international debt markets are too expensive to tap into right now, and China has a lot of foreign currency reserves. We have, in the past, used our internal debt (through the China Development Bank and Import-Export Bank) to service foreign debt but we have stopped that because it is inefficient. It will take a few years, but, in the end, our debt situation will improve considerably.

The employee challenge

We have recognized that improvements need to be made to our recruitment procedures so that we can attract good, talented people and we are taking steps to improve employee retention and performance. For example, we have recently introduced an employee compensation system that is linked to the Group's performance. But we have another problem right now: headquarters is finding it difficult to attract talent, as the pay level is much lower there than that offered by our profitable subsidiaries. We also need to localize the management talent in our overseas operations to capitalize on their local expertise and networks.

In the operating companies, a compensation committee determines compensation. For example, at CITIC Securities and CITIC Commercial Bank, the level of the general managers' compensation exceeds mine by three to four times. We also have a special policy to reward outstanding performance.

We hope that our employee compensation levels in CITIC Financial Holdings will match those of our competitors. By my estimation, the compensation levels at the four Chinese banks are much lower than ours. In general, compensation packages in China are far too complicated – take Hong Kong for example, where an employee's compensation is negotiated and if he or she performs well, he or she may get an extra bonus of a few months' pay, plus stock options if appropriate.

Employee training is another area in need of reform. We must increase the level of knowledge not only so that the company can become more profitable but also so that our people can build their own sense of achievement and personal commitment.

My future role within CITIC Group

I have already exceeded the length of my tenure at CITIC, as well as passed the retirement age. I will probably carry on for two more years, during which I hope to focus on the restructuring of CITIC Group and CITIC Financial Holdings, strengthening our core competency and competitiveness, and improving our financial health. Under the reorganization, the most important task is to regroup non-financial businesses into a holdings company, and to change the management style at CITIC, which has limited our development to a certain extent. We have the employee challenge which I am working to resolve and, lastly, the issues of the transformation of information and the way it is used here. That is also an urgent problem, and one that is faced by many traditional enterprises. I would like to put some effort into resolving this.

A positive brand reputation

CITIC was established early on in the implementation of China's reforms and became known across China as a window to its opening up. At the organization's fifth anniversary ceremony, Deng Xiaoping made a public speech citing the corporation as 'a window for economic development and mutual co-operation.'

This message was recreated visually by Rong Yiren, the designer of CITIC's corporate identity, who arranged the five CITIC initials inside a red circle in such a way as to simulate the shape of a gate being opened. The red circle was designed to suggest a rising sun – a symbol of prosperity and growth.

That mutual co-operation has helped shape a very positive reputation here in China and in the rest of the world. We were not handed a plan for how the company should develop because we were totally new in China, so we explored all the different investment opportunities. We couldn't limit ourselves. As a result, we were interacting with ordinary people from day one. That helped shape an image of CITIC among our customers and partners as being accessible and co-operative.

CITIC's strategy is to co-operate with any player non-exclusively. So, for example, our telecoms business could regard China Telecom as a competitor but in fact China Telecom could become a partner. Our aim is to establish orderly relationships with our partners and avoid vicious competition that would ultimately be detrimental to both parties. Telecommunications businesses need access to good financial services. Chinese society is an interrelated society – everybody has connections with everybody else – we could not have achieved what we have independently.

The CITIC brand also means reliability and trustworthiness because the repayment of debts has always taken priority and we have never defaulted, nor are we likely to default, on any repayments. We honour our duty to abide by the contracts we sign with our partners.

These two things, trust and co-operation, are the key qualities we bring to all our partnerships. The CITIC Prudential Insurance Company reflects this, having recently been hailed as one of the best joint venture insurance firms in China. It is the most developed and the fastest growing in the insurance arena and we are very proud of this subsidiary.

CITIC's responsibility to China

We believe that a good social environment is a prerequisite for the development of a company and its employees. The founder of our corporation, Rong Yiren, put into words what he called the corporate character of CITIC. It has 12 Chinese characters and, in the script, he emphasized the social, as well as the corporate, impact of CITIC. Throughout CITIC's life, we have ensured that this spirit is reinforced.

For example, we gave to our foreign competitors free and unlimited access to CITIC's property rights business to help them understand property rights in China. And prior to 1992, when CITIC undertook the financing work of the Ministry of Treasury, we helped a number of experts from around the world analyse China's economic environment. We even helped the government draft some of the new market economy laws.

In 2001 a 670-hectare forestation project was launched in the desert to the north-west hinterland of Beijing, the origin of sandstorms that afflict the Chinese capital in the spring season. CITIC will donate 5 million yuan to the project, which aims to cover part of Huangyangtan Desert with trees, bushes and grassland in three years.

Central government has also asked various state departments, ministries and large companies to help establish road-building and running-water projects in some of China's poorest regions. CITIC has taken responsibility for two areas: a very poor mountainous region called the Xishuangbanna Autonomous Prefecture of the Yunnan province at the border with Vietnam, Laos and Thailand; and the inhospitable Nyingchi Prefecture in Tibet. Each year we send someone to these regions to study the conditions and identify what needs to be done to best help the local people. That employee then remains in the region to manage and direct the project.

1. Hong, Zhaohui, and Yan, Ying, *Trust and Investment Corporations in China*, Economic Working Paper 9706 (1997), Federal Reserve Bank of Cleveland.
2. Kumar, Anjali, *et al*, *China's Non-Bank Financial Institutions: Trust and Investment Companies*, World Bank Discussion Paper Number 358, Washington, DC, The World Bank, 1997.
3. Chinese Finance Association, *Newsletter*, vol. 5, no. 7, 1998.

COMMENTARY

Trust is a key element of any relationship, but particularly in the one that exists between a financial services brand and its customers. In this sector, engendering a sense of trust in your customer is key to building sustainable brand capital.

Brands build trusting relationships by acting in the interests of their stakeholders. For CITIC that will mean acting with transparency, accountability and with a focus on value. However, China's financial sector brands have a history of none of these things: the general lack of transparency and accountability gives rise to a focus on market share and growth, rather than profits.

Many of China's conglomerates, like CITIC, are undergoing major restructuring, stripping away non-core assets and creating a business focus, in efforts to reduce inefficiencies and promote greater entrepreneurship. But such moves will be redundant if inefficiencies in corporate governance structures are not eliminated as well. These brands need an effective legal framework as well as independent supervision. They also need to begin to promote and enforce strong ethical values and standards internally and to nurture a culture of compliance. This is how the true value of the shareholder can be realized.

This will be one of the greatest challenges for brands like CITIC post-WTO entry and is the area in which much work will need to be done. But those willing to respond to the interests of the investor and promote transparency and sound corporate governance will attract the greatest rewards both from investors and joint partnerships. China's financial brands will need to start thinking about brands as relationships built on trust and will have to differentiate themselves with powerful propositions that resonate meaningfully with shareholders.

Introduction

Broad AC Co. Ltd is one of China's largest fully privatised enterprises. Based in Changsha, the capital of Hunan province, Broad is the world's largest manufacturer of gas-absorption air-conditioning, with branch offices in over 20 major Chinese cities and subsidiaries in New York and Paris. Its industrial, commercial and residential absorption air-conditioners use clean energy and safe refrigerants, and play a significant role in reducing China's summer peak-time electricity consumption and pollution emanating from coal-burning power stations and ozone-depleting CFCs in China.

Set up in 1988 by two brothers, Zhang Yue and Zhang Jian, with a mere US$4,000, Broad has grown rapidly and without government support. From 50 employees and total net assets of US$220,000 in 1992, it grew to 1,400 employees with total net assets of US$205 million in 2001. Continued royalties and careful running of the business have allowed the company to expand without taking on a bank loan. Broad has stayed loan-free since 1995 – a rare feat in China where most companies fuel growth with bank borrowing.

Broad's sales of gas-absorption air-conditioners have been ranked number one in China's central air-conditioning industry for the past six years, and its sales of direct-fired absorption air-conditioners have been ranked at number one in the world in this category for the past five years. Dominating 60 per cent of the Chinese market, Broad's products are also making their mark in international markets such as the US, France and Malaysia.

Zhang Yue, Broad's CEO, has been quoted as follows:

Fifteen years ago, I started this business. I never thought about who could give me extra support. I thought it would be great if no one bothered us. We should not rely too much on government support. If you cannot by yourself create the first wealth to dig out the barrel of gold, you will not be able to build a large private enterprise. If you cannot get the first batch of money and can only complain, forget it.

He has also said that access to too much money can have a negative effect on businesses because the possibility of failure is then much greater. Zhang Yue is known for believing that old-fashioned virtues such as self-reliance, hard work and common sense are the secrets to business success – that these basic principles can turn a pauper into a millionaire. Here he talks to us about the creation and growth of Broad and his philosophy behind it.

The origins of Broad

I started 16 years ago in the decoration and construction business. At that time I knew nothing about engineering or industrial sciences. In fact, I majored in Fine Arts at Chenzhou Teacher's College and I taught at Chenzhou University. My interests lay in social sciences and literature. However, my younger brother, Zhang Jian, was an engineering student majoring in thermal engineering and it all started when we came up with an inventive idea for a pressure-free boiler in 1989. It was to prove to be a historic event that would transform the boiler industry in China.

The mechanism is actually not difficult. You know the floating ball in those water tanks for the toilet? Our boiler is designed with an in-built floating ball. When the heat pressure builds up to a certain point, the floating ball will automatically block the water-in end of the boiler and activate the pressure-out end. With the floating ball, the boiler becomes an open system, eliminating any chance of explosions (a common problem with state-manufactured boilers at that time). We patented the technology, commercialized the production and licensed the technology to several clients earning 70–80,000 RMB or US $100,000. With that initial capital, we started Broad AC in 1988 when I was 28 years old. Also in 1992, we successfully developed the first direct-fired absorption (DFA) air-conditioner in China which, like the pressure-free boiler, transformed China's air-conditioning industry.

The Broad air-conditioner

What is so special about our product? The Broad DFA air-conditioner has a longer life span than conventional air-conditioners. It has a lower breakdown rate. It makes less noise and comes with better after-sales service. Every unit that is sold to our customers is connected to our central control network and subsidiary network via a telephone line. Our service personnel can fix and maintain the systems via computers. They can identify and forecast problems by looking at the screens, so that breakdowns are avoided more effectively.

Let me give you one example of how good our product is. A Broad customer who works in the hotel industry was once reported to have said: 'Oh! Is this a Broad central air-conditioning unit? Why didn't I know this or notice its existence before?' Apparently he had been contacted by a Broad representative to renew the maintenance contract and he could not believe that, in the three years following the installation of the Broad unit, they had never once had a problem with it.

Compared to conventional systems of the same load and capacity, the Broad air-conditioner is smaller in size. It uses a special salt (lithium bromide solution), not CFCs, as refrigerant and is driven by environmentally cleaner fuel, such as natural gas and diesel oil. Unlike CFCs, the salt refrigerant is not ozone-depleting. The Broad air-conditioner is also more energy-efficient than conventional air-conditioners. It performs three functions: cooling, heating and providing hot water. Broad air-conditioner systems are very flexible. They can even use the flue gas from the generators to cool and heat.

To support the production of this air-conditioner, we have a DFA technology centre, state-of-the-art research facilities, the world's biggest DFA unit test platform and the world's biggest DFA production line. I believe, however, that science and technology must cross country borders. So, although our DFA centre is regarded by the rest of the world as the centre of absorption chiller technology, we still value co-operation with foreign organizations (such as academic bodies, research organizations and other well-known enterprises) and we try to learn their advanced technologies. The importance of technological innovation to a modern enterprise is self-evident. A company has to continuously innovate to keep up with the accelerated progress of technology. Otherwise, it will not survive the competition.

Most privately owned enterprises in China start off with very low technology. Driven by their need to make a quick profit, they often overlook the importance of building up their foundations in technology and the capability to innovate. Then, when a new wave of technology arrives, these enterprises are unable to cope. At Broad, therefore, we are committed to continuous research, and the study of and absorption of new technologies. In that way, we can apply these new technologies to our products and services more quickly.

Despite all this, I still regard Broad at present to be a relatively small-scale enterprise. It has not developed enough for me to detach myself from daily logistics: 70 per cent of my time is spent on matters such as technology development, in which I am still actively involved, and I also have to compose and revise management documentation myself. Although I don't dedicate any time specifically to branding, I consider everything I am doing to be aimed at the awareness and reputation of the brand name, at building the tangible and the intangible value in the name 'Broad'.

Figure 4: **The Broad logo**

The Broad brand

The company's original brand name consisted of two Chinese characters and their Pinyin translation *yuan da*. In 1989 we adopted the English word 'Broad.' I had telephoned one of my friends in the US to suggest a possible English version to 'yuan da' and his spontaneous response was 'Broad' meaning far and enormous. I already knew about Broadway in the US – so I decided 'Broad' must be a good word.

If you look at our logo, you will see the letter 'b' sitting on a nicely shaped curve. The curve stands for the horizon of the world, the edge of the globe. It symbolizes the vision and the perfection we are pursuing. As to the two colours in the logo, the blue stands for the word 'far' and the orange stands for the word 'big'.

There are three key values in our brand. The first is the sense of honour that is achieved through innovation and invention. To be a creator is something that I value immensely. I have attached so much significance to innovation that sometimes I will innovate just for the sheer sake of it. From HR management to finance, production and technology, I want almost everything in Broad to be different from other companies, especially China's state-owned companies. There are to be no precedents.

The second value is in the recognition of our purpose behind doing business. For quite a lot of chief executives and enterprises, making money is the ultimate purpose for doing business. For me, the ultimate purpose is not just money; I am also trying hard to build an enterprise in its true sense – an enterprise that is effective, successful and sustainable. For Broad, the enterprise is a community of humankind. The ultimate goal is to create harmony between labour and capital, between employees, between the enterprise and its clients, and between the enterprise and society, people and the environment.

The third value is what I call the Law of the Farm. I treat it almost as a religion. How much you harvest from the land depends on how much you plant in it. Therefore I believe that before you can successfully harvest any land, you have to work hard at seeding and tilling it. One is rewarded in proportion to one's labours and one first has to labour before being rewarded. It is this law that makes us multiply our efforts in order to multiply our offer to customers.

These values translate into a 'principle-centred management philosophy' that underpins Broad's style of management. These values are not abstract concepts. We integrate the ideology into every aspect of our business activities. Being principle-centred, aiming at long-term, balanced and sustainable development, is what our success will depend on.

The management philosophy at Broad

What is this principle-centred ideology that I speak of? I feel that most privately owned enterprises in China lack a clear and long-term management ideology. Some companies even try to make their fortunes overnight through illegal practices. At Broad, we believe in running our business on principles. We are not just a company created to make products and generate money. We are also a community that needs to operate on principles. To give you an example, here are the principles we practise in our management, technology, transactions and after-sales service:

1 **Management**: to value long-term benefits; to not allow any short-term activities, decisions or personal benefits at the cost of the company's overall benefit and long-term development.
2 **Technology**: to base all technological development on improving indoor air quality and protecting the global environment; to satisfy the desire of mankind for civilized life to the maximum and to minimize the burden on the environment; to never make products with poor technology, poor functioning or poor quality.
3 **Transactions**: to protect a win-win business ecosystem; to make reasonable profit from customers legally and in a fair and open manner; to distribute part of the profit to suppliers to enable them to provide us with quality components and materials thus enabling us in turn to provide quality products and lifelong services to our customers.
4 **After-sales service**: to regard high-quality after-sales service as our obligation to our customers; to see any badly performed or rushed job or unreasonable profit as breaking the Broad promise to customers.

Many privately owned companies in China are also family-run businesses in which one or two family members have the absolute power to make decisions. In such circumstances, the owner can end up becoming a dictator, adopting a parental approach and making decisions on the basis of emotions. However, irrational and subjective management is no way to run a growing enterprise like Broad. Therefore, although we are ourselves a family business, we are trying to adopt a different management system.

This system involves using documents to create a process that guides how the company operates. All work that employees perform, for example, is governed by documents, from preparation through execution to modification. These documents cover everything from work rules to details on everyday routines such as instructions on the cleanliness of the environment, work ethics and personal grooming. I believe that the high standards set by these rules result in high standards of work and high-quality products. We have an independent committee that is in charge of the planning, composition and modification of these rules, but the members are open to suggestions from anyone. All documents are accessible to everyone instantly via the workplace computers and via mailboxes placed at work and in recreational areas.

I feel that this system has been critical to our success. Without it, we would have been destroyed by the rate at which we grew. Now, if I create a strategy for the company, it can be implemented smoothly and quickly without much need for explanations because everyone has a common understanding of how things work. So this system reduces our management cost and, at same time, increases our productivity. Most importantly it minimizes errors in communication and in the execution of strategies and plans. I am constantly working on making sure that this system penetrates throughout all layers of the company. It is not a perfect system nor fully complete yet, but it does ensure our stable development.

The Broad Town experience

As the founder and owner of Broad, I regard my business as my 'life career' and I approach it with a lot of passion. I would like every Broad employee to also regard his or her job at Broad as a 'life career', also to be approached with passion. Only with passion can people find enjoyment and fun from work.

That is the reason why I created Broad Town. An enterprise is not a good, sustainable enterprise if it only brings financial benefit to the employees. Besides material benefit, it has to fulfil a social and spiritual function for the employees.

Here at Broad Town I have tried to create the right environment to meet the social and spiritual needs of all Broad employees and, in that way, foster a passion for their 'life careers'. Besides factories, there are restaurants, bars, a heli-pad, condominiums and even a three-star hotel. Because we are a manufacturer you would expect this to have an austere factory-like atmosphere but, in fact, Broad Town is built to be a different world – a beautiful garden.

There are four spiritual edifices within Broad Town. The first – the Palace, which is our management school – is built in the style of eighteenth-century French architecture. Second, there is a research centre in the shape of an arch with a very modern design. The third is the pyramid, which serves as a Museum of Environmental Science. Entry to the Pyramid is free for all middle and elementary schools in the province. The fourth is a Mediterranean-style club for recreation. These four constructions together form what we call the Millennium Zone intended for the spiritual growth and enrichment of all Broad people.

In terms of style, the Palace management school stands out from everything else surrounding it, so that people who attend courses there will never forget what they have learned within it. Why did I choose the eighteenth-century classic style? Think of the most valued philosophical ideas on this planet – they all emerged in that period of history. Why? The architecture that the people of that time saw everyday and the constructions within which they lived must have had an influence. Both the Pyramid and the Palace mark the best periods in human civilization. In today's ever-changing, complicated, yet superficial, world, I feel we need some form of reminders as to the more profound and fundamental values of humankind.

If there is a juxtaposition of functional and aesthetic values in Broad Town, it is because I believe that the most functional is the most beautiful and the most beautiful is also the most functional. That is a law of nature. The smartest and most agile animals are the loveliest. Flowers with the best scents or most enhancing to the surroundings are the most beautiful. Functional value and aesthetic value therefore do not conflict. They work in harmony.

Broad Town works not just as an inspirational place for employees, but also as a branding and marketing tool for the corporation. We often have to entertain clients from all over China and the world at Broad Town. Their first impression of Broad is their sight of Broad Town and that must instil in them absolute confidence in our products and our brand. If Broad Town were to look like a provincial town, our clients would be doubtful of our technology and our expertise. They would not be prepared to trust our brand sufficiently to purchase an expensive item such as central air-conditioning from us.

Ultimately, in creating Broad Town, I am putting into expression a belief that I have about how everything in society interlinks. The quality of society determines the quality of enterprises, which in turn determines the quality of employees. The quality of employees affects the quality of products and their dominance of the marketplace. This last factor determines whether the company succeeds or fails. Therefore to control the quality of our company and our livelihood, we need to try to manage the quality of society. Today's society is ugly and full of problems. If we do not try to improve it, it will hinder the growth of our enterprise.

The employees at Broad

Here in Broad Town, I am actually practising the laws of nature – in particular what I call the Forest Law and the Farm Law. The Forest Law recognizes that only the strongest survive and that competition is needed to drive improvement in humankind. The Farm Law recognizes that there is a direct relationship between labour and rewards – something that I am very keen to inculcate in all Broad employees. These laws are manifested in our HR management and practices. We try to provide the right incentives for people to compete healthily and therefore progress.

There is no ceiling to the money that an employee can earn; it is entirely up to him or her to achieve his or her own goals. When we hire or promote, we look for employees who are down-to-earth and hardworking. We don't want people who talk big. We need people who can use their talent in every hardworking day. Attitude is very important. We believe that, no matter what you are capable of, you can always find the right role in Broad if you have the right attitude. We practise four Highs in our HR policies: high quality of staff, high pay, high level of responsibility and high level of workload.

Although our HR practices are centred on principles, when reality challenges our practices, we will adapt. At Broad Town, for instance, employees must undergo ten days of 'boot camp' where they have to run gruelling marathons to instil an esprit de corps. We have found that people who have impressive work track records may not be able to finish the marathon. We might lose some talent if we are too strict with the training, so we do adapt. Personally I always keep my office door 'open' to every employee. They can approach me with their ideas and suggestions at any time. There is only see-through glass between the offices at Broad, not cement walls.

But we do have one very strict rule at Broad: those who leave or quit Broad for whatever reason will never have another chance to join Broad again. It might sound cruel and it is true that some people who have left Broad for family or personal reasons were reluctant to go. But that's a rule.

There are basically two goals that I am trying to reach with employees at Broad. I aim to improve their quality by establishing the right atmosphere for them, by instilling in them the importance of integrity and character. My second aim is to ensure that all employees have a common ideology that provides the motivation for them to work hard at Broad. I believe that the right employees are a necessary ingredient for Broad to transform from a domestic enterprise into a world-class enterprise. Broad employees are very proud to be who they are. In Changsha, telling people that you are a Broad employee means that you are a capable person living and working in a modernized, progressive environment – so we must be doing something right.

Broad's vision – built on the laws of nature

I would like all Broad employees to have this brand vision: 'Treasure environment and love life.' If you read Chinese, you will find that these two phrases read like two lines in a poem. Our desire for a better life actually harms the environment. What we want to do via Broad is to minimize that harm. In our company declaration we say that 'Heaven has called us to a noble mission: to create the most desirable indoor environment but not at the cost of damaging the global environment.'

In China 40 per cent of pollution is generated from coal burnt at electricity power stations. Electricity generation has become an enormous burden for the national economy. Yet there are only one to two months in a year in China that actually demand a high load production. Many power stations have been built for peak consumption times that account for only 20 per cent of total capacity; 80 per cent of their capacity is therefore wasted. Unfortunately, even with so many power stations, the power shortage problems have not been solved. During the peak consumption period in summer, the enormous demand of air-conditioning systems for electricity still cannot be satisfied.

On the other hand there are abundant natural gas resources available in China that are not being used to full potential. Sometimes the excess natural gas has to be burnt off so that pressure does not build up from underground. Broad air-conditioning products are driven by this abundant natural gas resource instead of electricity.

Although this use of natural gas makes perfect sense, I've discovered through my business how strange the world is. The world is not driven by benefits, but by commercial profits. Despite all the disadvantages from overusage, the electricity-driven air-conditioner has lasted for 100 years. Too many stakeholders – that is, power stations, air-con manufacturers, power carriers, and so on – profit from the present state of affairs for the current situation to change.

To me, no artificial element is good for nature. If it is good, nature would have already provided us with it. If it is not natural, it is not good, not really functional, not really beautiful. That is the law of nature. This is the reason why, at Broad, we are committed to incorporating, in every aspect of corporate and social activities and lifestyle, *The Limits to Growth: A Report for the Club of Rome's Project on the Predicament of Mankind*. It is Broad's intention to be a leading force in the world environment protection movement.

We firmly believe that a pro-environmental spirit is desperately needed in the world in the future. Energy-consuming and energy-supplying devices have a huge negative impact on the environment, so the development of energy-saving technology and products is one of the most needed and most rewarding industries for human society. In the twentieth century, air conditioning improved the quality of our lives. In the twenty-first century, people will have even higher expectations for a better air-conditioner. It should use a cleaner fuel, a safer refrigerant and have much higher energy efficiency. It should use renewable energy and be aimed at zero pollution to ensure the sustainable development of humankind. This is the mission that Broad will undertake for the twenty-first century. Broad will always orient its business to the development and production of such energy-saving technology and products. This is one of the reasons why we came into existence and it will remain a strong driving force. For me, the name 'Broad' symbolizes this broad and far-reaching vision.

Broad's strength

The history of the market economy in China is short, which means that the history of competition in China is short. At present, the nature of this competition is not mature or rational. In my opinion, it is not very difficult for brands to become successful if you have a rational strategy.

We have a unique position among the competition. Some people think that Broad is a nobody because we make only air-conditioners and nothing else (unlike the large diversified Chinese conglomerates). But that is something we value. We don't want to compete irrationally. So many enterprises get loans from banks or rely on public listings to extend their investment and product portfolios. We don't want to do that. For the past eight years we have not borrowed a penny from any bank.

In fact, we have a 500–600 million RMB surplus in our bank account. Rather than irrationally expanding, we prefer to keep that as a cash reserve for crises. Broad produces air-conditioning systems and air-conditioning systems only. We are a financially conservative company and we believe that being financially conservative is a basic attribute of a sustainable enterprise. Therefore we will not enter into irrational loans, public listings or joint ventures. I have seen many privately owned enterprises in China go bankrupt. Like meteorites, they burn brightly but eventually burn out. They fail to evolve into permanent shining stars because they misjudge reality and expand too quickly without sound thinking.

Ultimately, we want to build in strength rather than size. That is why we believe in outsourcing. Instead of making all of our own components, we source 90 per cent of them from world-famous manufacturers such as Sumitomo, Fuji, Nippon Steel Corp., Dupont and Siemens. In this way, product quality is guaranteed and we can concentrate on what we are good at, our core technology and our core production.

In the non-CFC/gas-driven category of air-conditioners, there are only about ten companies worldwide that can claim to be our competitors. But these non-CFC/gas-driven air-conditioner brands spend all their time fighting each other rather than the electricity-driven air-conditioner brands. So much effort and hard work is wasted through 'internal competition'. By contrast, Broad is the only brand that is fighting the electricity-driven air-conditioner brands.

In what way do we do this? Most non-CFC/gas-driven air-conditioning companies try to attract customers who already intend to own a gas-driven model. They don't work with customers who favour an electricity-driven model. They walk away when they know that the customer wants an electricity-driven model. We are different. We work even harder on customers who want to own a traditional model to try to 'convert' them. We don't walk away. The market for traditional models is so huge in comparison to the slice left for absorption models that converting air-conditioner users to gas-driven models is, in our opinion, the most rational way to expand our niche market and grow the Broad brand.

The future for Broad is challenging, but we know how we wish to face these challenges:

We will always practise the principle of self-improvement and seek to be distinguished. We will not allow self-conceit or unprogressiveness. We must improve our spiritual as well as economic competitiveness every day. Only then are we superior in terms of industrial scale and reputation to our competitors and only then can we stay ahead of the competition in terms of technology and management. Only then can we sustain our corporation to benefit mankind, realize our Broad dream and bring brilliance to our brand.

COMMENTARY

With Broad, Mr Zhang Yue has taken brand experience and corporate culture development to another level. Many brands in the West have built their own 'towns' – for example, Nike and Disney with Nike Town and Disney World, but these experiential destinations are targeted mainly at customers. Broad Town, on the other hand, is a brand experience built specifically for an internal audience – Broad employees. Buildings and gardens have been designed specially to inspire the intellectual and spiritual enrichment of the occupants who live, work, play and learn there. A great deal of effort and expense has been made to combine aesthetics with functionality on the basis of Mr Zhang Yue's belief that the most beautiful things in nature tend also to be the most effective.

Mr Zhang's management philosophy is surprising when you consider that the main product this company manufactures is the air-conditioner – an item that the average consumer and the average employee would not find particularly interesting or inspiring. Yet, it is the extent to which his philosophies have been realized and lived out that has yielded benefits for the company – Broad employees are very proud to be who they are and Broad is a company that is extremely sought after as an employer.

If you consider that the success of today's companies will depend on the multiplicative effect of brand capital, intellectual know-how and internal commitment, then Broad is certainly doing the right thing by investing in its people. Building the right culture and corporate mindset builds loyalty and commitment among internal stakeholders, producing an exponential effect on the company's performance. Going forward, Broad intends to strengthen its internal management systems and processes to avoid becoming a 'dictatorship' – a danger that Mr Zhang sees many Asian family-run companies facing. A balance may have to be struck between the strong corporate culture that he is shaping at Broad and allowing sufficient individualism to encourage the innovation and inventiveness that he is trying to build.

Broad does not intend to diversify from the production of air-conditioners. This is quite unusual for a successful Chinese company. The company is instead driven by a very clear and strong vision – it believes in sustainable strength rather than size and it believes in the environmental benefits that its products will bring to this world. This is an inspirational story for companies in the West that are attempting to realize the rhetoric behind their corporate mission statements.

9 | Legend: Championing the Value Perception of 'Made in China'

Introduction

'Legend is what some in the industry call the biggest computer company no one outside of China has heard of' says the Los Angeles Times. *Perhaps the last bit of this quote should read as 'no one outside of China has heard of yet'. The company not only maintains a 30 per cent share of China's PC market and 13–14 per cent of the total Asian-Pacific market (excluding Japan) but also has an annual revenue of more than $2 billion and annual profits of more than $40 million. It ships almost double the number of units shipped by IBM and Compaq Computers, its nearest rivals, to the same region. Some say that this feat is all the more amazing because Legend has beaten its American competitors in the areas of marketing, customer awareness and after-sales service – all traditional American strengths. In addition, Legend has earned the reputation of being the most transparent of China's 'red-chip' companies, and its national sales and distribution network is unparalleled.*

Legend's development has also mirrored that of the Chinese economy in that it is growing from strength to strength. However, as the Chinese economy opens up, the true test will lie in whether Legend manages to make as big an impact on international markets as it has managed to do in China. Zhu Guang from the Brand Promotion Department of Legend Group describes to us the factors that underpin the phenomenal strength of this company, from its ability to learn from others to its brand values and the strong sense of responsibility that it feels towards the economic development of China. These are the same factors that will underpin its global expansion.

From humble beginnings to the number one PC company in China

Legend began in 1984 as an outgrowth from the computer development work being carried out at the Chinese Academy of Sciences in Beijing. At that time, under the national leadership of Deng Xiaoping, there was pressure on the Academy to find commercial applications for its scientific research. Liu Chuanzhi, our founder, was a researcher with the Computer Technology Institute at the Academy and he pushed for a licence to start a computer company. At that time, the company comprised just 11 people with 200,000 yuan of capital trying to be an independent and profitable business. Starting up was difficult – the company was so small that it was bullied. Apparently a business in Jiangxi province tried to cheat us of 140,000 yuan.

We first started using the name 'Legend' on 23 June 1988 when Legend (Hong Kong) started operations. Legend Group itself was officially established in 1989. The word 'Legend' in Mandarin means 'Lian Xiang' or 'Chain of Thought' and was actually the name of our famous product, Legend Style Han Character System or 'Han Ka', a Chinese-based computer system which had the capability to predict: hence the name 'Chain of Thought'.

Our business started off by distributing computers and printers for foreign companies like HP and IBM in China. Then, in 1990, we began to design, manufacture and distribute our own line of PCs under the Legend brand. In 1992, after spotting an unmet need for home PCs in the Chinese market, we became the first company to introduce the home PC concept to China. At that time, the PC market in China was already facing international competition because China had lifted restrictions on the import of information technology products and parts. We had to be very skilful in the way that we managed our channels, our products, our resources because if we lost control of costs, we would have lost the fight.

In 1994, alone, our Hong Kong company suffered losses of 100 million yuan. Yet despite such difficulties, we managed to turn our fortunes around. We started making PCs that were tailored to domestic users and this saved costs because we could cut out some unnecessary functions. In addition, the company restructured in the same year and, under the leadership of our chief executive Yang Yuanqing, managed to build an excellent sales distribution network. In 1996 a very important milestone was reached – our PC sales exceeded those of IBM, HP and Compaq for the first time and we became the number one PC company in China with a 9.6 per cent market share. Since then, the combined market share of our rivals has collapsed to less than 10 per cent whereas we have maintained our leadership position in China and seen our market share rise to 30 per cent.

By the time I joined Legend in 1998, the company's prospects were already very good. In fact, Legend has experienced steady growth continuously, since 1988. It was only in 2001 when the global economic recession hit that we decided to put on the brakes. With this recession, we have had to ask ourselves whether we are sufficiently agile to respond quickly to market conditions and yet continue to maintain healthy profits. This period is like an IT winter, but, in the circumstances, I think that we are doing pretty well.

Honesty, trust and management excellence make success

If you ask me why Legend has managed to become so successful, I would say that there are two factors. The first is our corporate culture. Our founder Liu Chuanzhi had a very strong entrepreneurial and innovative spirit, and this spirit has become an important part of the Legend corporate culture. Let me explain further. Our corporate culture at Legend has four components:

- customer service
- accuracy (*jin zhun qiu shi*)
- entrepreneurship and innovation
- mutual honesty and trust.

Each of these components has played a part in our achievements. The last component of mutual honesty and trust, for example, is a very important feature. Throughout our development, from a small company to the large enterprise that we are today, we have always been a company that behaves with a great deal of integrity. This is important when you are struggling to grow and you require a loan to support your development. You need to have a reputation and image of integrity before shareholders and banks will trust you with the necessary capital.

The second factor is management, which determined our ability to compete effectively against foreign competition. At Legend we place much emphasis on management effectiveness. We are always trying to learn more about management from internationally successful enterprises so that we can catch up. I think there is an extraordinary learning spirit and capability within our organization that enables us to adapt the management practices of foreign corporations into a form that suits both the Chinese markets and Chinese companies like ourselves.

When our vice-presidents recently worked on a project with international brand consultants, our team raised many challenging questions, and it was clear that they were keen to learn about the branding process. Our learning capabilities also translate into increased internal effectiveness. As we reinvent ourselves into a better organization, we are constantly breaking the norms, introducing change within ourselves, assimilating new concepts and liberating our thinking.

If you place these two critical factors together, you will see that it is a strong management and cultural foundation that will continue to guarantee Legend's future success. This will be important as we extend ourselves into new fields in order to develop into a multifaceted business in the IT industry. True success is not a sudden thing nor is it determined purely from good sales revenues. We feel deeply that our corporate culture should go beyond the superficial and that there should be a sound management foundation within the organization so that operations are structured and standardized. Our corporate culture has also had a critical influence on the brand's deeper content and character.

The core values and vision of the Legend brand

Work on the Legend brand is constant and ongoing. Currently we are trying to bring across certain values that form the core of the Legend brand:

1 **Innovation and vitality** When people think of the Legend brand, we want them to think of a company that seeks rapid development, is always breaking the norm and is always innovative.
2 **Honesty, integrity and trust** When people think of the Legend brand, we want them to be assured that we will always deliver what we promise, whether these are promises to shareholders, customers or employees. We know that a brand has to have a brand promise and, when you give your stakeholders a promise, you must be sure of how you can deliver on it.
3 **Superior professional service** Right now, a market study by Gallup has shown that Legend has very high after-sales satisfaction levels in the Chinese market. To continue to ensure that our brand stands for superior professional service, we are not only examining our after-sales service quality but also other aspects such as our IT service offering and the total solutions that we provide corporations. We basically need to have a very comprehensive service system.
4 **An honourable and good name** Our hope is that, through the Legend brand and through our hard work, we can make the benefits of the modern technological environment more accessible to people, making it easier for them to enjoy their work and their personal lives.

When you consider all of these values, you will see how they come together to form the vision for the Legend brand. We hope that, through our hard work (improving our service and our infrastructure), with our honesty and integrity and with our deep understanding of the IT market in China, we can make people's personal and professional lives more enriched, convenient and effective through information technology tools, products and services. This is the Legend vision.

Translating values and vision into reality

How do we translate our brand values into the reality of our business? One example is, when we build our R & D capabilities and our professional service teams, we try to build them on the basis of our brand values of honesty and integrity. Similarly, when we attempt to lead the trends in the market and when we seek to make our customers' lives more convenient and free, we do so on the basis of our constant innovative spirit.

Our brand positioning is a result of serious analysis. For instance, we do not mention 'high-tech' as part of our brand positioning now, even though you would imagine that to be a natural characteristic of a computer manufacturer brand. Because we cannot compete against companies like IBM in terms of technological advancement at present, we recognize that there is no advantage in making 'high-tech' a unique characteristic of our brand. But in the next three to four years, when we have caught up on that front, this will definitely change.

We also try to ensure that we offer the superior service that is expressed in our brand values. Last year, we decided to become even more service-oriented in order to provide more added value to our customers. We now have a dedicated IT management consulting services group which has just signed a very large contract in China. This IT services group will transform and diversify the mix of our current businesses.

Honesty and integrity, entrepreneurship and innovation – these values are all core parts of Legend's brand and corporate culture. As our work revolves around these principles, both work and values become closely intertwined. I feel it is important that our vision to make people's lives easier through technology is actually supported by real capabilities. Our PCs are able, for example, to help customers access the Internet with a one-touch button. This is what differentiates Legend from Dell in terms of PC design. Legend computers have much more software and user-friendliness because we sell to Chinese customers who are not as computer-savvy or knowledgeable about IT as Dell's customers. This is the kind of work that we want to continue doing, supported by our corporate culture and our brand values.

Knowing our customers

We have two main types of customer – corporate and individual. And this can be separated into a further four sub-segments – individual and family under the 'individual' category and large corporates and SMEs under the 'corporate' segment. For individual customers we provide products like PDAs and personal PCs. For families, we provide E-Home type solutions and family PCs. For big corporates/big customers and SMEs, we have corporate IT solutions that are appropriate to them.

Individual and corporate customers look for different things, so we have to stress different aspects of our brand and our products in order to meet their needs. Individual customers, for example, place more emphasis on the brand and on trends, and are more impulsive in their decision-making. Corporate buying tends to be more logical and measured. And corporate buyers are more interested in what we offer in terms of after-sales services and service systems. Furthermore, because they are more sensitive to price, they need to know the value that they are getting for the price that they are paying.

In the global corporate market we compete against companies such as IBM, HP and Dell. In the domestic market, we face companies like TCL, Founder, Samsung and Sony. I think the main way in which we outdo our competitors is through our superior understanding of the Chinese market and of the Chinese customers' needs. This understanding is something that other companies cannot match and allows us to offer localized solutions.

For example, through an in-depth study conducted amongst schools, we found that one problem faced by schools in China is the constant theft of the roller ball in the computer mouse by students. So we designed a mouse with a roller ball that cannot be removed, and sales of this product rocketed. Never underestimate the potential of such small innovations when they directly and effectively address the customers' needs. In this instance, Founder was selling a mouse that was much cheaper but, in the long run, it was more cost-effective for the schools to purchase a Legend mouse. We have had many years' experience in servicing and understanding the Chinese market, and our entire product design system taps in to this experience. Furthermore, our massive customer service system makes the benefits of this experience available to our customers.

Price is a delicate issue that every Chinese company faces. Our price is positioned higher than that of other domestic brands but lower than that of international brands like Dell. Research has shown, however, that one of our most prominent brand characteristics is 'value for money'. So, although our price may be higher than that of other domestic brands, the service that we offer – for example, after-sales service for PCs – is far superior. Underpinning this superior service are our brand values of honesty and integrity – doing what we say we will do. Therefore we offer a service guarantee in which we promise to respond quickly to any problems that the customer has with his or her PC and to fix those problems free of charge.

Legend does not engage in price wars. Look at the colour TV market in China. It is currently stuck in a price war that is not benefiting any of the manufacturers in the industry. Companies inevitably try to match one another in the market, but we at Legend do not follow the market. As leader, we have a market share that is three times that of the number two player – 30 per cent versus 10 per cent. If we wanted to, we could easily derail our competitors by reducing our prices. But we prefer instead to differentiate our brand in terms of quality, ease of use and true value for money. We are careful. Because we are not willing to reduce our prices, we make sure that we offer a better service. Ultimately, this is about making the Legend brand a high-quality, high-class brand, representing good taste – not the cheapest brand that everyone can afford. This way, our customers will be willing to pay the premium for our brand.

Communicating Legend the brand

There are many factors that influence our customers to purchase a Legend product, but I believe that our brand is the main factor. Legend is a very strong name in China. It is a brand that commands trust. It enjoys a very strong word-of-mouth reputation amongst consumers and that is one of the best ways to promote the company and its products.

We have a department that is focused on brand value creation. That is the department I belong to. We have two main responsibilities. The first is to promote the company's brands. We know that what each of our brands says needs to be integrated with what the company wants to do and its corporate strategy. We therefore communicate to target audiences, such as shareholders, the media and the government, our philosophy, our corporate strategy and our vision as well as the advanced technological products that are in the pipeline. All promotions and communications are focused on strengthening our brands.

We have a very comprehensive approach to PR. At the last launch of our new computer product, we made headline news in over 20 newspapers and journals in China. This is something that is difficult for other companies to achieve and is the advantage of being a national champion enterprise. We maintain very good relationships with the journalists of all of the major media companies – something that is quite unusual.

Our second responsibility is to oversee the marketing communications plan for the entire company. This is a very centrally controlled function. Why do we structure it like this? So that we have control over all our brands. Each business unit has its own marketing professionals with responsibility for a portfolio of products. However, we cannot let each product group have absolute freedom because it may affect Legend's corporate brand, so we set guidelines for them to follow on packaging, advertising and so on. This is our brand management system.

In the future, our work is going to revolve around the four brand characteristics that I described earlier. We will be organizing PR activities and advertising to increase awareness of these characteristics.

In the future we will be moving towards a more high-tech and service-oriented image for Legend. This is part of our plan to eventually transform ourselves from a staid and conventional manufacturing company to a more commercial IT company along the lines of Sun Microsystems and HP. We cannot afford to let people think that Legend is a company without technology.

To substantiate this transformation we will be increasing our investments in R & D to strengthen our R & D capabilities and build up our technological base. We intend to provide more front-end interconnectable facilities to unleash the power of the Internet and to allow our PCs, mobile phones, PDAs and cameras to connect seamlessly. Technology and service-related information about Legend are key items that we will try to report on the news and reflect in our advertising and promotions. With a good technological image we will be able to sell many other services. Therefore all our systems – PR, marketing, advertising – will need to support the communication of this technological image.

Marketing at Legend is organized very comprehensively and takes place at three levels: first, centrally, as I have described above, on a group and corporate level; second, at the level of the seven large regions where each will carry out localized marketing activities; and, finally, at the level of our dealers and distributors who also perform marketing activities with guidance from my department. They also localize their promotional activities.

Distribution like McDonalds and KFC

Marketing has to be linked closely to channel distribution. It is because we have an extensive distribution network that our marketing strength can be as massive as it is. Legend's products are not sold directly – another way in which we are very different from Dell – unless we are dealing with very large customers who want us, for example, to install their financial systems. In such cases, we do need to deal with them directly so that we can move fast and provide a solution that is customized to their requirements.

Otherwise, we have specialized outlets selling Legend products under the Legend '1+1' logo which you can see everywhere in the streets of China. These specialized shops are operated by our channel partners. We probably have around a few thousand of such shops in the country for individual customers and about the same number of outlets for corporate customers.

What are the advantages of having Legend branded outlets? Some people may think that this increases our cost base. But our philosophy is that we should have outlets that permeate all the regions in China – outlets where customers can buy our products, keep in touch with us and enjoy the IT services that we provide. It is a similar strategy to that of McDonalds or KFC which have outlets everywhere in the world in order to become part of the local communities.

To become a Legend channel partner is not easy. For each outlet, we have a very serious training programme. You must have sufficient capital, technological resources and a reasonable foundation in management. These channels will definitely change. There will be enlargement and also pruning of those that are non-performing. At present, however, very few have been terminated. Most of our channel partners have grown up with us. In the future, we see the provision of services to our customers as a joint responsibility to be borne between our channel partners and ourselves under the Legend brand.

In December this year, we will be introducing Legend World – an experiential space for our customers like that of Oracle World, which you may have heard of. It is part of our plan to help build an IT society in China. It will be like the IT equivalent of Nike Town.

Branding at the heart of our organization

The brand is the heart of our organization. Brand strategy affects corporate strategy at Legend. First, we determine the unique characteristics of the brand and its positioning to set the brand strategy. Then we think about how this brand should influence the work of other departments in the organization from marketing activities, channel sales, advertising, promotions to R&D and human resources. We also think about how we will use our brand values, philosophy and special characteristics to communicate with the rest of the departments within the organization so that we all understand conceptually how to approach our marketing.

Legend's founder Liu has had a lot of influence on our brand. As I have already explained, the values of honesty and integrity are important to us today because he emphasized them. He is the one who told us that Legend is successful today because it has shown honesty and integrity in its operations. Entrepreneurship and innovation are characteristics of the brand that are also largely attributed to Liu's personal charisma. Liu himself places a great deal of importance on branding. He feels that many of the brand issues need to be discussed at board level.

For example, it was the board that decided that our logo and the Chinese characters for the word Legend should be placed side-by-side. As Liu is now chairman of the company, it is our chief executive Yang Yuanqing who has ultimate responsibility for the brand. His strict and prudent, but innovative, style is enriching the content of our brand just as Liu's leadership did. I feel, however, that the success of our brand is not just one person's work. Defending the brand is everyone's responsibility. Every employee represents, in some way, the Legend brand and image. The only difference is in the magnitude of that responsibility. This is why each value that forms part of our brand and our corporate culture has been comprehensively described, so that our employees know how things should be done to achieve consistency with the Legend brand and corporate culture. This is a way to guide the behaviour of our employees and also to ensure that our brand is protected.

Legend's promise to employees

The Legend brand is our best tool for attracting talent. A recent survey of university students revealed that Legend is one of the most preferred employers in China. This is not because of what we guarantee to pay in salary. Rather, it is the Legend brand promise that draws them. What is this promise? We tell them that after they join us, we expect them to constantly improve and innovate. If they are stagnant, their position in Legend will be at risk. They will be required to constantly accept and integrate new ideas and thinking into their work.

However, we promise that their progress in Legend will be 'ceiling-less'. We tell them that we are not in need of capital. We have more than sufficient funds and what we lack is talented leaders for our troops. We tell them that we have a business with very good prospects – a business that needs to be developed by talented people such as themselves. So, if you have an idea, you will be given the capital and the freedom to implement it within Legend. This is a very attractive proposition and is the reason why we have been able to attract many students who have studied overseas and gained fantastic academic credentials, as well as the top engineers from China's elite universities.

Legend has seen very rapid growth both in revenues and in size in the last decade. There are both positives and negatives to this. When a company is stagnant, regressing or merely maintaining the same rate of growth, its culture will lack rejuvenation. If your salary is being cut and people are being made redundant, it is very unlikely that you will pay much attention to corporate culture. High-speed growth and development allows employees within the company to 'feel' the company's hope. They can 'see' the future and their own personal development in the future development of the company.

Therefore, I think that high-speed growth has the advantage of stimulating employees to pay attention to corporate culture. At the same time, high-speed growth means constant change. This makes it difficult for the company's corporate culture to mature, because it needs time. It does not develop overnight. Let me illustrate it this way. With high-speed growth the number of staff will increase rapidly, with each member of staff bringing his or her own set of values. The difficulty lies in integrating each staff member, and through training, to encourage him or her to accept Legend's corporate culture as quickly as possible. If an employee does not find a fit between his or her own personal values and the values of Legend, then he or she should leave.

Allowing brand equity to grow

When people ask what brand management lessons we have learnt through our experiences, I have one point that I believe is worth making. In the IT business, we introduce new brands every year. Each time we launch a brand, we spend a lot of money. What we underestimate is the brand's ability to generate its own value over time. In introducing a brand, we tend only to explain the product's capabilities without giving sufficient focus to the brand's characteristics and values. Also, in the past we have introduced too many brands, some of which have now disappeared. We have not given our brands sufficient time to stabilize and accumulate brand equity.

Similarly, every year we introduce slogans. For instance, we had one that said, 'Every day, every year, we are improving.' Then this year we introduced 'As Legend becomes closer to you, technology becomes closer to you.' The problem is that the slogan changes too frequently. In the future we want a more consistent and coherent message in our slogans so that the message accumulates and reinforces itself over time in the consumer's mind. Again, this will increase our overall brand equity. This is especially important for our corporate brand.

If you look at our current brand structure, it basically emphasizes one brand as our strategy. What we hope to do is to channel more resources into the main corporate brand in order to drive the effectiveness of the product brands. At the same time, we want to develop our business and product brands so that they are able to express more clearly the products and services we have on offer. In future our business structure may change, but I think it will largely remain a 'one brand' strategy. This means that it is important to let the Legend corporate brand accumulate its value over time and not keep changing what it is about.

At Legend we do not place much emphasis on measuring the financial value of our brand. Of course, I have seen that other companies like Coca Cola, IBM and Microsoft have done so. You could potentially look at sales volume, relative price differences between your products and other products, comparative industry profitability, manufacturing scale and stock prices to calculate this valuation but there will always be a subjective element in the method. If we do it in-house it will be even more impossible to be objective. I think it is more important to measure our marketing effectiveness. For instance, what kind of message is our brand conveying to the consumers and what kind of image of Legend is being formed in their minds as a result? When we do such an analysis every year, I will have a better idea of how to improve the brand.

Five years' time

I hope that in five years' time, when we look back to now, we will have progressed so far that it will be like looking back from now to 1984 when we started with only 11 people. Although there is such a big difference between us and the large IT companies in the world today, we are going to grit our teeth and persevere – to become a Fortune 500 company by the year 2010. I am very optimistic about Legend's future. If you want to buy shares, I will recommend you Legend shares. Many people have become rich buying Legend shares. Our profits are increasing all the time. As an employee, I am full of confidence.

One major challenge for the future is, of course, how we are going to improve our technological base. At the moment, we are trying to enhance our technological know-how to match companies like IBM and HP. We know that, for the future, we will need leading core technologies if we are to have a stronghold on the market and increase our market share. On the other hand, we do have a very spirited and dynamic group of employees as well as a good cultural and management foundation. This will attract even more talented people to come to work for us and help us develop faster.

Entry to the WTO will not have that great an impact on us. The tax in high-tech industries in China is low anyway. We were already a very open industry in the 1990s compared to, say, the automobile industry, which was very protected. And because we have been competing on a global level, any new competition now is not going to scare us. In fact, we welcome WTO membership. It is only in an intensely competitive environment that we can continuously train ourselves to develop beyond the borders of China.

This development will come through alliances and mergers and acquisitions. Our brand and corporate values of honesty and integrity are going to be key when we attempt to work with other companies in such alliances. For example, when we wanted to expand our IT service business, we realized that we could not develop it from scratch, so we acquired Han International Consulting Company. This locally renowned company is an information-intensive company whereas we are a manufacturing-intensive company. But we acknowledged the differences that were going to arise in our corporate cultures and we embraced them. We allowed for difference and encouraged it.

Also, when we partnered with AOL, we allowed a new corporate culture to develop in the joint venture. We did not expect ourselves to completely adapt to AOL's culture nor vice versa. Rather, we sought to come to a joint solution.

Carrying the flag for China

Legend is a national brand and a national champion enterprise in China. I think this carries with it certain strengths. If I, a Chinese person, am working for IBM or HP today, I may work hard to prove my worth in the company and will, in the process, make IBM stronger, but I may not find that sense of achievement that comes through having a national identity. If I work in a national enterprise, however, I will feel very proud to be part of it and will do my best to make it a stronger enterprise so that it can defend itself better against foreign competition. Legend can wave the national enterprise flag because we are striving towards achieving benefits for our country. There is a pride in our Chinese roots. And this spirit has, and always will, urge our employees on.

Legend's biggest contribution to society is not just in providing IT information services and products that will help speed up China's development into an information-based society. There are other social responsibilities that we carry. For a nation to be strong, it needs a group of reputable, well-known companies to represent it. These companies will set an example – a benchmark for other companies to follow. They will share their experiences and management expertise with their fellow companies, pushing forward every company's development and ultimately bringing progress to the entire country. In this sense, China badly needs companies like Legend and Haier. I believe that it is this sense of responsibility felt within each of our employees towards our country that has pushed us to go that little bit further in our efforts. In China, although it may not appear to be so, there is real support for national brands from both customers and the media. I think our number one position in the Chinese market is related to the fact that we identify ourselves as, first and foremost, a Chinese national champion enterprise and one that will be a pillar for China's economic development.

Being a Chinese brand can have its disadvantages. Our market study conducted in Europe and the US showed that the 'Made in China' label connotes poor quality in international markets. But I believe that the positive factors far outweigh the negative factors. And, besides, negative perceptions of Chinese manufacturing will definitely change – it is only a question of time. In the 1950s and 1960s when Japanese cars were entering the US market and other Japanese products were entering Europe, the perception of their products and brands was similar to that of Chinese brands today. But because a group of excellent Japanese companies led the way, innovating and assimilating advanced technologies from other countries, they managed to achieve high-speed growth and development. Today's top Japanese brands like Sony and Toyota have become as internationally well-known as the leading Western brands.

In the 1980s and the 1990s, the success stories were brands like LG and Samsung. In the West, these brands are not as well regarded as Sony but they have nevertheless made definitive steps forward. Their market share is increasing and their prospects are good for the future. Step-by-step, I believe that, one day, we will see the emergence of brands in China equivalent to the Sonys and the Samsungs.

Of course, emerging Chinese companies like Haier and ourselves would need to tidy up our internal organization first. Thankfully, China offers a massive market that will provide many opportunities for growth and exploration. It will be a good training ground for the exercise of business management skills and corporate culture development. There is a chance for us to learn to do things in a more structured manner with proper procedures so that, in future, Chinese companies will be able to compete against international brands. One day, equipped with the experience and the strength from all this training, Legend will achieve for China what Sony has achieved for Japan.

COMMENTARY

Think of Germany and one thinks of the famous brands of Mercedes, BMW and Audi – three of the world's top makers of luxury cars. The development and success of these icons of German engineering excellence have certainly put the German automobile industry at the forefront of the global car industry, contributing to the overall development of the German economy. Similarly, as Mr Zhu Guang mentions, Sony has achieved much international credibility for the Japanese electronics and technology industry. One wonders at the drive and dedication with which these German and Japanese companies sought to re-establish their respective countries on the economic world stage after the Second World War.

In the same way, Chinese companies feel very passionately that it is now China's turn to take centre-stage. What is striking about Legend is how strongly it regards itself as playing a key role in this national endeavour. It is a 'national champion enterprise' – a company that is flying the Chinese flag high for all other Chinese companies to follow. Together with other champions like Haier and TCL, it intends to learn best practices from foreign competitors, disseminate this critical knowledge to its fellow Chinese corporations, improve on it and pave the way to future internationalization and global dominance.

Furthermore, this sense of national identity is a driving force felt within each of its employees. They are not working just for their own profit, but also to make sure that Legend can defeat its foreign competition – and this surely gives Legend a competitive advantage over Western companies whose employees do not feel such an acute sense of battle.

Moreover, this national spirit seems to extend to other stakeholders. Legend feels that it has the support of its investors, the media and Chinese consumers, giving it further competitive advantages. But perhaps it is not so much 'Made in China' but 'Made by Legend' that makes the difference, and this may have something to do with the way in which the company upholds its values of honesty and integrity. Growing the residual trust that Legend has built up in its relationships with its stakeholders will be critical to building sustainable brand capital for the future.

The challenge for Legend is whether it will be able to replicate its success internationally. At present, it has a clear advantage in that it has a deep understanding of Chinese customers and their needs, but what about non-Chinese customers who are more computer-savvy? Legend's marketing power, based on its large distribution network, stops at the Chinese borders. How is it going to reach out to overseas markets and become part of their communities? These are the important issues that Legend is going to have to address. Nevertheless, at least on its home turf, it will continue to be a champion among champions.

10 | AsiaInfo: Setting Standards in Corporate Governance

Introduction

AsiaInfo Holdings Inc. (Nasdaq ASIA) is a provider of total network solutions. Co-founded by James Ding in 1994, it began as a small Texas-based Internet content provider (ICP) selling information about China to US investors. The following year the company moved to Beijing, taking with it a vision to help China link up to the Internet and to the world. Today, AsiaInfo is China's leading telecoms network integrator and software provider, having built most of mainland China's Internet infrastructure and with sales in 2000 reaching $176 million.

AsiaInfo's chief executive, James Ding, tells us about the rise of AsiaInfo and his vision of building a multinational corporation. He explains the five key challenges in achieving this aim and also the critical role of corporate governance. He firmly believes that, to attract shareholders, any listed company has to have in place processes and structures for administration and governance that are sustainable and meet international standards.

For businesses in China, this presents the greatest challenge because lack of transparency and inefficient regulatory structures have been the norm. Through its US connection and by taking learning from overseas, AsiaInfo has achieved a great deal of success in this area, with many of its top leaders being asked to speak on corporate governance issues around China. James Ding is considered something of an expert on the subject and he hopes that, through these knowledge-sharing opportunities more local entrepreneurs and government departments will come to understand and appreciate the importance of corporate governance.

Ding attributes AsiaInfo's success to its efforts to reconcile the needs of all its stakeholders – not just its shareholders but also its managers, employees and customers. For example, he has introduced steps to ensure a good fit between the corporate values and those of new management and employees.

And for the customer, Ding makes sure that the company follows an approach that is consistently solutions-focused. Prior to AsiaInfo's arrival on the scene, systems integration (SI) advice to the customer tended to be biased in favour of the hardware supplier who could supply the SI company with the cheapest products. That meant customers did not always get the products that were right for them.

AsiaInfo fought hard to establish a position of neutrality that would demonstrate true integrity towards customers and their needs. This approach initially caused friction because AsiaInfo would not stock products unless they truly met customer needs. However, by sticking to these principles, AsiaInfo has grown into a highly trusted and respected brand in China.

Getting off the ground

I am one of the co-founders of AsiaInfo Holdings Inc., who had the vision to help China build its Internet. It was around 1988 and I had just arrived in the US where I was studying for a Masters degree in information systems at the University of California at Los Angeles. I am interested in information systems and how information is distributed, and the Internet represents the perfect medium for that. I began to think just how powerful a country the size of China could be if it could get its Internet network off the ground.

In 1993 I met Edward Tian, who is now the president of China Netcom, and we talked about the possibility of starting a business that could help China link up to the Internet. That was how AsiaInfo's predecessor, BDI, began. I was 28.

In the early days, we concentrated on the distribution of information. It was the early 1990s and, since China did not have an Internet infrastructure, we set up in Dallas, Texas. Back then, our aim was to sell business information from China to users in the US. While we weren't helping China build its own network directly, we were helping to bring information about China to the rest of the world. The problem at the time was in getting users to pay for the information, since most were either students or professors. We had no venture capitalists behind us, unlike companies such as Yahoo, so basically we couldn't sustain the business.

We returned to China to see how things had changed and found that the telecommunication carriers had started to think about building China's Internet infrastructure. We knew we could help, but by contributing our technology expertise rather than our information-related services. So in 1995 we moved the whole operation back into China and began to concentrate on telecoms network integration. We set about recruiting more technology people and started to bid for contracts.

With the shift in focus, we decided that we would have to rethink the parent company structure and how we could separate the technology side of the business from the information side. We discussed the possibility of having a logo and one idea was to use the @ symbol. However, we decided against this, having seen IBM spend millions of dollars in its efforts to promote the 'e'. Instead, we took advice from a PR company which told us that a symbol is less memorable than a name.

It was then that we dropped the name AsiaInfo Services, which we had used previously to promote our information services business, and became known instead as AsiaInfo Holdings. We took AsiaInfo for the parent because of its simplicity and its functionality and also because it translates literally as the same in Chinese.

Our first project, for China Telecom, was to design and build the country's first national commercial Internet backbone. It was the largest network-building contract in China, and it got AsiaInfo off the ground. Since that project, we have constructed national backbones and provincial access networks for all of China's major national telecoms carriers, including China Mobile, China Unicom and China Netcom. We have also built China's first provincial Internet backbone, GuangdongNet.

First steps

When we began, none of the founders, myself included, had any experience in running a business and we made many, many mistakes. But that is part of the learning curve. Growth comes from learning from your own and others' mistakes, and it is very important that we support that.

That lack of experience has meant that, at times, we have had to hire specialists in certain areas, such as for setting training programmes for our employees. We have also hired management consultants from time to time. And when we went public in 2000, we hired branding experts to help us position the company for the investor audience, focusing on the qualities of transparency and honesty.

Having relocated to China with a new business focus of network integration, we set out our first five-year business plan. That was created using only our common sense and, although it was very vague, many of our predictions have turned out to be pretty accurate.

Our initial focus was telecoms network integration because that is like a consultancy service and required the least capital to get started. We then predicted that eventually we would be making software and developing the products side of the business, which is exactly what we have done. In 2000, we restructured operations into two strategic business units: Network Solutions, which offers Internet and telecoms infrastructure construction, and Software Products which develops billing and customer care, messaging and network management applications. Since then, we have invested heavily in software and R & D, developing and branding our own software products.

The final part of the plan is to become more vertically integrated, which is our present long-term strategy for growth. That strategy also involves broadening our focus to begin selling more software products outside China, although China will remain our priority market.

Achieving our vision

Our vision in the short term is to become the leading provider of world-class software products and network solutions in China, which we aim to achieve through harnessing our strengths. If we continue to grow as we have, then I believe we have a good chance of achieving this.

In the long term we are aiming to become a large multinational corporation with an internationally recognized brand. Can the Chinese build such a thing? An editor of a journal once told me that capitalist blood flows through every Chinese person. Indeed, the Chinese have achieved outstanding results in the global economy bringing diligence, intelligence and talent to the world throughout history. So the answer is: of course we can build successful enterprises.

In the high-tech sector, I believe that we will soon see the emergence of international enterprises founded and managed by Chinese people. It may not necessarily be AsiaInfo or Legend or whoever is out there right now. In terms of global recognition, we are like infants taking our first tentative steps. But I am confident that AsiaInfo can quickly bridge the gap to become a large-scale multinational – the foundation stones are already in place.

Success is not easy; it has an element of randomness to it. It does not necessarily follow that you will be successful if you have done everything right – a minor hitch outside your control can easily foul things up. That is why I like the ex-president of Intel Andrew S. Grove's philosophy that only extremely dedicated and focused 'maniacs' can survive.

There are many potential traps on the road to success so I am cautious, always wondering what dangers are lurking ahead for AsiaInfo. Of course, if I couldn't cope with this state of mind, then I wouldn't have founded AsiaInfo or become a successful manager. I have to believe that the journey is also the reward. To me, an extremely dedicated and focused 'maniac' is a manager who possesses the ability to anticipate the dangers and respond swiftly.

Five challenges on the path to becoming a multinational

The personality challenge

Founding a business and turning it into a success does not merely require a clever brain. An entrepreneur and founder has to have two qualities: an innovative spirit which includes the ability to entertain concepts and ideas that others fear; and passion.

AsiaInfo's innovative spirit is like a magic weapon, enabling us to play a leading role in our industry. Once we had a competitor who used us as a learning model. After four years, he realized that our market share was growing while his company's was shrinking. After attending a management course at Beijing University, the company's management realized that, because they were always following in our footsteps, they were destined to lag behind. Because we are constantly innovating, we are always one step ahead of them.

I am not a particularly passionate person, but I do have a very passionate partner, Edward Tian. In AsiaInfo's early days, it was Tian's passion that helped the company grow by enabling me to harness my innovative spirit and ability to think independently.

But for an entrepreneur, passion is not enough, although without passion it is impossible to start a business. A practical person will not want to start a business, as he or she will invariably wait until the probability of success exceeds 50 per cent before making a start. But the probability of success in founding a business is definitely less than 50 per cent.

The operations challenge

Operations is actually a conceptual problem. We come from a generation that grew up in a state planned economy and so have no notion of market economics – for Chinese people, earning money is not something to be proud of. It was not until I went to the US for further studies that I started to understand the notion of a 'market' and experienced the meaning of competition. Of course, today's Chinese business founders have improved their way of thinking about market economics.

The basic fundamental of founding a business lies in operations. If you have a good concept, but do not know how to manifest it commercially, then founding a business will be akin to building castles in the air. If you do not have healthy operational thinking, it will be difficult to continue the fledgling business. In the wave of a networked economy, we have seen many once-prominent companies fade into oblivion. I think the main cause is problems in operations.

Take AsiaInfo: the business was founded on the idea that we would be an Internet content provider and sell information about China and Asia through network stations. However, at that time, our operating environment restricted us, and the market did not accept our business concept. That was why we turned around to focus instead on system integration and producing technology software.

From 1996 to 1997, the Internet became a sizzling hot item. At the pinnacle of Internet fever (1997), we received venture capital investment and had a major debate on AsiaInfo's operational thinking. Some people suggested that we should go into Internet content provision because we had the best network infrastructure system and the best technicians who would be able to use our software to help customers set up three network stations per night. I decided against this, as I felt that it would not be a profitable move and, furthermore, our core strengths did not lie in content broadcasting. Consequently we did not pursue the Internet bubble and that decision has since proven to be the right one.

The operations challenge can destroy 90 per cent of a company, simply because there are so many potential paths to take, few of which lead to success. I have a 30/70 rule. In the fiercely competitive international market, our most important goal will always be to satisfy market needs. However, market needs are not always obvious. To really understand market needs, the operations management staff need to thoroughly analyse the information they have. If you do not have control of 30 per cent of the information available when you are making decisions, you are making wild guesses, and that is very close to gambling. But when you have 70 per cent of the information, and you are still waiting for more information to understand the market even more, then the market share may as well belong to someone else. When you have food in your mouth, swallow it quickly. Otherwise, the food is not yours.

The management challenge

I think that one of the greatest challenges for young Chinese people looking to set up business in China concerns their general lack of understanding of business management in a capitalist system. The younger generation have been educated in a socialist country, and their understanding of other economic systems is weak. Once education improves, I think we will begin to see more and more young Chinese entrepreneurs building well-managed, sustainable businesses.

In AsiaInfo's early days, we did not necessarily use the best management practices. With only limited resources, we could only focus on satisfying customers' needs and discovering new potential market opportunities. In terms of internal administration, we did not adopt the management styles of big companies, as the cost was too high. We concentrated instead on proving our business model to investors and convincing customers of our service and product guarantee.

However, as the company grew to a certain size, the cohesiveness of the team became a critical factor. We went through a very long, painful learning curve and we have now reached a stage where we must keep growing.

Technology, strategy, human resources and capital all need to be managed successfully. To this end, we use both our own experience and learning from Silicon Valley with its team of professional managers. In our interaction with our offices in the US, we learn an immense amount.

This throws up another problem – the clash of corporate culture with professional managers. In 2001 we had a major shift in AsiaInfo's top management. A chief executive, a general manager and four high-level executives left the company. I feel that we had placed too much emphasis on these professional managers' skills and abilities whilst failing to integrate them into our corporate culture. AsiaInfo is a young, high-tech company that demands practical action and passion – qualities that were lacking in these professional managers. In future we hope that managers will be able to complement our corporate culture.

Part of our current vision is to become China's best-managed company and, today, there are four qualities I always demand in my managers: honesty and integrity; passion for innovation; team spirit; and respect and responsibility for the job. In addition, all our senior managers are native Chinese with first-hand knowledge of the local market, most of whom have worked or studied abroad, becoming conversant in international management practices. By encouraging open communications at all organizational levels, we are then able to tap the management experience of our employees.

The growth challenge

Growing up is like climbing a bigger mountain. As chief executive, I must use investors' capital wisely so that I can grow the company in scale and meet Wall Street's earnings expectations. But, notwithstanding the pressure to grow, the time frame must be realistic. The speed of growth must achieve a balance between not outgrowing ourselves and, at the same time, not being too slow to invest in areas with the most potential.

The international challenge

A product-focused company must become international because only then can the cost base be reduced. I can use mathematics to prove this: the cost base of Chinese companies is one-third that of foreign companies, but our market scale is only about one-sixth of theirs. If you analyse this you will see that, in reality, the cost base of foreign companies is really half that of Chinese companies. Even if they lose money in China, they can always recoup in other markets. If we only have the local Chinese market, there is no way in which we can compete with them because, in the long term, our cost base is too high.

Of course, the risks of becoming international are very high. Moving from China to a more developed country immediately presents the challenge of a higher cost base. There are also cultural and social differences to be dealt with. So going international is not a short-term move, but requires long-term planning. It is always easier to make money from your front door than in other people's territory.

At present, we are introducing our mature software products into international markets, because the software R & D costs have already been recouped and the cost base is relatively stable. Selling in international markets can strengthen our competitiveness, as well as raise the level of our technological skills through valuable feedback from international customers.

AsiaInfo is a provider of total network solutions. The development of our products must be our first priority in our strategy to conquer global markets. In future we plan to maintain a good pace of development – the internationalization agenda is already set. If we do not do this, then we cannot consider ourselves successful.

The importance of corporate governance

Corporate governance is a central challenge in the development of China's enterprises. A company must be able to develop in a way that has long-term sustainability, so it must be able to reconcile the interests of shareholders, management and employees. There are comprehensive laws outside China that clearly specify the roles and responsibilities of the board and of management so that there are no conflicts of interests or irresponsible behaviours. To develop, a company must adhere strictly to these rules in operations and in practice. Even if you are chief executive, no matter what percentage of shares you own, you should only exercise your rights as a chief executive.

AsiaInfo is very different from many traditional Chinese state-owned enterprises and privately owned companies. For example, since its inception, AsiaInfo has been developing internationally and, in the telecoms industry, it has always competed with international players.

AsiaInfo's development in the telecoms arena is such that our management model is helping the globalization of all Chinese enterprises. Looking ahead, it will leverage its competitive advantage, develop more global and comprehensive resources and capitalize on the foreign venture capital investment to aggressively nurture China's high-tech industry and continue to focus on the development of China's telecoms industry.

The three taboos of corporate governance

In terms of culture, corporate governance should not be viewed as limiting, as a good administration structure is an essential support for an entrepreneurial company. If you do not have a system to protect the rights of minority shareholders, for example, then they will not invest in the company.

As a NASDAQ-listed company, AsiaInfo applies high standards so that it can fulfil the requirements of listed companies, and it applies the same standards in administering the management of the company. In fact, we spent a long time studying the needs of shareholders and the concepts of honesty and transparency came out as key. Since then, AsiaInfo has been named as a world-class transparent company in Asia and we are very proud of our work in this area. In fact, some of the top management, myself included, have been asked to speak in other countries about corporate governance. AsiaInfo is one of the very few companies listed on NASDAQ and it is very successful and trusted by our shareholders. This has had a favourable impact on our maintaining our competitive advantage and achieving growth.

In terms of management, I wish I could have the final say in directing the company's operations and strategy. However, again, I do not wish to override the administrative structure to forcefully implement what I think is the right strategy for the company. As a chief executive and part of the management, I need to seek ways within the administrative structure to persuade my shareholders and my board of directors and gather support for my proposals.

In terms of operations, I think the taking of shortcuts is a big mistake, as this may breach the company's rules and regulations, adversely affect shareholders' trust and exacerbate the problems.

Chinese companies need to strengthen their administrative structures

I was a recent participant in a forum 'Administration of Chinese Companies' held in April 2002, which was concerned with building a transparent, fair, just and modern corporate system with clear lines of responsibilities. This signifies that Chinese enterprises are maturing, and that Chinese businesspeople are bridging the gap between their own knowledge and that of other world-class corporate leaders.

The concept of company administration or corporate governance is relatively new to Chinese enterprises. In a narrow sense, it refers to a company's internal management system. In a broad sense, however, it encompasses the relationship between the company and society. A company's administration is a system to ensure that a company is able to operate efficiently.

Many Chinese businesspeople make the common mistake of thinking that problems in a company's administrative structure are shared by big companies or state-owned enterprises only. In reality, the administrative structure should be a much more important consideration in smaller companies and companies in their early stages of development. Once the building is built, it is very difficult to make changes to its foundation. The best and most important time to consider the foundation of a company and its administrative structure is when it is still being developed. Special consideration ought to be given to the entire company administrative structure and the relationships both between shareholders and between shareholders and management.

Frankly, Chinese companies have inherent disadvantages. We emphasize 'face' (loosely defined as 'status' or 'self-respect'), personal relationships and lack of contract culture. Also, most founders are inexperienced first-timers, and hence administrative structures conceal many underlying problems. In China we also lack a comprehensive, detailed company administration law and set of regulations and, when problems arise, we do not have effective ways of dealing with them.

In the early stages of a company's development, if you discover problems in the administrative structure, you must act to resolve them as soon as possible. At the same time, for listed companies, the interests of the company and all its shareholders must be aligned. As a member of top management my job should be to look after the shareholders' interests, especially those of the individual. And as chief executive and a major shareholder, I must put more effort into this, because otherwise the company will not be successful, and my own reputation will be ruined.

WTO entry and its effects on the competitiveness of Chinese companies

In a recent university debate Professor Zhang, assistant dean of the Business Management Department, Beijing University, expressed optimism about the competitiveness of Chinese companies nationally, but was pessimistic about their global competitiveness.

China's entry into the WTO places immense pressure on Chinese enterprises, giving them great impetus to reconsider their core strengths and competitiveness and directly focus their efforts on achieving profitability on a global scale.

On the back of gradual deregulation and the resulting increased competition in the international telecoms market, AsiaInfo will put greater effort into helping China's telecoms companies become more competitive. Because the telecoms industry is one of the core strategic industries in any country's development, it is also the bridge between the people and the IT industry. Once people have bought their PCs, they do not want to spend more money on acquiring IT skills. These costs should be carried by the telecoms companies by providing the customer with the IT software, skills and technology.

That is why, with China joining the WTO, the degree of deregulation in the industry and the potential of foreign companies holding majority stakes in Chinese companies is a problem that has yet to be solved. Giving away too much control in the telecoms industry will equate to giving away the IT industry as well, because the two are tightly linked and the telecoms industry has strategic value for the development of a country's IT industry.

When a multinational telecoms company enters China, it will bring with it its partners and customers. If we do not defend the telecoms industry, then the IT industry will suffer an even greater loss.

Since its foundation in China in 1995, AsiaInfo has been very concerned with building its own core competitiveness. This is because AsiaInfo is the result of winning a battle against foreign international competitors, and because it has become the leader in China's telecoms market. Our core competencies of possessing an in-depth knowledge of the telecoms industry and its development and our ability to provide advanced telecoms equipment, skills and customer service are becoming more pronounced. Joining the WTO has not changed the competitive rules in the marketplace, but the market that AsiaInfo serves has changed. China's telecoms companies now require partners with core competitive advantages that can provide high-quality service.

Building trust and respect in the customer

We won all the major contracts in China because of our technological know-how. That knowledge is one of our core competitive advantages. It enabled us to be the pioneers and set industry standards in both high-end systems integration and Internet software solutions for the country's leading Internet service and content providers.

Our other source of competitive advantage lies in our commitment to our customers and our desire to win their trust. For SI companies such as Asia-Info, the hardware margin is a major revenue earner. But many suppliers, particularly the foreign ones, simply want to offload as much of their hardware into China as they can. They try to entice companies like ours to stock their products by offering discounts and other incentives. Signing to one supplier effectively disqualifies you from selling another's products. Unfortunately, the vast majority of SI companies operating in China go along with this approach, but AsiaInfo is different. We will not limit ourselves to any one single supplier because we want the best for our customers.

However big or powerful the supplier, we have consistently argued that we wish to remain impartial and we will not distribute products unless they meet our customers' needs. Initially, suppliers would refuse us a discount, but with pressure from our customers, eventually they would sell to us at an acceptable price without us having to compromise the neutrality of our position.

As a result, we earned the trust of the customers and, ultimately, the respect of the suppliers. If AsiaInfo recommends something, it is because it is genuinely good, not because we have our hands tied behind our backs.

We battled with the big companies like CISCO and HP but we stood firm. I recall a time when one company that had been particularly dominant in China refused to add a small feature to its products – one that our Chinese customers wanted very badly. I talked to the company's chief engineer and said, 'It will only take you two weeks to add the feature – please – otherwise you will have problems.' He replied, 'No, we are not going to add one feature just for China, no way.' So I talked to another, much smaller supplier and asked, 'Will you do it?' They said 'Yes', and, in about two months from when we had first made our proposal, everything began to change. The smaller company got all the sales and, within four months, it had secured 60 per cent of the market share. That proved to everyone that demand in China should not be taken lightly.

Now we are trusted implicitly and our customers listen to our viewpoint because we have consistently demonstrated our solution-focused approach. That sets us apart from our competitors in the industry and has helped us grow a very strong and loyal customer base.

Living the values

It is very important to us to promote internally those values that have helped us build our loyal customer base. For example, when we hire new people, we look out for qualities such as integrity and honesty and do our best to foster them in our day-to-day work. We have company videos and we have monthly newsletters with stories about the company and our beliefs. We also run new employee orientation programmes as well as team-building programmes.

A credible brand provenance

Being a technology company in China may not give us as much credibility in the eyes of the world as it might if we were located in, say, Silicon Valley or in certain parts of India, but I believe that this situation is beginning to change.

Since August 2000 we have been based in the Haidian District of Beijing, which is increasingly becoming known as China's Silicon Valley, not just in

China, but also in other parts of the world. The area is actually called Zhong-guancun which means 'village' in Chinese. In this small area live the largest technology companies in China, such as Stone, Legend and SINA. We also have China's most famous universities, including Beijing University, Qinghua University and also the China Academy of Science. So intellectual credibility was established here long before the high-tech companies moved in.

I recently saw one of the Chinese engineers working in Silicon Valley paste a picture of a Chinese face on the front cover of a brochure from a very high-tech US company. He was joking but, at the same time, this is something which we all believe will happen very soon.

Bridging the knowledge gap

In terms of a wider remit, from the outset we have wanted to help China link up with the rest of the world, and we take great pride in the role we have played in building China's Internet. That was basically why we started the business in the first place. Our goal derives from our belief in the role information can play in empowering the individual and strengthening the overall economy.

We have become involved in raising money for the Hope Project to give poor schools in rural areas access to better teaching facilities and books. We encourage our employees to get personally involved by asking them to donate voluntarily and the company matches the total collected. It's an enormous project and it helps bridge the knowledge gap nationally as well as internationally.

COMMENTARY

James Ding is one of a core band of young entrepreneurs who have returned to China to set up world-class companies that are becoming models for corporate transforma-tion. By drawing on his experiences overseas, Ding is setting standards in corporate governance for the whole of China. Today, AsiaInfo boasts a market capitalization in the region of US$500 million. Such an achievement is due in part to Ding's recogni-tion of the critical need to protect the interests of the small shareholder and, with that, a deep commitment to achieving the highest standards of corporate governance.

AsiaInfo is a force for change in China, but Ding is well aware of the challenges that companies face in efforts to improve their own standards of corporate governance. It is not easy to build good management and operational practice in a country where such things have historically not been rewarded and where, as a result, legal and reg-ulatory structures are not able to play a fundamental supporting role. In emerging economies like China, businesses will have to go it alone until laws and regulations are improved – at least for the time being.

But there is another challenge that Chinese businesses face in establishing good corporate governance. The organizational structure that dominates the corporate landscape is hierarchical. This can create an internal culture in which competition, rather than sharing, prevails. Good corporate governance, on the other hand, demands that every employee takes responsibility for achieving certain standards of ethical behaviour in areas such as transparency, accountability and operational quality. Such a culture is easier to establish in a flat organizational structure because such a structure encourages openness and sharing and creates a sense of empowerment at every level.

The key, according to Ding, is to nurture ethical behaviour right from the outset. That means building a culture of commitment to protecting the interests of the small shareholder. But eventually, once an effective legal framework is set, laws will need to be strictly monitored and enforced, and this will be necessary not just in China but across the globe.

11 | Erdos: Valuing the Origins of a Brand

Introduction

North China's Inner Mongolia Autonomous Region is famous for cashmere. Boasting over 3 million white cashmere goats, the region is China's largest cashmere producer. Most of the goats thrive on the plateaus of this region and one plateau in particular – the Erdos Plateau – is home to a breed of goats believed to produce the highest quality cashmere in the world.

It is perhaps not surprising that from this region has emerged the largest cashmere processing enterprise in the world, aptly called the Erdos Cashmere Group. Erdos Group currently holds a 40 per cent market share in China and a 25 per cent market share in the world. Nicknamed 'The King of Cashmere Products' in China and with such a strong position in this industry, what further challenges does this company see itself facing? Mr Wang Linxiang, president of Erdos Group, clearly does not believe in complacency. Here he traces the development of Erdos and its continuing challenges.

The development of Erdos

'Opening to the outside whilst invigorating the inside'

It was the year 1979 and we were all guided by the Chinese Communist Party's new economic policy of 'opening to the outside whilst invigorating the inside'. At Erdos we wanted to take the opportunity to play an active role in turning around the cashmere industry which, at that time, was producing low-value processed wool and using very basic equipment. Our bold step, taken after serious study of the market, was to import the most advanced processing equipment of that time from Japan into our factory.

We became the first enterprise in China's textile industry to have totally foreign imported technologically advanced equipment. You might say that this was the first critical step in our transformation. In the 20 years of development since, our production of cashmere products has increased from 300,000 pieces per year to 5 million pieces. Today, we continue to ensure that the equipment in our factories leads this industry worldwide and that we are more advanced than our competitors in Italy or in the UK. We have been able to produce products that are not only of the highest quality and light in weight but also environmentally responsible.

With cashmere processing as our core business, we have evolved to become a true Chinese conglomerate with interests in electronics, pharmaceuticals and construction materials. Our brand has developed alongside the development of our enterprise. The two are closely linked, as will become clear below.

The brand's international development

Conveying an image of elegance and class, cashmere definitely belongs in the category of high-end luxury goods. Because of this, our early years were focused on pure export, targeting developed countries as our main market.

One difficulty was that, prior to 1988, the cashmere producing companies in China had no authority to export cashmere, and the right to distribute internally within China was also restricted. Erdos, at that time, was forced to sell via an export company on an OEM basis. There was no opportunity to build the Erdos brand. Nevertheless, during this period, as our sales strategy was based on high volumes, we began to establish a total quality management system. Within the first three years of operations, our OEM KVSS product of de-haired wool won international praise as China's number one de-haired goat's wool and was commended as the 'Gem Amongst Fibres'. In 1986, 90 per cent of all of Erdos' exports to its Japanese customers was accepted without inspection, further validating the high quality of our wool.

After October 1988 we obtained the right to export our products as well as set up our own distribution network within China. This was a move from indirect distribution towards a more direct relationship with the customer and consequently the need for a new brand to interface with customers arose. Our initial solution was to pay 40,000 yuan per year to the Weaving Import and Export Authority of the Inner Mongolia Autonomous Region for the right to use a mark called the 'Double Fish'. Eventually, we changed this to the Erdos brandmark. At one stage, we had to use both brands in parallel because the company's trading partners only recognized the Double Fish mark. Following improvements in product quality, international customers began to prefer the Erdos brandmark. That's when we stopped using the Double Fish.

We also began to send representatives to Europe and the US to initiate commercial discussions and market research, with the object of improving our position in the international market and broadening our sales and marketing channels. After 1991 the Erdos brand was registered in the US, the UK, Japan, Hong Kong, Singapore, France, Switzerland and other countries (over 40 in total) and Erdos began to establish its own sales companies and retail stores in major markets around the world. Internationally, our brand was on its way.

The brand's domestic development

Meanwhile, the development of Erdos' domestic market took a different turn. In 1988 a trade war broke out in the goat's wool market and many cashmere companies shut down. There was a drastic reduction in demand and international clients collectively withdrew their orders. Political turmoil in 1989 added to the industry's woes.

Faced with this downward spiral of the industry, we came to this realization: the international marketplace is far from our factories; it is full of risks and hard to manage. The domestic market, in contrast, comprising 1.2 billion consumers offers great potential, is close to our factories and will provide market feedback much faster. We decided to adjust our sales strategy, from mainly export-led to balancing both domestic and export markets. Not only did we start consolidating and strengthening our international presence, we also planned simultaneously to proactively conquer the domestic market.

In 1989 we capitalized on the rise of the Chinese advertising and fashion industry to launch the first Erdos Cashmere Wool Fashion Show in Beijing's People's Cultural Palace. The ten-day event attracted an overwhelming response and was hailed by journalists as 'The Erdos Tornado' that hit Beijing. Erdos was set to become a household name.

From 1989 to 1990 we advertised on prime time CCTV, using slots on the film channel through to slots during the weather forecast for Inner Mongolia. From 1991, we started to establish distribution networks in all the major cities in China and, from 1994, we established retail chain stores – boutiques with eye-catching branded storefronts bearing the Erdos name. We even organized seminars to educate the Chinese public on the basics of cashmere. As the business expanded, so did awareness of the Erdos brand. Erdos began to win award after award, from 'China's Most Satisfying Product' through 'The Most Competitive and Most Influential Product' to 'The King of China's Cashmere Products'.

The domestic development of our brand reached its peak in 1999 when we were recognized by the state Industrial and Commercial Administration Bureau as 'China's Most Famous Trademark' – the only company among China's 2,200 cashmere processing enterprises to receive this honour. This designation gave us not only legal priorities and protection in the use of the Erdos name but also conferred on the company an intangible value. We can now say that we have built a brand that is known on a nationwide basis, enjoying a high level of reputation and awareness. The value of this brand has actually been assessed by the Beijing Brand Evaluation Centre at 3.8 billion yuan. It is the best-known brand in China's fashion industry.

Significant decisions and Erdos' willingness to challenge the status quo

Several significant decisions made during the past 20 years have been critical to the successful development of our enterprise. The first was our strategic decision in the early 1990s to transform ourselves from an export-only business to an export plus domestic sales business. Another was our decision to keep to the system of having one core industry (in cashmere processing) with support from sub-industries. Even to this day, our core business still accounts for 90 per cent of our value.

Third, we made the 'revolutionary' decision to go public. Cashmere has a unique production cycle. Raw material purchase occurs only once in the year and there is no futures market in cashmere raw materials. This means that capital or cash flow is critical if a company wants to increase its market share. In addition, Inner Mongolia is a poor and underdeveloped region subject to capital restrictions – a factor that can quickly stunt the development of an enterprise. We at Erdos were faced with a situation where our bank loans were not sufficient to support our purchase of raw materials.

So in 1995 we became the first company in the Inner Mongolia region to become listed by successfully going public in the Shanghai B-share market. In 1997 and then again in 2001 we offered additional shares on the A-share market. In this way, we raised the 2.4 billion yuan we needed to fuel our growth and transform us to our present state.

The fourth significant decision concerns the ownership of the enterprise. In the late 1990s the rapid introduction of market economics led to intense competition in the cashmere industry, which exposed the weaknesses inherent in many state-owned enterprises (such as politically motivated decision-making and lack of clear lines of responsibility). There was a perception of instability and an outflow of talent. Erdos, basing its decision on the Communist Party's 15 Principles, resolved to improve the situation by giving employees share options under the principle: 'If you are a worker, you will have shares and if you are able, you will have rewards.'

Today, most of the company is owned by staff and management in the following proportions: one-third belongs to decision-making management, one-third to technical or middle management and one-third to staff. Almost half of our 21,000-strong staff are owners of the company. This reformed ownership structure has really helped us build a company with longevity. It has proved a very effective way of motivating our staff, retaining talent within the organization and keeping the company growing.

Finally, since 2001, we have been restructuring in order to build a market-focused, highly responsive and motivated organization. Because the Erdos group now consists of 52 enterprises and 21,000 staff, we think our large size slows us down. The reorganization will enhance our efficiency, in particular by flattening our organizational structure.

Some say that the success of Erdos can be attributed to the advantages we have had in terms of access to raw materials, technological superiority and low cost. I disagree. I think Erdos' 20 years of success has been due primarily to our ability to constantly outperform ourselves and not remain complacent. We have always moved with the times, constantly seeking to build a yet more superior organizational system. As a result, our internal operating departments are very responsive and creative. From the early 1980s, when we were faced with the introduction of government policies on labour and allocation of resources, to the 1990s property rights reform and the 2001 policies of enterprise restructuring, there has been change every year. Because of these changes, we have been able to continuously abolish old schools of thought that inhibit our progress and build, within the organization, the capabilities to adapt and support development. We are continuously innovating, initiating the self-destruction of the current status quo so that we can attain a higher-level status quo. Through this repeated cycle of stability – innovation – stability, our competitiveness, as well as our capability for dynamic development, has been increased.

I also feel that the personality and management style of top management has had a very significant impact on the development of the Erdos brand. The values, vision, decisiveness and nature of the person in charge combine to become like a strong wind that shapes the Erdos brand. However, Erdos' success is not entirely due to one person's capability or intellectual capacity. Rather, our brand success comes from the work of three teams: our professional management and technical team with its diverse experiences; our general staff who are well trained, ingrained with a fighting spirit and able to withstand hardships to work tirelessly; and our business strategy management team who are adept at planning and decision-making and have a far-reaching vision.

Significant lessons learnt and the challenges that will follow

Throughout our period of development we have learnt much. For instance, in 1988, in response to a price war among China's cashmere manufacturers, we marked down our prices. However, even though we managed to reduce our inventory levels, it severely affected our image. From this we learnt an extremely important lesson – that, as China's foremost branded cashmere manufacturer, we must never participate in unstructured and unprincipled price wars. Our brand speaks for superior management, technology and culture and our prices must reflect this.

We learnt another significant lesson when the department store in Zhenzhou Henan province went bankrupt. We lost 3 million RMB. From then on, we decided to take distribution into our own hands using a system that guaranteed the least amount of loss to ourselves. We have 'Erdos Corners' in 500 department stores and, with each of these stores, we have set up a minimum threshold of 1 million RMB in sales. If the department store cannot reach this threshold, we withdraw our Corner. This is important in the current climate in which the market is shifting towards giving more bargaining power to the department stores.

Our goal throughout these difficulties is to become the top brand of cashmere in the world. Although China is one of the biggest cashmere manufacturing countries in the world, there are as yet no internationally famous Chinese cashmere brands. This is why we want international consumers to one day equate the name Erdos with 'best cashmere in the world'. Yes, we already hold quite a large market share both in China and internationally. In fact, even if the market share of all our competitors is added up, it is still smaller than our market share.

However, all this means is that our biggest competitor is ourselves, and our biggest challenge is to avoid becoming conceited and complacent. *The Art of War* by Sun Tze says that only when you are fully knowledgeable about your competitors can you win the war. Despite our leading position, we will never cease to 'know' ourselves and to 'know' all aspects of our competitors' businesses.

Erdos' vision – to warm

Our logo tries to convey all our hopes and desires. First, it resembles the initial 'e' from the word 'Erdos' but it also has the shape of a goat's horn representing our core business's reliance on the cashmere goat. The three lines in the right-hand corner symbolize how the many business interests of the Erdos conglomerate co-exist. And the bold red colour symbolizes our fighting spirit, the upward tendency of our growth and development, our competitive nature and dynamism.

The outer boundary of the logo is a circle denoting that Erdos started from nothing but has experienced a spiralling expansion and development. The lower part of the circle resembles the waves of the sea depicting the sea of changes and reforms that the company is continuously undergoing. It can also be likened to the earth, suggesting the globalization of the company's business and brand. The circle is not closed, emphasizing our philosophy of openness to change and improvement rather than the guarding of a status quo.

The Erdos brand vision is to warm. Like the warmth of a fire, we seek to perform a service for humankind. We want to bring warmth to consumers, warmth to shareholders, warmth to staff and warmth to society. Our brand is about making the best efforts to offer care to all stakeholders and about fulfilling our dream to become a top global brand. Over the past 20 years we have obtained much support, care and attention from the Chinese government and the public at large and we feel that we have a duty to ensure that our development will have a positive knock-on effect on Inner Mongolia's economic development.

For instance, we have invested considerable funds into restoring Inner Mongolia's grass plains and protecting the environment. Recently we also donated 30 million yuan in aid of disaster victims and to promote Project 'Hope' work. In addition, we sponsor scholarships to ease the financial burden of children's education among the farming community. Then, in 2000–2001, Erdos donated 2 million yuan towards the building of ten Erdos Hope primary schools in ten cashmere production provinces, tightening the ties between Erdos and the cashmere production provinces.

This year, the company has committed to a long-term plan of building five new Hope schools each year, with each school receiving an annual grant of 200,000 yuan. Finally, we have directly invested in building new factories in the cashmere provinces, helping to solve the unemployment problems of the farming community. All of these actions have yielded many economic and social benefits.

We hope that, in the process of becoming bigger, stronger and better, we will simultaneously raise the standard of living of the entire cashmere farming community. It is really part of our brand vision to first bring warmth to the lives of these 13 million people whose destinies are so closely linked to ours and then ultimately bring warmth to the world.

Management with the brand as its very nucleus

History has shown that, if a brand collapses, the whole company could collapse. Many of the world's largest companies go bankrupt because they become overconfident and believe that they are protected by their sheer size. They do not pay sufficient attention to crisis management and brand management. At Erdos we have no such misconceptions. I often warn my colleagues that a brand crisis could be our biggest crisis if we are not prepared.

For this reason, we have adopted a corporate development strategy that has the brand as its very nucleus. We have specialized departments for brand management – for example, an intellectual property department focused on brand registration and the management of our trademarks and patents. We have our own advertising company responsible for brand image, advertising, promotions, communications and planning. To protect the massive investment and effort that has been put into the Erdos brand, we have established a 24-hour crisis management system that enables anyone in China and throughout the world to have direct access to our corporate headquarters or even to me, as president. Each of our 30 subsidiaries in different provinces is obliged to report any risk of any crisis to our brand.

We even have an in-house legal department responsible for protecting our brand and an 'anti-fake office', as we call it. Counterfeit products have a definite impact on our brand reputation. Members of the public are offered a handsome reward to alert Erdos about fake products and we maintain a good relationship with the consumer associations and quality inspection departments so that we can react as quickly as possible once such products are detected.

As I see it, counterfeiting is part of the chaos that comes with a new market economy. Although it is not a state of affairs to be tolerated, it is understandable. However, as long as globalization progresses with China's entry into the WTO, counterfeits will have no chance in the market. Honesty and integrity will become the lifeline of most enterprises and products and, eventually, the protection of intellectual property rights in China will be enhanced and strengthened.

Erdos' corporate culture is the brand

Managing a corporate brand is really about managing a type of culture within the enterprise. A successful product on its own is not sufficient to build a company that is going to survive successfully in the long term. What is more important is for the company to have its own management philosophy and the right corporate culture.

At Erdos, it is our corporate culture that has enabled us to develop a revolutionary new understanding of the business that we are in. For example, we have a corporate philosophy that states that all outcomes are dependent on the actions and efforts of men and women, not of the fairies or of the gods. This has given us the courage and daring to pursue our vision of bringing warmth to the entire world. Particularly while we are undergoing a period of restructuring, we need to strengthen the enterprise's spiritual essence, not just its material aspects.

In philosophical terms, we say that one 'tendency' tends to overshadow another 'tendency'. Twenty years ago, before the opening of the market, China had overemphasized the spirit of making sacrifices to such an extent that it almost caused the collapse of the Chinese economy. However, when the reform policies caused us to shift our focus on to economic pursuits, not enough attention was paid to spiritual and cultural pursuits. That is why I say one tendency tends to overshadow another. And this can be very detrimental to both the development of society and individuals.

Erdos' success is owed to our awareness that this can happen. Even during the economic construction-centred and material benefit-centred stage of China's development, we realized that material demands will never be entirely satisfied. I have a saying, 'We cannot live without the enterprise. But the enterprise should not be our only purpose in life.' Striking the right balance and making this balance clear to all our staff and leadership is very important. If this conflict can be resolved, we can pull everyone more closely together.

At Erdos we have our own Corporate Culture Book in which we express and explain the essence of our culture to each of our 21,000 employees. The Erdos philosophy permeates all levels of the organization and, in that way, creates a deep and lasting effect on our employees and our brand.

One of the consequences of this has been the respect that the company has for knowledge and for talent. Many foreign companies consider the Erdos region to be unfit for a business; it is not a place that attracts talent. At Erdos we insist on treating all our employees as valuable capital that will generate returns, on assigning people positions that will unleash their potential, on promoting the young and capable. We have also changed the way in which we remunerate our employees. For example, we have increased our compensation package for graduates so that we can attract, retain and deploy talent, creating at the same time a more vibrant and dynamic environment within the company. As more talent enters the company and integrates into its culture, the nature of that culture broadens and deepens. This culture develops even as the enterprise develops (similar to the brand) and it becomes a strong driving force behind the company's economic pursuits.

To give you an example of the impact of our philosophy, we value three qualities. The first is loyalty – meaning sincerity and integrity in the context of the new market economy. The second is responsibility – being responsible to the enterprise, to customers and to society. The third is valuing ideals, which applies to each Erdos employee – not just the ideal of a better enterprise or of better pay but also the ideal of a greater contribution if needed. For example, the months of July, August and September are our busiest periods for goods delivery. There is no time to waste. An eight-hour working day would be too short. It has to be 12 hours. It would be unimaginable for our people to not be willing to contribute this extra effort.

We therefore need to have a common understanding from top management to the front-line workers on the need for this extra effort, and that is an understanding that is achieved through culture building. Things like sit-down strikes that occur at some old state-owned enterprises have never happened here. It isn't that our employees have nothing to complain about, but rather that we put serious efforts into managing our relationships properly. I recently remarked to my colleagues that there is a need for balance within a company otherwise it cannot develop in a stable fashion. To reach this balance, you have to negotiate amongst the different parties involved. But balance alone is not enough; it has to be accompanied by a breakthrough that is usually achieved through denial of self-interest. When you break through to new ground, you build a new balance. Only through this repeated break–balance process can a company make long-term progress.

Erdos' future in the cashmere industry

At present, the global cashmere industry is indisputably 'looking at China'. Cashmere remains the world's best knitting and weaving raw material and, because of its high price and the lack of a viable substitute, the potential in this industry remains tremendous. Take China, for example: making a conservative assumption that one in 100 consumers will purchase one cashmere product in a year, the market potential is 13 million pieces. For the international market, let us estimate that one in 300 consumers will purchase a cashmere product in a year and we will have a market potential of up to 18 million pieces, making the total global market potential 31 million pieces. Based on estimated annual global cashmere production capacity, only 22 million of these 31 million pieces of standard cashmere products can be manufactured. There is therefore demand for 9 million pieces that needs to be satisfied.

Within China's domestic market, as people experience a period of sustained economic growth and stability, their appetite and demand for cashmere products will rapidly increase. This is very likely to have a positive impact on the development of the cashmere industry, as will the development strategy of China's western regions, where massive investments are being made into improving the rearing of cashmere goats.

With this potential, it is clear that Erdos will continue to focus on cashmere as its mainstream business. In the next ten years, should our sales income hit 10 billion yuan, we hope that cashmere will account for 65–70 per cent of it, with sub-industries taking up the remaining 30–35 per cent. In terms of sub-industries we have decided to venture into food, specifically the dairy industry where Inner Mongolia has a competitive advantage. In addition, we have invested 70 million RMB into a joint venture with a Canadian bio-pharmaceutical company. That is how we see our future – in clothing, food and medicine. So long as humans live, they will need food and medicine. And as long as the global climate keeps to the climate of winter following summer, we will need warm clothing.

Of course, these new ventures will have an impact on our brand architecture. At the moment, we have a unified brand structure in that we use the Erdos brand for not just our core cashmere business but also for all the other businesses such as ceramics, electronics and pharmaceuticals which are carried on the brand's reputation and awareness. At present we do not think that there are any conflicts arising from using a single brand for such diversified businesses. However, with development, conflicts will arise and we are thinking of planning a multi-brand strategy. We may use Erdos exclusively for cashmere and weaving/knitting-related businesses but will build new brands for the other businesses.

The world is looking at China

In the old China, dominated by the centrally planned economy, brand strategy, brand management and all these branding concepts did not exist. Such concepts were impossibilities. But now, as China shifts from being a seller's market to a buyer's market, the buying patterns and behaviour of Chinese consumers are changing significantly as well, particularly in terms of how price, quality and brand affect their product choices. In the past, Chinese consumers would buy goods on the basis that they were cheap, practical and durable but now they are buying on the basis of the brand behind the goods. To Chinese consumers, it has become a question of brand choice and, to industries, it has become an issue of brand competition.

I believe that a brand refers not only to the product logo or the company logo and trading name but also to the whole of the company's image, reputation and competitiveness. A brand is an indispensable component of any product and is even more important in the context of fashion-related goods. In the fashion industry, the brand speaks of the quality and style of the fashion item, its product positioning and personality and is sometimes even a status symbol. Some people believe that wearing clothes is equivalent to wearing a brand.

Using one's brand to develop a market is therefore about implementing a brand strategy. First a brand should seek to excel in three areas, compared to its competition: (1) product quality and product development potential; (2) market share and expansion potential; (3) corporate philosophy and cultural strength. Market share is the brand's external performance in the market, product quality and development potential are the brand's intrinsic strength and corporate philosophy is the brand's foundation. A brand does not exist or operate in an isolated environment. Rather, it evolves from, and through, market competition and is then 'recognized' by consumers.

To implement its brand strategy, a company should engage in comprehensive planning along the following lines:

1 Examine your product quality strategy. Quality is the stepping stone to the creation of a branded product. For fashion goods, the main principle to follow is technological brilliance, superior quality and design and reasonable prices.
2 Examine your corporate image and logo strategy. The main idea is to perfect the corporate image, particularly the special characteristics of the company's behaviour and philosophy and the brand's look and feel, using the right imagery, colours and words.
3 Examine your sales and advertising strategy. This includes product and price positioning, target market, sales methods, sales materials, public relations and so on.
4 Examine your capital deployment strategy. The expansion of a brand should not be pursued only along the traditional path of 'increasing the number and the size of stores' because this may require longer building and production times and may also lead to a situation where you reinvent the wheel.

For instance, many of Hong Kong's and Taiwan's mass consumer fashion brands have been very successful in China, but the companies have kept their investments in factories in China very small. Their strategy is to capitalize on existing local production facilities, enhancing them to manufacture products that suit their brands rather than building completely new plants. There are numerous examples that point to the fact that combining efficient capital deployment with one's brand is the road to success.

To develop a regional brand into a national brand and then ultimately into a world-class brand requires an extraordinary amount of hard work in the long term from every single person in the entire company. The development of such a world-class brand will, however, not only bring to the company that owns it intangible value but will also become representative of the country's image and power. For this reason, brands should definitely receive protection and affection.

Building a brand in China comes with definite advantages. First, the commercial opportunities are limitless. China is huge, with a lot of land, and has a massive 1.3 billion population. It offers the potential of being the biggest market in the world. Second, China currently has very few well-known brands internally and even fewer Chinese brands that are well-known throughout the world. There is, therefore, a great deal of potential to develop a brand in China. Third, branding in China is at a very immature stage, and it is this immaturity and the immaturity of the market that offer great opportunities. Those of us who can capture the branding opportunities first in this market will emerge as the winners.

Of course, there are certain limiting factors that you cannot ignore. Foreign enterprises need to familiarize themselves with, and immerse themselves in, Chinese sentiments and culture. Chinese enterprises, after China's entry into the WTO, will find that the international competition is close at their heels. There is a significant gap between domestic and foreign companies in terms of management, technology and marketing strategies. Brand awareness in many of China's enterprises is not very strong and this will affect and limit their creation of international and domestic brands.

For instance, consider the negative effect of the 'Made in China' label. In the US last year, we sold 1.5 million pieces and in Japan 0.6 million. Although there have been no problems concerning the quality of our cashmere products in the past 20 years, the fact that we are 'Made in China' is still not very well accepted by international consumers.

Nevertheless, I believe that China's pursuit of deeper reforms, the development of a freer market and the improvement of the quality of the labour force, coupled with the traditional Chinese values of 'self-improvement, getting your household in order, governing the country and global peace', will one day, inevitably, result in the launch of world-class Chinese enterprises with world-class brands on to the global stage. Our own growth and emergence has been the catalyst for the development of the Chinese cashmere industry. The world is now looking at China. We, at Erdos, have forged a path for Chinese enterprises to become international.

COMMENTARY

Erdos' mission to become the top cashmere brand in the world stems from its argument that, although China is one of the world's biggest cashmere manufacturing countries, there are as yet no internationally famous Chinese cashmere brands. The natural competitive advantage provided by the plateaus of Inner Mongolia is but one factor in the equation to becoming a globally successful brand and business. Erdos has been quick to realize this and has tried hard to ensure that it does not become complacent.

In fact, the company's location has presented particular challenges. For example, Inner Mongolia is not the most attractive place to work. In response, Erdos has transformed its ownership structure so that the company can be partly owned by employees.

This progressive move on the part of a Chinese state-owned corporation supports, with real action, the value that the company places on the importance of human capital and helps to retain and attract talent. Similarly, the company's investment in the local cashmere farming communities demonstrates its awareness that its destiny is very much linked to that of the people of Inner Mongolia. In these times, when a corporation's social responsibilities so often come under scrutiny, it is heartening to know that Erdos regards its vision of bringing warmth to the world through its products as beginning with sustaining and improving the livelihoods of its cashmere farmers.

In branding terms, we see two areas of potential development for the Erdos brand as it goes global. The first is the possibility of incorporating a social ideology into the brand. Since the company does already have a social responsibility agenda, this may mean communicating more fully to stakeholders (whether employees or customers or the financial community) the two-way relationship between the success of the brand and the social development of that region of China. Having such a social ideology may prove to be a competitive advantage for the brand in the long term.

The second is whether the company has considered utilizing the provenance effect of the Inner Mongolia region to positively impact on its brand. To consumers in the West, the word 'Mongolia' conjures up images of a remote hinterland in China, wild grassy plains once roamed by warriors on horseback and romantic windswept deserts. The potential that this holds for Erdos should it consider developing into a full fashion brand remains to be seen. Could Erdos develop a premium designer sub-brand, the Missoni of the East?

With foreign demand for cashmere currently on a slowdown because of the sluggish economies of developed countries, it is also a good time for Erdos to concentrate on stimulating local demand for cashmere garments in order to maintain domestic sales. As Mr Wang Linxiang himself says, the potential of the Chinese market is huge – on population numbers alone. However, cashmere is a luxury product that is traditionally exported. This may mean that the company needs to increase efforts to make the brand more relevant to, and perhaps aspirational for, the average Chinese consumer.

12 | Yanjing Beer: Choosing the Right Path for Growth

Introduction

Local heroes in China beer

China is believed to have been brewing some form of beer by the twenty-third century BC, although for almost four centuries beer was considered to be an inferior beverage to rice wine and other liquors. It wasn't until the end of the nineteenth century, when China's first commercial brewery appeared, that China began to get a taste for beer. The first half of the twentieth century saw breweries spring up across the nation. And, while the economic hardship of the 1960s saw many of them close down again, the industry was to make a comeback under the economic reforms of the late Deng Xiaoping.

With the reforms came both a change in patterns of consumption and a shift in trading behaviour: consumer spending power rose and more barley was imported into China. The market for beer began to grow at an astounding rate and breweries reappeared throughout the country. By 1995 beer accounted for 61 per cent of China's total output of alcoholic beverages and by 2000 that figure had risen to 78 per cent.

Today, China is the world's second largest beer producer, just behind the United States. With a growth rate of 6 per cent per year it is set to take the first position over the next few years. Yet current per capita annual production stands at almost two-thirds of the global average – lower than in any other major beer-producing country – so there is still a huge potential for market growth. The most successful in China will lead the world, but who's who in China beer?

The sector is complex, with wide regional variations and, despite two decades of consolidation, it remains highly fragmented, with hundreds of small-scale, local breweries dominating local markets. In fact, China's ten largest brewers hold just 40 per cent of the total market combined, and the top two, Tsingtao Brewery and the Beijing Yanjing Brewery, hold less than 20 per cent. Even today there are few truly national beer brands, with every city having, as its leading beer, the one that is brewed locally. So in Guangzhou it is the Zhunjiang Brewery, in Qingdao the leader is Tsingtao, and in Beijing it is the Beijing Yanjing Brewery.

It seems that China's beer consumers prefer their local brand not simply because it engenders in the drinker a sense of community pride, but because the beer is of fine quality and is cheap. China's historically prohibitive transport infrastructure, while making defection to other brands difficult for consumers, has allowed brewers, free of distribution overheads, to keep prices down. A 640ml bottle of Chinese beer often retails at just above one yuan – cheaper than mineral water. No wonder local beer is the choice of nine out of ten Chinese beer drinkers – the so-called 'common drinkers'.

The 'drink local' attitude of China's beer drinkers is not an easy attitude to shift, as many international players were to discover at their cost. The late 1980s saw more than 60 brewers arrive from overseas, lured by the promise of profit and market share. These producers included Anheuser-Busch who make Budweiser, the German Bass Group, the Japanese Asahi Brewery and Carlsberg, one of the few to set up a wholly owned beer plant. Within a few years of setting up in China, many were forced to close or at least scale down. The problem was in their approach, which involved spending vast amounts on advertising to target the 10 per cent high-end of the market.

One player, South African Breweries (SAB), was, however, able to remain profitable because it implemented a truly 'think local, act local' strategy. Its approach was to cast a net over a tiny area in north-east China where demand for beer exceeded brewing capacity. Then it dealt with further expansion by tackling each region as if it were a discrete market. Its domestic partner, China Resources Enterprises Ltd, was able to take advantage of the foreign capital, the technology and the managerial experience made available to it by SAB while strengthening its own presence. The partnership has bought significant benefits to both sides and, today, China Resources' major brands, Snowflake and Keller, have a strong local presence.

Now that China is set to become the largest beer-producing country in the world, overseas producers are showing renewed interest. In 2001 Belgium giant Interbrew signed a preliminary agreement to purchase a stake in the wealthy Guangdong province's Zhujiang Beer Group. Also, Tsingtao, China's largest producer, is holding talks with Budweiser producer Anheuser-Busch. And, as trade tariffs relax, more imported brands will appear on the market.

The upshot will be a fiercely competitive market comprising three types of competitor: the domestic brands, including Tsingtao and Yanjing; the foreign brands produced by joint ventures between international and local beer makers; and the imported brands. For the domestic players, the government's message is: consolidate or be forced out of the market. Moreover, experts are predicting that soon there will be no small-scale producers left – that's 60 per cent or so of all China's beer producers – leaving just a handful of large-scale, super-brewers with national and increasingly international market strategies. How will these giants fare in a market that likes to 'think local, drink local'?

Quingdong province's Tsingtao Brewery and Beijing Yanjing Brewery have long been the stars in China beer production and both are pushing a national, as well as an international, presence. But both have struggled to reach the market beyond their founding cities, despite countrywide acquisitions and sales and distribution networks in place.

Tsingtao is China's largest producer and its second oldest. Since 1996 the company has been buying up China's small-scale brewers in an effort to achieve a large slice of national market share. More than 40 small breweries have been acquired, the more significant of these being the famous Beijing Five Star Brewery and Beijing Three Rings Brewery. And the company wants to buy many more. Tsingtao also has a controlling share in a number of joint ventures with foreign brands to help it raise funds for future acquisitions and to gain a better grasp of international trading behaviour. But, despite Tsingtao's efforts to be China's national leader, its national market share remains relatively low, at 12 per cent, and still lags behind some very tiny brands in some of China's cities.

The other leader, and the focus for this story, is the Beijing Yanjing Beer Group Corporation. Backed by its parent, Beijing Enterprises, Yanjing has followed in the footsteps of Tsingtao in acquiring a host of local breweries to help it achieve a nation-wide presence. These include the Shangdong-based Wuming Brewery Co. and Sankong Brewery Co. and, more recently, the popular Guilin-based Liquan Beer. But while Yanjing holds almost 90 per cent of the Beijing beer market, its national market share is only 8 per cent.

Brand provenance as a symbol of authenticity

The 'drink local' mindset of the Chinese people can be understood by looking at the beer-drinking aspirations of consumers in other parts of the world such as the UK. Here it's not about where the beer is brewed, but whether its claimed provenance carries a credible beer-making heritage. Consider UK-brewed Cobra beer, which recently took the premium Indian restaurant sector by storm by positioning itself as an Indian thoroughbred for diners on Indian food. Today, it is the biggest selling bottled beer in that sector, winning Gold for the second year running at the 2002 Monde Selection Quality Awards. The beer's 'Indian-ness' cannot be doubted – Cobra was first brewed in Bangalore 12 years ago and is still brewed to the original Indian recipe. But it's not brewed in India. In fact, 90 per cent of all foreign beers on sale in Britain claim a false provenance, including the UK-brewed, bottled and labelled Carlsberg Export and Kronenbourg 1664. The success of a beer brand is a function of, amongst other things, the perceived brewing capabilities and beer-making heritage of the town, city or country from which the brand claims to originate.

The towns and villages around China have been building a strong reputation for high-quality beer-making over many years and, as China opens up to the outside world, that credibility will continue to drive China's beer consumption. But as non-

local and then non-Chinese beers begin to penetrate the China market, perceptions that local is best may begin to shift.

Initially though, for the likes of Tsingtao or Yanjing to achieve a solid nationwide presence in the face of the 80 per cent or so of China's small-scale local producers will demand pursuing a discrete branding strategy in which the corporate brand remains in the background and the local brand can enjoy its loyal and trusty following.

Mr Zhang Er Jing, vice-director of the Beijing Yanjing Beer Group Corporation, now tells us how Yanjing has risen to the challenge of expansion and how the company plans to achieve its vision of becoming one of the top ten beer manufacturers in the world by 2005.

The Beijing Yanjing Beer Group Corporation

Beijing Yanjing Beer Group Corporation developed out of the former Yanjing Brewery in September 1980. Today, the corporation's total assets are worth in the region of 2,500 million RMB. In 1997, having completed a shareholder restructuring, the group established the Beijing Yanjing Beer Co. Ltd as one of its subsidiary companies. Others include Beijing Yanda Crown Corks Co. Ltd, Beijing Changyi Ginseng Drinks Co. Ltd., Beijing Shuangyan Colour Printing Works and Beijing Hangxing Flavoring Limited Liability Company. The corporation is 54 per cent owned by Beijing Enterprises Holdings, the Hong Kong-listed investment arm of the Beijing government.

Yanjing has enjoyed continuous growth since its establishment in 1980 and, by 1999, production had reached 1,040,000 tonnes. The group is now the largest brewery in China as well as one of China's 100 biggest beverage producers. Beverage products include nectar juice, ginseng juice and syrups, mango juice, cola and mineral water. The corporation also produces bottle and can labels, flavourings, yeast powder and animal feeds. But the main product is beer, accounting for 90 per cent of total sales. Yanjing produces nearly 50 different kinds of beer such as the Yanjing Special Beer 11°and 12°, the Refreshing Beer 11°, the Dry Beer 10°and Yanjing Draft Beer. But most popular by far is the 'common' Yanjing beer: 560,000 tonnes of this beverage are sold every year.

Yanjing beer is famous for its clarity and mellow taste. It was one of the first beers to be awarded a quality certificate by the state and it has been nominated as the beer of choice for state banquets. It is also the chosen beer for Air China. Our beer has won more than 30 prizes in domestic and international tasting competitions and can be found in almost all parts of the country.

The company is equipped with the most up-to-date technical processes and modern production systems, as well as the necessary facilities for testing and quality control. All products are produced in accordance with international standards, and new techniques and processes are regularly introduced. The company also co-operates with the Chinese Fermentation Research Institute which provides a source of insights into the development of new products.

Our vision is to become one of the ten largest brewers in the world within the next five years. Our annual beer production is currently at 1.75 million tonnes, which we fully expect to increase by 12 per cent to 1.9 million tonnes by the end of 2002, and then again to 2.5 million tonnes by the end of 2005. We will achieve this growth by continuing our strategy of mergers and acquisitions and by making the necessary adjustments to methods of production.

Though headquartered in Beijing, our market covers the whole of China. In 2001 alone, we bought 11 breweries across the country. We also have a presence in 20 other countries and regions in the world, but these markets currently contribute only a small part of the total sales to date. We are hoping to increase our international profile, particularly in markets such as the US, UK and other parts of Europe.

The history of the Yanjing brand

As I have said, the enterprise was established in 1980 at a time when China wasn't filled with brands like other countries. Most of the enterprises in China were under the planned economy: we were simply an enterprise producing different types of products and had no understanding even of the basic concepts of brands.

This situation lasted until 1983 when the former minister of light industry, Mr Huchu Ha, suggested that an enterprise should be given a name, just like a baby is given a name. In Beijing there were already some quite influential enterprises also producing beer, such as the Beijing Five Star Brewery. Our factory was named the Beijing Beer Factory. We didn't have the name 'Yanjing beer' at that time.

Later on, we decided that we needed a more distinctive name so we looked at the names that other beer enterprises had chosen. They all referred to their city of founding – even the Five Star Brewery suggests its city of founding, Beijing, in the sense that Beijing is a five-star city. Yanjing was the name of China's capital city, Beijing, more than 3,000 years ago before China was unified. It was called Yanjing before Ming Dynasty officials renamed the city Beijing in 1403. So that is why we chose Yangjing as our name.

Prior to 1988, 90 per cent of our production was sold through a monopoly called the Municipal Sugar, Tobacco and Wine Corporation of Beijing and we were only allowed to sell one bottle of beer for every ten bottles we produced. Moreover, China's state-owned enterprises had very little under-standing of brands and branding nor did they have the inclination or knowl-edge to build a company brand, so Yanjing did not have the brand advantage that it has today.

Up until 1989 every enterprise in the beer industry used the unified plan for purchasing and for sales, but Yanjing entered the market using a contract agreement because we recognized the value and importance of people's awareness of the brand. We also decided to focus on a market that we knew would be solid – the 10 million permanent residents of Beijing.

Yanjing was the first true brand on the market. Even the meaning of the word 'market' was unknown to ordinary Chinese people in the early 1980s. But by 1988, it had become part of our language, and it was around that time that Yanjing began to promote its brand as a beer for the everyday Beijing resident.

By around 1993 most of the enterprises in China's beer sector had wit-nessed a surge of foreign brands into China and, through that, had acquired a great deal of foreign capital, either through joint ventures or through mergers and acquisitions. At that time, our own annual production was in excess of 50,000 tonnes and we had about 61 enterprises, 54 of which were either joint ventures, or the result of mergers or acquisitions.

The problem was that most of these enterprises did not know how to factor into the purchasing or joint venture deal the value of their brand. They only paid attention to the value of their tangible assets, such as their equipment or their plot of land.

This mindset wasn't confined only to enterprises – the majority of people in China had little knowledge about brands or branding. This was true for all brands in China, not only beer enterprise brands. Later, with more extensive reforms and deeper opening up to the outside world, and as China's economy came more into line with the global economy, people gradually became aware of the importance of brands.

The same is true for Yanjing which, at the end of the 1980s and in the early 1990s, became aware of the brand and its importance. For example, in the 1990s when there was an influx of foreign capital, Yanjing belonged to the cat-egory of enterprises characterized by the state as having the potential for rapid growth. This meant that it was relatively easy to attract foreign investors, and a considerable number of foreign brands had their eye on Yanjing. Consequently, a whole host of world-famous foreign beer companies visited us to explore our potential – for example, Budweiser from the US, and others from Germany, New Zealand and the UK.

It was during negotiations with these different breweries that we became aware of the potential value of our own brand. There was hot debate on who should have the controlling share in the joint venture and we couldn't reach an agreement. Finally, Yanjing decided that it should grow on its own and develop its own brand.

Yanjing was growing more or less as soon as it began. In 1991 we were one of the top ten enterprises in China's beer industry; by 1992 we had moved into the top five; by 1993 we had jumped to third place; by 1994 we were second; and by 1995 we had reached the top of the list. So it took us only five years to develop from a relatively small enterprise to a big and renowned enterprise in China. Furthermore, for seven consecutive years Yanjing has maintained a leadership position in both production and sales and for five consecutive years we have been the leader in terms of sales revenue.

By extending our scale of production and also our market scope, we became very influential in the beer sector. The value of our intangible assets – that is, the value of our brand – was increasing.

In May 1997 Yanjing was listed on the Hong Kong Stock Exchange, and an asset evaluation company in Beijing valued our brand to be worth 520 million RNB. In 2001 a second brand asset evaluation firm in China valued our brand at 552.9 billion RNB.

Achieving geographical expansion

In 1998 we formulated our market strategy which consists of the following objectives: to maintain and strengthen our position in the Beijing market; to enlarge our presence in northern China; to maximize our potential throughout the country; and to enter the international market. With another increase in the group's production, we can now claim somewhere between 85 per cent and 90 per cent of the Beijing market and 30 per cent in North China; nationally, we now have close to 10 per cent; and last year we exported around 6,000 tonnes to overseas markets.

The beer export total for China beer is very large because both the US and the European markets are currently saturated. We entered international markets because we wanted to build brand awareness, but in order to gain access to these markets, we decided that we should first enter Hong Kong and Taiwan because they have closer links with the Western markets. Entering these two markets first helped us increase our brand awareness in these countries and then to expand further west.

Today, our total export to Hong Kong is 2,000 tonnes. In fact, in June 2002 one of the biggest supermarkets in Hong Kong identified Yanjing as one of their consumers' top ten favourite beers out of a possible 10,000 beers on sale.

In 2002 we entered Taiwan, a move which served to open up their own market, and now Taiwan is exporting 2,000 tonnes of Taiwanese beer per year to China.

Before we entered the Taiwan and Hong Kong markets, we already had a sales agreement with the US market, the European market and also the market in the UK. But international practice is very different from the practice here in China so, although Yanjing beer has a presence in these markets, it is actually very tiny. We are in the process of improving our knowledge of international trade and we hope that, soon, Yanjing will become as famous internationally as it is nationally.

On future planning

With regard to the future, we have some basic plans. For our fifth five-year plan – that is, from 2001 to 2005 – we expect our own production to reach 3 million tonnes. If we achieve this, we will be one of the top ten beer manufacturers in the world.

We are also actively exploring the domestic and the international markets in order to position the brand Yanjing among the internationally famous beer brands. We know there are many difficulties to overcome, but we are willing to work very hard to become world-famous.

To this end, we are sponsoring the Beijing Olympic Games in 2008 which is a good opportunity for us to raise awareness and recognition of the Yanjing name. This is a rare opportunity for us: such an event happens only every four years so we have jumped at it.

The path to success

I believe that the increase in the value of the brand, and its power and influence in China, is not only dependent on the profile you build in other areas, it is also closely linked to the knowledge and experience of the internal management, as well as the effectiveness of quality control, technology and production techniques.

We strive to use the best equipment available and to ensure that our technological capability is equivalent to, or close to the equivalent of, the state-of-the-art technologies used by our counterparts in the international community. We do this so that we can guarantee the quality of Yanjing beer. It also helps us be a more efficient producer.

Over the years, Yanjing has invested nearly 1.7 billion yuan in acquiring the world's most advanced technology, testing instruments and production facilities. For the saccharification process, we use equipment imported both from Germany and New Zealand. The beer-brewing and bottling equipment all derive from Germany and our testing and analysing equipment is from famous manufacturers in Switzerland and Sweden.

From the very beginning, Yanjing was described as a place of technological reform – a tag we achieved by being the first beer brewery in China to implement a vat fermentation technique instead of the traditional two-vat method. Compared with the traditional method, a single vat technique saves much more energy and physical production space. It is simpler and better for modern, large-scale production. So, in 1995, Yanjing established its own technology development centre. Today, Yanjing's entire production process is computerized.

But superb technology and the latest facilities aren't all you need to make a modern enterprise. While other companies can equal Yanjing's technical expertise, they cannot replicate Yanjing's unique management concept and ethical code, which we are developing according to market-led principles.

A great product

Yanjing is a very popular and well-liked brand throughout China. One reason for this is the product quality and taste which are due, in part, to the mineral content of the water with which it is made. That mineral water derives from a unique water resource here in Beijing, and there is an amusing story behind its discovery.

The mineral water actually flows right underneath the enterprise, 200 metres down, and we have been extracting and using it right from day one. But it was not until later that we discovered the superiority of its mineral content and its particular suitability for beer brewing.

Around 1992–93 the consumption behaviour of the people of Beijing underwent a shift and mineral water suddenly became a hot product. This was the first time that such a product had been so in demand in China. Our factory began to look everywhere for a mineral water resource so that we could add a mineral water product to our portfolio. We didn't realize we had that resource running under our feet.

Every year we would have to provide a water sample to the quality inspection bureau for analysis. There are many different tests to identify water content, and a number of these will show whether or not the water is adequate for beer brewing. The more tests that you request the higher the cost, so to save costs we asked only for the minimum number to be taken.

Had we paid more and had all the tests done, we would have discovered that our water was not only mineral water – which we did not know – but also that it had a very high concentration of strontium and silicic acid, the two most important minerals for brewing beer. In fact, the content of these minerals in our water is two times higher than the state requirement. The concentration of these two minerals relates to the quality of the beer and the taste.

In fact it wasn't even us that uncovered the exceptional quality of the water we were using; it was another beer factory – a competitor. This beer factory was already using mineral water in its beer and it wanted to compare the taste of beer made using mineral water against beer made without mineral water. They took as their samples, Tsingtao beer, Five Star beer and Yanjing beer. But, after the initial tasting, we stood out as the best. After that, we took a water sample to the inspection bureau for a full analysis and we discovered the truth about our water. We now have a mineral water product as part of our range and can boast about the why Yanjing tastes so good in our brochures.

Our mineral water now has approval and certification from a number of ministries including the Ministry of Light Industry, the Ministry of Health and the Ministry of Internal Trade.

The other important factor in making great beer includes using high-quality rice, malt and hops. The hops we use are in the highest quality category and come from Europe.

How do we know that our product is good? In 1991, and then again in 1995, the China Brewery Association and the Beer Association conducted a national grading of all the major beers in China in order to create an evaluation standard against which to test. Twice they sampled from eight large beer manufacturers, using 40 beer experts, and on both occasions Yanjing beer was chosen as that evaluation standard.

Setting the standards in NPD

Before China's economic reform, China's production enterprises were not connected in any way with research and development. They simply made products for the people and the state. It was the Research and Development Institute that would develop and test new product ranges. But, because the Institute would not then make the products – that was the role of the production enterprises – there was a clear disadvantage in the sense that any new products developed by the Institute would have to be patented prior to commercialization by any enterprise. This was not an efficient way of getting new products out into the market.

Yanjing sought to change this by inviting scientists from the Institute to come to the enterprise and carry out the research on-site. At that time, the Research and Development Institute was funded out of the country's central budget. Having invited the scientists to come to Yanjing and work for us, we took responsibility for paying all the fees. We also didn't ask for the exclusive patent rights, only that we would be given the chance to commercialize the products before any other enterprise. That gave Yanjing a big competitive advantage.

In fact, China's first beer expert was actually a scientist from the Research and Development Institute who came to work for us in Beijing many years ago. He is still with us today. He also was responsible for writing the first-ever brewery production guidelines. Today, Yanjing boasts a strong force of scientists. Out of its 11,000 employees, 25 per cent are scientists or technicians.

Yanjing – the people's beer

At the heart of the Yanjing brand is the concept of beer for the common man. The brand logo for Yanjing consists of a drawing of a swallow. This is a very positive symbol in China and is suggestive of spring and good fortune – the early spring swallow ready to conquer the world. The yellow symbol indicates superior scientific management. And the depiction of hops and rice – a symbol of harvest – suggests a welcome for everybody – a common person's beer.

Our TV commercial and press advert for magazines and newspapers sum up the Yanjing brand, describing Yanjing as 'the great people-brand'. We have another message that we use on the labels: 'Yanjing people make everyday people feel the best.'

The internal culture

To develop, an enterprise must have its own culture and that culture must double as a way of improving the enterprise's competitive advantage. I also think that a healthy company culture increases employee cohesion.

For the past 20 years we have had five core values for Yanjing – the Yanjing Spirit. These values are as follows: 'the spirit of devoted contribution'; 'the spirit of hard work'; 'the pioneering spirit of originality'; 'the spirit of co-operation for the good of the whole'; and 'the leadership spirit of being the top of our trade.'

These five values have helped us to guide the company and improve our enterprise's teamwork. They are at the core of the company's success and the success of each individual employee. These values, along with Yanjing's administrative style as well as its superb technology, have helped create a formidable brand in today's competitive beer industry.

Building consumer understanding

We have three channels for gathering insights about the consumer: every year a market research company and a university department help certain enterprises, including Yanjing, carry out market research. This is one channel for us to get information. Our second channel is the Yanjing beer group itself: we sell millions of tonnes of beer so we have our own sales network. This network also gives us some feedback in terms of consumer needs and also on quality issues. In addition, we have all the general statistical analysis of all this feedback information. Our third channel is our special market research department which can assess consumer demand and also changes in consumption behaviour. A comprehensive analysis of all this information provides a pretty good basis for decision-making at the management level.

The research practised in China is usually quantitative in its nature – qualitative research is rarely practised here. But the feedback we get from these three channels helps us make a final decision about the kinds of product we should produce. We currently have different categories of beer – some are very fresh, some are very light. Because China is a vast country and people have different tastes from region to region, we tailor our beers accordingly. So the product that we mainly sell in the south of China has a light taste, whereas in northern parts it's heavy. The same applies to cost. Cheaper beers sell better in the poorer regions.

China's local beer

In 1998 we formulated strategies for expansion, but, of course, one factory was insufficient for expansion nationwide. To resolve this, Yanjing acquired many local breweries across China through mergers and acquisitions. The Beijing Yanjing brand is the core brand but there are many sub-brands that have a loyal local customer base.

While consolidation is now very important for Yanjing in areas such as the brand, the market, the culture and various other aspects, it is a time-consuming process and we must be very cautious. Currently, the sub-brands are the preferred brands locally. If we changed their names all of a sudden, people wouldn't recognize them. Eventually, though, all the acquired enterprises, cultures and everything else will become Yanjing.

A responsibility to society and to the economy

Yanjing stands for the best-quality products for consumers, the best value and the best service. It also means responsibility.

In our production process we have made use of many social resources so, in return, we have to act very responsibly towards society. We have recently initiated a programme to become the most environmentally friendly enterprise in China. Under this initiative, we give donations to help build schools, and we also construct and build hospitals. We help create and manage green areas in some of the cities in China, and we pay for public information films, as well as educational films, for children. This work is carried out across China, not only in local areas, and, through these activities, Yanjing can reinforce its credibility as the 'beer of the people'.

COMMENTARY

Yanjing has taken a slightly different path to achieving growth than other big breweries, such as Tsingtao, in that, despite the lure of foreign capital and expertise, the company has decided to go it alone.

In the short term, remaining 100 per cent Chinese could give the brewery an advantage over Tsingtao: it may enhance the perceived craftmanship and authentic heritage of its beer products. But once international beer brands have built up their own credibility in China for quality and for taste, will the desire to remain independent become a burden?

One reason for finding a partner is to accelerate technology-driven competitiveness. But Yanjing has already established a name for itself as a place of technological reform. And it continues to lead the sector in technological innovation. There are, however, other reasons for partnering. Accession to the WTO is placing new demands on China's business leaders, who will need to adapt management styles to new market conditions to survive and build their brands.

Perhaps, for Yanjing, the finding of a foreign partner for market-led insights is not a question of if, but when. In the past, overseas players have been eager to enter China on their own terms and successful brands such as Yanjing have often been undervalued. Yanjing did try, in the past, to set up joint ventures with these brewers, but both sides failed to agree on who should take the controlling share.

With the new wave of international interest comes a new way of thinking about what to look for when choosing a Chinese partner. This time around, the foreign brands will need to focus less on company credentials and more on brand capital and capabilities. For a company like Yanjing that understands the value of its own brand, establishing a foreign partner could bring significant and mutual rewards for both parties.

13 | Yue-Sai: Influencing the Course of Social Change

Introduction

Yue-Sai Kan Cosmetics is China's leading cosmetics firm. Established in Shanghai in 1992, the company was the result of founder Yue-Sai Kan's frustrations at not being able to find cosmetics that suited her Asian skin tone and facial features. She gave the company a mission – to develop and distribute a brand of cosmetics designed especially for the Chinese woman. Since then, the company has expanded to 18 regional offices around China, including offices in secondary markets such as Harbin in Heilongjiang province and Kunming in Yunnan province.

In 1996, as the leading cosmetics brand in China, the company entered into a joint venture with Coty, a Paris-based cosmetics firm that is a division of the German consumer goods company, John A. Benckiser GmbH. Through this joint venture, it set up a US$20 million, 300,000 square foot cosmetics manufacturing facility in Shanghai's Pudong Area, manufacturing beauty products for the Chinese market.

Yue-Sai herself was voted the 'Most Influential Person in the Beauty Industry' in the year 2000 by the Beauty and Cosmetics Industry Association in China. She has been called the 'Queen of Cosmetics' and has been heralded by Forbes *magazine as 'the woman who changed the face of China one lipstick at a time.' A household name in China, her face, it is estimated, is recognized by 95 per cent of the Chinese population.*

The following tells the story of the Yue-Sai brand, the vision that helped it grow and how Yue-Sai, the woman behind the brand, brought colour to China.

Celebrating Asian Beauty

For years I had been living all over the world – in the US, Hong Kong and Africa. And yet, in all of these places, I was not able to discover a single cosmetics company that really catered to my needs. None of them was able to say to me: 'I understand you are different. I understand that you have black hair, black eyes and a yellow based skin tone.' None of them was able to say: 'I know you, I care about you and I want to create products just for you – products that will make you equally, if not more, beautiful than anyone else in this

world.' None of them was able to educate me: 'I can teach you make-up techniques that will make your unique features even more beautiful. And give you
colours that are modern so that you are not just going to be a gorgeous
woman from the Tang Dynasty of China but a gorgeous woman anywhere,
whether walking down the streets of Paris, London or New York.'

It was this failure to find such a cosmetics company that led me to set up
Yue-Sai Kan Cosmetics. My company had, and still has, a specific vision: to be
the Asian beauty authority.

Back in the early 1990s, the concept of using cosmetics was alien to the
average Chinese woman. She was like me when I arrived, as a fresh-faced
teenager, in Hong Kong and then the US. I was bewildered by the multitude
of colours to be used for clothes and make-up, and I made mistakes. Knowing
that half a billion Chinese women would be facing this same predicament, I
wanted to create a line of cosmetics and products to help them, to teach them
the magical, transformational power that colour can have on us.

Before I came along, the world had an image of femininity and of beauty
that was Caucasian in origin. White women dominated the covers of fashion
magazines setting a standard of beauty for Asian women that was impossible
to follow. I wanted to present to the world our own beauty standard and to
foster a sense of pride in our physical being. I wanted Asian women to start
believing that being Chinese or being Asian is beautiful in itself. We don't
have to copy anyone else in order to be beautiful.

'Doing it the way you do it in the US'

I was born in Guilin, China, and grew up in Hong Kong in the 1950s and
1960s. My mother, who died in 1994, ran a theatre company. My father is a
famous Chinese painter living in New York.

At the age of 16, I left Hong Kong, having won a scholarship to study
music at Brigham Young University in Hawaii. I studied at the university for
four years during which time I took a number of jobs so that I could support
myself financially. One of these was teaching the piano to younger children,
which I adored. In those days my only desire was to be a great concert pianist.

After college was over, I moved back in with my parents in Hong Kong and
began to work for my uncle, then head of Hyatt Hotels Asia, as a trainee telephone operator for the Hilton. I remained at the Hilton for about six months,
switching departments and ended up as an assistant in the PR department.
Soon after, my uncle launched the Hyatt's flagship hotel in Kowloon and he
invited me to come to work there.

It was a very interesting time in my life, and I certainly learnt a lot about
public relations but I was being carried further and further away from my real

love – music. So I made a decision to go back to graduate school in Hawaii to take my masters degree in music.

The next year marked a major turning point in my life as slowly it began to dawn on me that I would never be the great pianist I had dreamed about. I was simply not talented enough. I was bitterly disappointed and, after my last concert in Singapore, I vowed that I would never touch a piano again. I left for New York, not really knowing what I was going to do with my life and arrived on a freezing cold January 1st morning with $150 in my pocket. I was wearing the warmest dress that I had in Hawaii, but when I got into New York it was snowing. I had no coat. Nothing. It was really scary. I knew only one girl who I went to high school with, but I hadn't seen her for years. I used to sleep on the couch of her apartment but I loved New York City so much, I decided that I would stay. These were my very humble beginnings in New York.

I embarked on a career in broadcast journalism and soon found my own tiny apartment to rent. After a time, my parents gave me the money to put down a deposit on my first apartment in New York – a small, but very beautiful studio flat. My parents were always there at the important times in my life and I feel very fortunate. Next, my mother sent me a piano. Because I had spent all those years studying music, she knew the immense joy the piano could bring me, and in her wonderful way she was right. I still love to play the piano. In fact, for the company's tenth anniversary I composed a love song to capture the spirit and feeling behind my brand and to show Asian women that I really do want them to feel beautiful.

While in New York, it did not take long before I landed a job hosting a TV show in English and Chinese on a local cable station. Things began to happen for me very quickly and, by 1978, I had produced my first documentary series, *Looking East*, created to give Americans new insights into the cultures of the East. Then, in 1989, I won an Emmy award for the ABC documentary, *China Walls and Bridges*.

Being given an Emmy for any kind of work in television is like being given an Oscar in the movies. It is a great honour. But, ultimately, what is important to me is how I feel about myself and all that I have accomplished. The question I must ask is: have I changed the perception that Chinese women have about themselves – the way they look at colour and at style? And have I changed the way they look at the outside world? I think that both my television programmes and my books have helped to do this. But I also have to ask: have I really helped China in its opening up to the outside world? Through my work I believe that I have and this is what really counts – receiving recognition is immaterial.

I had achieved fame in the US but, despite this, I was still relatively unknown in China. That was to change in 1986, when I began hosting the

China-based documentary series *One World*, which ran twice-weekly for a year on China's only national network, the Chinese Communist government television station (CCTV). This series was to give Chinese viewers their first snapshot of Western lifestyles and cultures, and it was a great success. It was the first-ever programme produced and hosted by a foreigner and it made my face famous.

At that time, psychologically, China had just woken up to the idea of aesthetics. Until then, people had no aspirations to be beautiful. China was drab. Imagine the reaction when I hosted this programme dressed in Fendi, Ungaro and all the beautiful designs of the day, with gorgeous make-up colours – a complete contrast to my predecessors who had looked very serious and severe. It was a radical move which, in fact, had been suggested to me by the minister of television at CCTV. At that time, I was so nervous of doing a show in China that I didn't dare use too much make-up. I didn't dare do anything. How could I possibly be sure that China really wanted to open itself up? So I hosted three pilot programmes for approval wearing grey clothes and very little make-up. Afterwards, the minister said, 'Yue-Sai, these are fabulous programmes but is this how you look when you do television in America?' I said it wasn't. He replied, 'In that case, why don't you just do it the way you do it in the United States?'

It was also during this period that I started puzzling over why certain colours that looked fabulous on my Caucasian friends looked ghastly on me. It struck me that my skin tone and features were uniquely Asian but the standard of beauty that I had been following as a presenter was a Western standard. Consequently, I began to adopt a whole new approach to fashion and started to wear clothes and cosmetic colours that enhanced my overall look. Asian hair and eye colouring is distinctive because it is so dark and contrasting. Cosmetic shades should flatter that contrast. The same rule applies to clothes: make-up should not only complement our features and skin tone, it must work with the outfit as well.

Yet all around me I continued to see very chic Asian women wearing exquisite outfits that actually emphasized the sallowness of their skin or using clashing shades of lipstick or nail polish. This started me thinking – wouldn't it be fabulous if I could devise a colour palette that could instantly help all of us who have yellow skin tones to choose the most flattering colours for our wardrobe and make-up? Such a tool would also help women avoid wasted time and costly mistakes. It would simplify life by giving us fewer, but better, choices. This palette could give Asian women the confidence to know that they have at their fingertips a foolproof guarantee for looking fabulous all the time.

Starting Yue-Sai Kan Cosmetics presented me with the perfect opportunity to implement this idea.

Creating the 'colour palette'

The process took two years. I adopted a very systematic and scientific approach to the project. With the help of two top colour consultants in New York, Justine Blair Carroll and Diane C. Schwartz, we draped the shoulders of hundreds of pan-Asian women with every conceivable fabric colour. The women were of all ages, came from countries ranging from Indonesia to Japan, with skin tones that varied from extremely dark to very fair. We rejected any colour, clothing or make-up that failed to flatter the model.

During the tests, we found that the wrong colour actually emphasizes the wrinkles and dark spots to which Asian women are prone, while the right colour can brighten the skin and make it appear healthier and more radiant as well as dramatically enhancing the dark hair and dark eyes.

Colour is basically light so it casts a reflection on the skin affecting its tone in a way that can be profound and has the power to transform a woman's overall look. For example, the reflection of brown makes Asian skin look pale and sallow. Certain muddy greens reflect dark light and give Asian skin a greenish tint. Both colours contain yellow undertones that automatically add to the natural yellow base tone of Asian skin. On the other hand, a clear bright pink has the opposite effect because it has blue undertones and these complement Asian colouring, enhancing the brightness of skin, the whites of the eyes and the teeth.

I found over 50 colours that are truly beautiful on Asian women. I divided these into three colour groups: the orange family, the pink family and the neutral family. The neutrals include the dark, dark green and dark, dark charcoal brown. The face and the outfit should be complementary. For example, a pink dress should not be worn with an orange lipstick, but a neutral dress can be worn comfortably with any of the make-up shades in the colour system.

Within the three colour families, I created lipstick colours to match, in dark, medium and light – every one flattering to Asian skin. The woman simply has to decide two things: which colour outfit and the brightness of the lipstick to go with it. The lipstick then leads everything else, such as cheek colours and nail polish. My blushers, for example, always come in a compact with two colours, one from the orange family and one from the pink family, so that, depending on the outfit and the lipstick, the consumer knows immediately which cheek colour to use.

For enhancing the facial features, I have a special product called three-colour contour powder. This contour powder consists of a dark brown, a light brown and a white. I use light brown to shade the sides of the nose and I put white along the ridge so that the nose lifts a little more. In the same way that women use a highlighter for their brows to play off the shadows cast by the eyes, we have created products that work for the features of Asian women.

With this colour palette, I have created the first Asian colour co-ordinating system. I believe that one cannot sell cosmetics without understanding colour. In our palette we have 'classic shades' – a small number of cosmetic colours that will always flatter Asian women of any age group in any outfit. It took two years of testing to arrive at these classic shades. But the end benefit to the consumer is worthwhile, because she cannot go wrong with it. A system has been set up to allow Asian women to understand colours and use cosmetics easily. And the philosophy driving all of this is that my cosmetics are truly and especially made for the Asian woman.

Yue-Sai's unique points of difference

Yue-Sai is a personality-driven brand. Just look at my company logo. The words represent my name and were written by my father. The picture is a monochrome photograph of my face because I came into cosmetics with a face made famous from television. It was reworked by Andy Warhol who added a splash of bright red lipstick. This is a logo that is recognized by practically everyone in China and, in that way, has helped create the company brand. It has also added warmth and personality to our corporate brand.

As 'the Asian beauty authority', I want Chinese women to realize that I am just like them. It is not a Caucasian making products for them, it is Yue-Sai making products for them. So, unlike the major cosmetic companies that sell Asian women make-up colours that are fashionable but only look great on Western women, we find colours that both complement her and keep her up to date. Fashion colours change every season, but a seasonal colour can exist in a hundred shades or more. This means that, whatever the colour trends on the catwalks of Paris and New York, Yue-Sai Kan Cosmetics not only has the most beautiful colours to match, but has also identified the most flattering shades for Asians. In this way, our lines are both 'made for you', in the bespoke sense, and are also 'making it for you' in the sense of enabling the Asian woman to be beautiful in a totally contemporary way.

For the Asian woman, there are a number of other benefits. First, she saves time. Once educated, she can go straight to the shades that complement her outfit without worrying whether or not they will suit her. She saves money since she no longer buys colours that she finds do nothing for her. But what cannot be measured is the psychological effect. Her confidence in her look grows and that can transform the way in which a woman interacts with the world. We feel that no other company has empowered Asian women in this way.

This deep commitment to empowering Asian women is our brand 'soul' and it is what makes us truly unique. It also means that in everything we do – from ingredients used in manufacturing to the way in which we package and market our products – we try to be true to this soul and to find a way of expressing this commitment. Our advertising, for example, has never used a model who is not Chinese. This reinforces to our customers the idea that being Chinese is enough to be beautiful.

Our product formulas combine Chinese wisdom that has been passed from generation to generation over thousands of years with the very latest Western technologies. We have lipsticks that contain green tea and we have a skin-care range that contains a concoction of traditional herbs that Chinese people have been using for 5,000 years. We have a whitening line that is based on a reformulation of the precious pearl – something that the Chinese have been using as a whitening agent for centuries. We also have a skin-care range with patented formulas, one of which contains ingredients that act like magnets, activating the cells under the skin and encouraging them to regenerate. The phenomenon of magnetism was a Chinese discovery.

We also combine the use of the products with traditional Chinese rituals. For example, we put certain scents into our night and day creams. One aids slumber; the other stimulates wakefulness. We teach pressure point stimulation to induce sleep so that, at night, you use a particular cream with a particular smell and a particular ritual. All our therapies and rituals flow from our commitment to teach Asian women how to enhance their beauty.

In this way, we ensure that we are not just any brand of cosmetics in the market. If you ask anyone what differentiates the Yue-Sai brand, I will wager that 95 per cent of Chinese women will say 'they have made it especially for me'. This is a very powerful and relevant message that we have managed to communicate to our market. But the bigger challenge is how we are going to translate this extraordinary 95 per cent brand awareness into real purchases.

This will depend on our operation. How do we operate in a way that is true to the brand and maintains its integrity? For example, are we ensuring that the style of our advertising supports our message? How do we translate the brand message into a compelling reason for people to buy our products? Let me tell you a story. A woman once approached me and said, 'When you first launched your line of products, my sister, my mother and I gathered our money together so we could buy our first Yue-Sai lipstick.' Now, that is compelling.

Yue-Sai has been around for eleven years. Is the woman who bought our lipstick eleven years ago still using Yue-Sai today? Is she still loyal to the brand in the face of rising competition? That is the other challenge. We may be the biggest cosmetic company in China with a major distribution across the country (in fact we have 10 per cent of the department store distribution channel business in China) but I think there is still a lot of work that needs to be done.

Work in progress

Yue-Sai Kan Cosmetics is work in progress. One of the things I am trying to do is to drive this message of being committed to the Asian woman deep into my organization. I want to provide good training all the way down to my sales girls such that when they sell my lipstick, they don't just sell it as 'the most popular lipstick' but as 'this is the most fashionable colour of the season and this is the most flattering shade that is made for you'. This is a proposition that we can own. I also want them to be able to teach consumers how to use the products effectively, making it simple for consumers to understand cosmetics and understand the core values of the Yue-Sai brand.

It is an education process that we are involved in. Why do you think cosmetic companies all over the world have make-up artists at the counters? Because there are techniques that we can teach to our consumers about how to use new fashion colours and how to apply them to almond-shaped eyes. Previously, consumers who came to a Yue-Sai counter were invited to view an hour-long television programme that provided them with everything from product information to the understanding of colour. We have discontinued this now, but we are still striving to find a way of creating that special experience that would differentiate us from other make-up counters.

In terms of product development, we are always trying to improve on our existing products. We have three skin-care institutes around the world, one in each of the cities of New York, Monaco and Shanghai. All the testing is done in Shanghai because we are only interested in Asian skin, but we have the advantage of utilizing resources from the other institutes, especially the latest Western skin-care technology that is developed in Europe. Asian skins are unique in many ways. We are very allergy-prone because our skin is so sensitive and we react differently to the sun than peach-based skin tones. Skin cancer is extremely rare because the melanin under our skin, which tints it yellow, also protects us from UV rays. But dark spots indicate that Asian skin is damaged. All our research is aimed at helping us understand these sorts of differences between Asian skin and Western skin so that our products can target this difference.

What I want to emphasize is that there is real research and thinking behind our line of products. I believe that, as a cosmetics brand, we cannot be all things to all people. Perhaps when you advertise, you can be flexible with your emotional content. You can feature a blonde woman and the young Chinese girls of today may still aspire to that image but, when it comes to using the products, you cannot compromise. Yes, we do try to sell the best of what is fashionable in cosmetic colours to our consumers, but they are all made with a real understanding of Asian skin.

Yue-Sai's challenges

Our success in China has also presented us with our challenges. When we first launched our products in Shanghai in 1992, cosmetics, while not taboo, were not used by women. We effectively created the cosmetics market in China. Prior to us, there was no supporting infrastructure. For instance, it was impossible to find people to employ who had a good knowledge of cosmetics. In fact just about anything related to cosmetics manufacture, distribution and licensing simply did not exist. To make a delivery from Shanghai to Beijing I had to send a man over to the train station who would then spend a week negotiating for a container to be sent to Beijing. Even finding a truck to go from Shenzhen, where my first factory was, up to Shanghai, was impossible. Can you imagine a 40 year-old woman coming up to me, holding a lipstick in shaking hands and saying half-apologetically, with a look of desperation in her eyes, 'Yue-Sai, I have never used cosmetics before. I don't know how to use it.' So we were the pioneers, but we also ended up opening a path for competitors to enter this market. We made it easier for other companies to sell to the Chinese consumer because she was no longer facing the first lipstick of her life.

And the competition has been fierce. The foreign multinationals that enter China are only interested in market share and they try to get it at any cost. To achieve visibility, they will throw money at their investment – by advertising, for instance – without concern for the returns. This makes it difficult for companies like us to compete.

Furthermore, we have never had government support. Just because I know Zhang Zemin does not mean that I have a successful business. I applied for a licence to sell just like everyone else. And just because I obtained the licence does not mean that my products will sell. The success of my business depends on my convincing millions of Chinese women to use my products, not just once, but over and over again. Sometimes when we have a product that needs urgent approval from the health department, I go there personally so I can obtain it ahead of time, but such advantages are nominal. The government gives us no special privileges. We compete on the same level with international companies like L'Oréal and Shiseido.

The other problem we face is that of perception. When Western cosmetic brands started appearing in the Chinese departmental stores, the Chinese consumer looked at them and thought, 'Oh they are international, they must be good!' Yue-Sai, on the other hand, is not international yet. As a result, the Chinese consumer prefers whatever is international without regard to how suitable the product actually is. This is frustrating because our products are every bit as good as the foreign competition's.

The Chinese market is undoubtedly huge and, if we manage our business well, there is an unlimited potential for us within China. But I do realize that we have to build our brand overseas. No matter how big or small, we need an overseas presence so that, when our consumers go travelling, they will see us not just in China and Taiwan, but also in New York and Paris. Perhaps this is a feature of the development of Asian brands. Look at Issey Miyake or Kenzo. They succeeded overseas before gaining prominence in their home markets. The famous Chinese film director, Zhang Yimou, was much more highly regarded after he achieved success at the Cannes Film Festival. Gong Li, the Chinese actress, was never very big in China until she made it at Cannes and then returned home.

Of course, the bigger we grow, the harder it will be to control the company. At the moment, I personally approve everything. But I used to be so much more hands-on. I used to tape every video that teaches my sales girls how to sell, but I can't do that any more. In the past year alone, we grew 21 per cent, which makes improving our training, product development and overall control very critical indeed. Yes, the company is growing healthily, beautifully, but this is also the point when we have to be sure that we are growing in the direction of the vision into which we were born. There is no room for complacency because I do not just want to be a bigger company, I want to be a company that is going to lead and dominate the market.

As an 11-year-old company, we are not a young brand. We have to constantly evolve our products, our advertising and our packaging design. A great deal of trust is placed in the Yue-Sai brand and we have to live up to it. Otherwise, we will not survive. When I launched the company back in 1992, there were two other famous Asian women, both actresses, who created their own cosmetic lines. Neither company survived because they did not really have a raison d'être. They did not have that overwhelming commitment that my company has to our market.

The Yue-Sai impact

Education is something to which I am passionately committed. I have combined that with the brand message by setting up a scholarship fund at Beijing University, the premier university in China. The scholarship supports outstanding female students from each province.

I also launched a doll company to create a positive role model – to help Asian children develop confidence in the way they look and in their differences to Western children. The first Asian fashion doll, the Yue-Sai Wa Wa, went on sale in 2001. I am running initiatives, as part of the doll business, designed to teach children social responsibility and environmental issues. For example, we give the children a small accessory, such as a handbag or shoes, if they return a certain number of batteries for recycling. Alternatively, if a child brings a book to the counter that she has read, we will swap that either for a doll accessory or another book.

As a UNICEF ambassador, I have been responsible for raising awareness about UNICEF throughout China through the 'Say Yes for Children' campaign. The campaign is the start of a global movement that aims to transform the way in which the world treats children. At its launch in April 2000 we had less than 100,000 signatures. Through setting up signature collection points at every Yue-Sai sales counter in every store across China, we were able to increase that number to over 20 million signatures which we recently presented to the UN.

I think how the company and I myself have impacted on society can be summed up as follows: I was in a hospital the other day and a doctor came up to me and said: 'Yue-Sai, you know you have influenced all three generations of my family. You influenced my father and mother because they all saw your television programmes. I learnt English through you. My wife is using your cosmetics and my daughter now is playing with your dolls.'

I hope to continue to have a positive impact on society. Yue-Sai Kan Cosmetics caters to three common qualities: black eyes, black hair and a yellow-based skin-tone, and with that, a belief that being Asian is enough to be beautiful. That message is empowering Asian women throughout the world and is helping to bridge the gap in the understanding of what constitutes beauty. Our company was the first to use Chinese models. Even Shiseido at that time did not use Asian models. We led the way for that positive change in fashion magazines and in editorial policies. Even our understanding of the differences between Asian skin and Caucasian skin is a breakthrough for society.

Where do I go from here? I think that there are many areas in which my name could be very relevant – for example, health-related products. If you think about cosmetics as outer beauty then why not a line of Yue-Sai products related to inner beauty? In fact, anything to do with women, from underwear to jewellery, clothes to accessories. I would love to work with a major design company with the manufacturing capabilities to create a line of clothing tailored towards the Asian skin tone. There could be products for children now that I have the doll company – children's clothes, for example.

All of these things are very relevant to what the brand name can do. And that does not necessarily mean that we cannot come up with anything for men either. Yue-Sai Kan Cosmetics could certainly have a line of cosmetics for men. I have so many ideas. The only limitation is in finding the right people to help me implement these ideas, to cross the hurdles of licensing and distribution in China. Think about it – the Yue-Sai brand is known to 95 per cent of 1.3 billion people here in China. How far can we take that?

COMMENTARY

Yue-Sai Kan Cosmetics is China's most famous personality-led brand. Yue-Sai's vivacious personality lends colour to her brand just as her cosmetic products bring colour to the face of China. Like Virgin in the UK, Yue-Sai, the brand, is an expression of the personal vision and passion of its founder. Yue-Sai takes it one step further than Virgin, however, because the logo of the company is Yue-Sai's face and the name of the company is her name written in beautiful calligraphy by her own father.

Taken positively, this makes the brand highly distinctive and unique. The story of the brand is the story of her struggle to find a range of cosmetics that suited her skin tone and would bring out her beauty as an Asian woman. Female consumers in China will find it impossible not to identify with her as more and more of them are introduced to international fashion and cosmetic trends, and they attempt to find their sense of style. In the course of enhancing the natural beauty of Chinese women, she has been a beacon of hope for millions of women who were seeking more self-confidence in the early years of reform.

The challenge that Yue-Sai Kan Cosmetics may face in the future is how to develop the brand's ideology and image so that it is able to exist and grow independently of Yue-Sai the person. The brand needs to be institutionalized so that it can develop successfully beyond Yue-Sai's prominence as a Chinese celebrity. Yue-Sai herself is already facing some of these challenges. As the company grows, she is unable to be as hands-on as she would like to be. Brand awareness is very high, but will this continue into future generations? Will she continue to be perceived as representing what is modern and fashionable? Will she need to find other spokespersons for the brand – other Asian female role models from around the world who can perhaps personify the Yue-Sai brand in different ways?

As Chinese society modernizes and as the brand attempts to seek an international audience in Chinese communities overseas, Yue-Sai Kan Cosmetics will need to evolve to stay competitive. It may need to draw on the strength of its founding vision – to change the standard of beauty in the world, from its focus on fair skin to a recognition of the diversity of modern society and the rising prominence of Asians. An American-born Chinese teenager, you might say, is born holding a lipstick. For her to select Yue-Sai's beauty products over the range of American and European brands on offer will ultimately depend on how much she considers Yue-Sai's brand proposition of being the 'Asian Beauty Authority' to be truly relevant to her.

14 | Phoenix TV: Becoming the Media Brand King

Introduction

Phoenix Television began broadcasting the Phoenix Chinese Channel on 31 March 1996, setting up a TV station that developed rapidly into a window to the world for the Chinese global community. China has always been seen as a place where private media companies never existed but, through careful management and lateral thinking, Phoenix has been pushing its way through the heavily guarded Byzantine pathways of the Chinese media industry with remarkable success. Liu Changle is a key figure in the future of Chinese media freedom, and a breath of fresh air in Chinese television.

With a fifth of the world's population speaking Chinese, China is full of virtually untapped potential telly-addicts. China is the only regional market where one will see significant advertising inflation in the next few years. TV advertising, almost nil in 1990, has grown at a compound annual growth rate (CAGR) of 35 per cent for the last ten years. Television developed from nothing to 50 per cent of total advertising in ten years and is set to grow faster than overall advertising for the next five years. This is despite the fact that almost all programming is run by the state. Since Phoenix reaches 45 million of China's 320 million television households, or about 60 per cent of total cable households, the influence that Phoenix will have over the next few years is obvious.

Liu Changle, the founder, chairman and chief executive officer of Phoenix Satellite Television, was born in Shanghai in 1952 and was a teenager at the time of the Cultural Revolution, which broke out in 1966 and during which he served in the People's Liberation Army. He left the military at the end of the Cultural Revolution and joined the Central People's Radio Station, after which he studied at the Beijing Broadcasting Institute. He then returned to Central Radio as a reporter, news editor and commentator, eventually becoming the manager of the section responsible for covering military affairs. He is known for being 'an extraordinary master at the guanxi game' and, in a country where the boundaries between the tolerable and the prohibited are media grey areas, Liu has a remarkable capability to see the danger points – and a talent for getting away with stepping across the lines from time to time.

The restrictions on who can legally receive the Phoenix signal illustrate the narrow confines of China's media opportunities. Their coverage rate in China is only 40 per cent, while China Central Television has an 80 per cent coverage rate. Yet Phoenix has the second highest ratings and the fourth highest commercial revenue among the 44 TV stations, making Phoenix a phenomenally successful television station. Criticism of the Communist Party and coverage of sensitive topics like the Falungong crackdown are still no-go areas, but Phoenix viewers do get uncensored glimpses of life outside China in movies, travel shows and access to talk shows that focus on sex and gossip, all of which would have been unthinkable a few years ago.

From one channel, Phoenix merged with Rupert Murdoch's Star TV and built up a multinational platform – 'When the dragon flies, the phoenix dances', as an old Chinese idiom goes. Today, Phoenix channels include the Phoenix Chinese Channel, the Phoenix Movie Channel, the Phoenix North American Chinese Channel and the Phoenix CNE Channel, which broadcasts in Europe. Liu's next test will be the competition from other joint venture satellite broadcasters hoping to imitate his model. Former Phoenix star anchor, Yang Lan, began broadcasting her Sun TV into China last year and others are on the way, including Beijing-based Five Star TV, which plans to begin broadcasting entertainment programming similar to Phoenix's by the end of this year.

The beginning

I was one of the first Chinese to engage in private business. I based myself in Singapore and traded petroleum before expanding my business activities to include real estate and infrastructure projects both in China and overseas. I was privileged in that I was a private citizen, yet still had good government connections, so I began to contemplate using my established commercial base to launch a Chinese-language television broadcaster that would be politically neutral and use modern technology to broadcast Chinese around the world. Phoenix Television's inimitable approach caught on very quickly in China and its rapid development exerted pressure on competitors. The pressure factor was not only that Phoenix occupied a major share of the advertising market, but that it was undeniably famous.

At this point, Star TV, which started broadcasting in 1991, was looking to localize its strategy. News Corporation bought Star TV in 1993, but it became apparent that, since it broadcast primarily in English and had a highly educated audience, it was not reaching the critical mass. Rupert Murdoch, head of News Corporation, made the mistake of prophesying that satellite TV was 'an unambiguous threat to totalitarian regimes everywhere' – a phrase that sent shivers down the spine of the Chinese Communist Party headquarters. He thus began to find himself facing a number of setbacks and was advised to link Star TV more tightly with China itself. It was too much to hope that an Australian businessman could simply wander into a different political and social structure and achieve instant success. All this meant that

News Corporation was looking for a Chinese project that would draw in the critical mass. Both Phoenix and Star TV could see that their competition came from each other so, for the sake of our mutual development, Phoenix merged with Star TV, giving us a total of five channels.

Our first impact on China is often cited as being the Hong Kong handover in 1997, when Phoenix was the only channel to give unbiased footage of the ceremony. Although China Central Television boasted numerous cameras, its hands were tied by the government and its cameras focused almost continually on President Zemin, which significantly muted the symbolism of the event. Phoenix was able to show a more neutral vantage-point, giving equal coverage to both spokesmen, Mr Jiang and the then Governor of Hong Kong Chris Patten. After this broadcast, word spread that an innovative new channel had hit China and, for five consecutive years, annual growth rate has been 67 per cent, with advertising revenue in the founding year standing at US$3 million. Advertising revenue is now US$100 million, and the brand has even acquired a commercial value, with the price of residential property rising if it has access to Phoenix Television.

The brand

Phoenix has a very clear and accurate idea of how to position the company. Although the logo was my idea, we spent $300,000 and invited Americans to design it. The Phoenix mythology is an essential force in the spirit of Phoenix Television, so we wanted the logo to be faultless.

The Chinese Phoenix or 'Feng Huang' first appeared to the Chinese emperor, Hung Ti, around 2600 BCE. Feng Huang only appeared in times of peace and prosperity, usually when a new benign emperor ascended the throne. The phoenix and the dragon are two revered symbols of prosperity in the minds of the Chinese people, so our logo has a positive internal force. The phoenix has long stood for perseverance and fighting spirit, which is apt considering the political environment that Phoenix TV encounters on a daily basis. Our logo inspires Phoenix Television to thrive even in the face of adversity since, when the phoenix fights with fire, it refuses to die, but rises from the ashes to fight another battle.

In China we have this expression: 'Feng wei bai niao zhi wang', meaning 'the phoenix is king amongst the birds'. We have analysed the internal meaning of this ancient Chinese symbol so thoroughly that each member of staff works with the characteristics of the phoenix in mind. One of these characteristics translates for employees as the ambition to make the programme the best it can be. According to mythology, the phoenix's song was the basis for the Chinese musical scale. On earth the phoenix nests in *wu t'ung* trees and it is believed that if one plays a musical instrument while sitting under these trees, the phoenix will bless the musician with further musical gifts. The phoenix is therefore a symbol of inspiration and vision, always flying in front of the other birds and leading the way.

Unlike the phoenix of Western mythology, the Chinese legends describe the phoenix as two different birds: *feng* represents the male and *hwang* represents the female. The male is the yang and represents the solar cycle and summer, while the female is the yin, the lunar cycle, and a symbol of the Chinese empress. This *taiji*, or yin-yang relationship, equates to the balance of East and West within the Phoenix brand and our partnership with Star TV. The two birds of our logo share the same crown, which looks like the penetrating eye of the Phoenix and these swirling circles create the eye of a camera. The open circle refers to how Phoenix Television has a free-thinking approach to media television.

Phoenix's star quality

Phoenix is successful because it is unique. Our first gamble was in deciding to take the 'star approach' to media television in China, which had never been done before. We recruited renowned journalists, commentators and reporters who were excited by the idea of a more open-minded approach to current affairs. It was obvious to us that, in order to cultivate an unbeatable television channel, we needed to involve exceptional personalities.

Other Hong Kong-based television stations are afraid to make this commitment, possibly because they are under the impression that the stars will resign as soon as they become famous. So far, only Yang Lan has left Phoenix Television and this was because she was craving to go into business herself. There is an extremely simple reason why our stars do not leave – it is basically because if a star, such as Madame Chen Lu Yu, decided to change jobs he or she could not go to Taiwan because the audiences are so much smaller nor could they go to China Central Television because they would not be able to express themselves in the way in which they can with Phoenix. At Phoenix we see our relationship with these well-known media personalities as one of equals, so we cultivate and train each presenter in such a way that they are given opportunities, promotion and creative space that they would find nowhere else in Chinese broadcasting. In return, our team of presenters has helped consolidate our position as the most powerful global Mandarin-language television network.

Recently there has been a heated debate as to whether reporters and hostesses ought to reflect their own personalities in what they broadcast. At the Beijing Broadcasting Institute, the reporters are taught exactly how to act.

China Central Television, like the BBC, requires that the announcers should adopt a formal, relatively stiff presentation style, and reflect the position of the country through their intonation. The BBC has now changed its format somewhat, but the reporters used to merely be mouthpieces, each with the same uniform approach to news reading. There was no excitement or personality in these commentaries, but only a tired 'parent to child' attitude, as if the presenter was instructing the audience on current affairs. The intonation and style lacked the energy and the animation of our Phoenix reporters.

Each Phoenix personality has characteristics that draw the audience into experiencing and involving themselves with the reporter's observations. Chen Lu Yu has her own morning programme and she does this without the aid of numerous preprepared papers to read from. She has read the newspapers and news items and then she creates the programme. At Phoenix we always try to take a different and more innovative approach than our competitors. For example, we have a host by the name of Dou Wen Tao who chaired a very special programme, captivating the audience by being one of them.

This is the distinguishing feature of Phoenix hosts – they work to create empathy with the audience in order to communicate the message. While the BBC and American broadcasting have started to use beautiful, smart and opinionated stars, Phoenix remains distinctive because, in essence, we are a Chinese-language broadcaster who chooses hostesses with the traditional virtues of Chinese women. Shirley Wu, Xiao Li and Chen Lu Yu are all shining examples of women with traditional Chinese virtues. Our rationale is that our programmes ought to be for the people and so reflect the character of the people.

Bridging different cultures

Our slogan is 'Phoenix shortens the distance between the Chinese around the world'. Parallel to our star-quality approach is our 'Greater China Concept', both of which help make the Phoenix brand special. Phoenix is different from mainland channels, different from Hong Kong channels and different from those in Taiwan. We have created a singular 'Made in China' brand, meaning that we package ourselves as a common link between all the different Mandarin-speaking societies.

Most of the staff are local, from Hong Kong, but we also have people from mainland China and Taiwan and, although these two countries are not on good political terms, Phoenix is a special environment in which people from three very different regions can work harmoniously together. The headquarters are based in Hong Kong because it is a paradise of freedom driven by a booming commercial market, but we have retained the purity of a mainland China company. Phoenix seeks to transcend the various components of greater China and offers Chinese viewers a media service that is global in outlook and independent of local political attachments.

Since 2000 Phoenix has been listed on the Hong Kong Growth Enterprise Market and our two largest shareholders are News Corporation and Today's Asia, which is now largely owned by me. These two corporations own over 75 per cent of Phoenix and public investors own 16.4 per cent. Mainland China is a very special market so, despite being a public company free from the control of any government, we are restrained by the mechanisms of this party-controlled social system in which media is regarded as an organ for the party. Striking a balance between the censorship and monitoring functions of the government and our popularity among audiences is like walking on a high wire. We stick quite closely to the correct political line, to the extent that Premier Zhu Rongii once announced that he often watched Phoenix Television. The key to success in China is not to challenge outright the Beijing leadership view of the world. However, if we were to meet all of the government requirements, our ratings and revenue would fall and, if we went too far in the other direction, we would be taken off the air. Like the yin and yang balance of our logo, Phoenix Television aims for a sensitive equilibrium between censorship and freedom.

I am strongly influenced by strict Western accounting rules and corporate transparency. There are loopholes – for example, the Enron case – but nevertheless this system has operated successfully for a few hundred years. Our chief financial officer is a UK graduate, originating from Hong Kong, and therefore has both a Hong Kong and UK certificate for his field of work. Western accountants such as PriceWaterhouseCoopers audit our company and our legal department is made up of experienced people who are also qualified in both Hong Kong and the UK.

As mentioned earlier, our headquarters are in Hong Kong and our production centre is located in Shenzhen, where the labour cost for staff with the same expertise is one-tenth of that in Hong Kong. Phoenix is a listed company in Hong Kong, which means that our company management is regulated. The reason why we started operating in Hong Kong is because Hong Kong has two faces – the face of freedom and the face of structure and regulations. Hong Kong gives us a great deal of ideological freedom but, commercially speaking, it is highly regulated and, in terms of business management and corporate governance, it is quite institutionalized. Phoenix is considered as a foreign satellite with restricted business, so Hong Kong is one of the few places in the East where we can enjoy freedom and consistency. Although we broadcast to China, we work according to the comparatively lenient Hong Kong rules.

Our business management is influenced by the Western systems, but our core ideology is strongly rooted in Chinese culture. Star TV brought a popular technical aspect into Phoenix Television's style of broadcasting, but the content is very much Chinese. When we first began, viewers were overwhelmed by how our articulate, traditional presenters were dressed up in a Western way and although, commercially, we are a company engaged in the news media sector of China, in terms of business management we set our own standards. The Chinese way is too simple and the Western way is too pedantic, so we have extracted the best aspects of each system and created a new way of working. Phoenix Television is an amalgamation of the best of the West with the best of the East, giving us a distinctive niche in the world market.

Corporate social responsibility

Ever since I started my business in China I have done a lot of work in the area of Buddhism. I started the first computer database for the Buddhist culture in China and if you go to this website, you can get very detailed information on Buddhist history and all related aspects. I do not do this out of a religious belief, but simply because I consider Buddhism as an inherent part of Chinese culture and believe that if you can understand Buddhism you will have a deeper appreciation of the Chinese culture.

We were personally involved in the process of taking the Buddha stone from Xian to Taipei, Taiwan. Phoenix was instrumental in the inception of the idea and we covered the entire procedure, starting from the moment when the stone left the temple in Xian to the point when I myself received the stone in Taipei. Phoenix reporters were in fact the only reporters that went on the plane accompanying the stone.

In October 2000 a very famous Phoenix reporter, Liu Hai Ruo, was hurt in the Hertfordshire train crash in the UK. British doctors thought she was beyond saving, but traditional Chinese doctors kept her alive. There were many critical comments clouding this issue, because people said that we were milking the situation to sensationalize the event and attract more publicity. I remember one of our commentators being very angry when he heard this criticism, since he argued that Phoenix is a brand and Liu Hai Ruo was an important character within this brand. Since Liu Hai Ruo was part of Phoenix, why shouldn't we have worked hard and spent a lot of money on bringing her back? It is perfectly natural that we went to so much effort for her.

From the grassroots level to management, from bottom to the top, it is important to us that all Phoenix employees are full of love towards other people. This is the cultural heritage of Phoenix and also part of our management strategy. Phoenix has two types of management model: first, using a Chinese way of managing people; and, second, using a traditional Western way. The Liu Hai Ruo case is a perfect example of the traditional Chinese way of managing people since the Chinese model emphasizes personal feelings, emotions and personal care, while the Western model manages by law, rules and regulations. This special combination gives Phoenix an unusual cohesiveness among the staff, which is reflected both in the way in which we conduct our business and in the way in which we carry out our social responsibilities. Our reporters show love and caring in all the programmes that they do and this gives Phoenix Television a strong and unusual character.

Another project with which Phoenix is involved is the affairs of handicapped people in China. We have many connections and joint activities with the China Handicapped People's Committee. Last year a handicapped performance troupe from China visited the US and one of our star reporters, Chen Wu Lu, looked after the troupe and covered the event. On Christmas Eve 2002 Phoenix also participated in the China Handicapped People's Committee performance in the Great Hall of the People and, since January 2003, Phoenix has been sending the Chinese handicapped delegation to perform in Taiwan. Similarly, Phoenix broadcasts a programme called *Ambassador of Love*, which helps young children with blood diseases get bone marrow transplants. Last year we did live coverage of a case where people in Taiwan donated bone marrow to a girl living in Suzhou, saving the girl's life.

All the people working with Phoenix carry out public responsibilities within their scope of business. In the coastal areas of China there are numerous Taiwanese investors and if they want to set up their businesses in the Chinese coastal regions, they want to bring their families with them. However, examination results in China and Taiwan are not mutually recognized, so if their children attend local Chinese schools, their results would not be transferred to the Taiwan University. Since Taiwanese children cannot therefore be enrolled in the mainland schools, the mothers have to stay behind in Taiwan to look after them. The Taiwanese businessmen sometimes find mistresses in China and this causes a potential danger to the family units and there is a higher chance of them splitting up. Phoenix reporters made two reports on this issue and the tone of the reporting was so serious that the central government took notice and asked the Guangdong provincial authority to find a solution.

Approval was eventually given for the Taiwan people to set up a school for their children in Dong Wan Town in Guangdong province, where they use teachers and textbooks from Taiwan. As a result of our work, many Taiwanese families were saved and the board of directors of this school paid me a personal visit to say how grateful they and the headmaster were for Phoenix's input.

The future

Phoenix always tries to think outside the box, which is often difficult in China because of the deep-seated impact of socialism. Although many mainlanders in Hong Kong are exceptionally clever, Chinese politics run so deeply in the society that it is potentially difficult for the Chinese to think without restraint. Phoenix is trying to modify this mindset. In January we launched our new Information News Channel and, although it is not making much money at the moment, we believe that it is an important programme in terms of bringing honest, immediate news broadcasting into the Chinese arena. Once the mainland authorities give their consent, it will be huge.

The environment in China is changing, and Phoenix has a pivotal role to play in helping to bring China the media freedom that is a natural consequence of China's economic reforms. The 16th session of the Central Party's Congress is going to change the way in which we work, since China's situation is likely to become more benign and open. This meeting will signal an optimistic new stage in the development of Phoenix Television. China's entry into the World Trade Organization will also gradually open China up to the outside world, especially in the telecommunication and cultural sectors. Although we anticipate that the expansion of news and media will be the last item on the agenda, Phoenix will play its part in accelerating this essential transition. The previous five years have been a foundation for the future, marking only the very beginning of our adventure in Chinese television.

COMMENTARY

Media brands are notoriously difficult to manage: the brand values are delivered by a team of people working under intense pressure, to be received by the consumer in the form of a programme or publication that, of necessity, changes by the hour, day or month. Strong media brands always have a distinctive look/feel/tone of voice, which is often instinctive to those who work within it. They also have a strong sense of what they are not ('We wouldn't run that story', 'We wouldn't talk like that') as well as what they are.

Phoenix is helped in this because of its unique position as a permitted alternative to the state broadcasters run by the government. It is easy to develop a refreshing tone of voice when the alternative is stilted, orthodox or boring. However, its existence is based entirely on the government's willingness to continue its permission. So it has to run a fine line between pushing the boundaries (which maintains its consumer franchise) and not overstepping the mark (which removes the government's tolerance).

It is evident that Liu Changle has a very clear grasp of how to create a strong brand and how to use Western branding skills to deliver it. From logo to presentational style, here is a brand that many Western broadcasters would love to emulate.

15 | Wall's: Global Brand Capital, Local Application

Introduction

Wall's, part of the Unilever Group and the best selling ice-cream producer in the world, hit the streets of Beijing in China for the first time in the summer of 1994. Unilever itself had been present in China for almost 100 years and is the company behind a wide range of consumer goods with brand names such as Dove, Knorr, Omo, Lux, Hazeline and Lipton. Six months later, Wall's (China) Co. Ltd broke the record for the first six months of sales for all start-up Unilever ice-cream operations. In just one summer, Wall's managed to outcompete all domestic ice-cream brands. Using branded refrigerated vending cabinets in combination with a strong point-of-sale programme and relatively modest advertising support, the Wall's brand quickly became well-known throughout Beijing.

Encouraged by this success, Wall's rapidly expanded to the 70 largest urban clusters in China. It was a defining moment for the brand because it gave Wall's a first-mover advantage. But it was also a leap of faith as the company had not had time to acquire sufficient knowledge about each of the different regional markets in China. The period of 1994–99 was spent building and rebuilding the operations in many territories where the company faced operational control issues due to a roll-out that had occurred too quickly. In 2000, Wall's took its second defining step – it made the decision to move from a distribution-push to a brand-led business model. But it was the right thing to do. Since 2001, the sales volumes of Wall's ice creams have ranked the best in all areas where it has decided to operate. Wall's is currently market leader in all key urban ice-cream markets in China, holding a strong 30–40 per cent value share in the key Beijing and Shanghai markets. Peter Ter-Kulve, Wall's CEO in China, speaks about the lessons that Wall's learnt through those years.

The challenge of China

Business in China for most multinationals is extremely challenging. The key success measurement for any business, even one that is entering China, should still be profit. For sure, setting up in China is a strategic investment but strategic intent cannot be an excuse for not making money. In the rapidly changing environment of China, having a business plan that promises returns in five years' time is not good enough. When you cannot make money next year (at the latest), you really should be considering whether you are doing the right thing. Do you really have the right business model? Wall's has been struggling for a long time to find the right business model. We are not alone though. Pepsi didn't make money in the beginning and after 20 years is still not making money. McDonald's has a huge operation on the border of profitability and loss. There is something about this market that makes it difficult. I cannot imagine that all companies that enter China are incompetent or that they send incompetent people to China. The question is – what is it about China that makes it such a challenge?

For me there are two elements about China that make it more complex than most other markets of the world.

Complexity in diversity and size

The first thing that makes China different is that it is huge and extremely diverse. There is not 'one China'. When people say they have a China strategy, they mostly don't know what they are talking about because the country is too diverse for that. What you need to have is a Shenyang strategy, a Harbin strategy, a Beijing strategy, a Wuhan strategy and a Guangzhou strategy. The list goes on.

The Chinese find it funny that it is taking so long for foreigners to make money in China but I have the following analogy. Imagine that you work for a very successful Chinese company with a really popular ice-cream brand in China. As part of your expansion plans you come to Europe, starting in London. You launch your product and get an immediate positive reaction. Your product is so different, so unique that all the early adopters jump on it. You send enthusiastic reports to the head office saying 'Hey, the market really likes what we do, it likes the quality, it likes our new approach …' And your entire board says, 'This is fantastic, this "Europe" is a fantastic place.' They tell you to roll the business out from London to the 100 largest cities in Europe. You go to Moscow next year, to Lisbon, to Rome, to Amsterdam … And then things go totally out of control. You find that replicating your initial success in London is not that simple.

Now every Chinese person will tell you that this is exactly the situation in China because the differences between the north and south are as large as the differences between Norway and Greece. China's very size makes it complex. There is local competition, local trade structures, local consumers with local preferences, all of which need to be analysed and understood territory by territory. How does the government work in Russia and how does the government work in the UK? Very differently – and likewise in China. One cannot learn all about the European market in one or two years. That would be unrealistic, especially for a business that is based on consumer and customer understanding. Similarly for China, how can a European who does not speak any Mandarin expect to acquire intimate knowledge of a territory substantially larger then Europe in two years? Companies that enter China with this analogy and understanding in mind will do much better than those who come in saying 'Yeah! We're going to "do" China.'

Furthermore, Wall's is in the food industry where there can be enormous differences in what people prefer in terms of both taste and flavour. I remember the time we introduced a taro-flavoured product. (Taro is a sort of Chinese sweet potato.) We developed a fantastic product in Shanghai that was received very enthusiastically. We brought it to Guangzhou and the people there said 'This tastes awful! This is not taro, what is this?' Apparently the taro in Guangzhou is completely different to the taro in Shanghai. These are the sort of small differences that make the consumer business, and particularly the food business, tick.

On top of all this, you have to organize yourself to operate over a very large territory in terms of supply lines, cost structures, manufacturing, buying and so on. Especially when starting out, you will have to manage a relatively small business that is spread out over a continent larger than Europe. And to cover this territory, you have to staff your business. Where do you find the equivalents of your brilliant 'Russians, Greeks, Spaniards, Italians' and how do you get them to work for you?

So, to conclude, there are consumer insight issues, there are regional government issues and there are operational issues. And the one thing that creates all these difficulties is the enormous size and diversity of the country.

Complexity in rapid change

The second element is that China is such a rapidly changing environment, especially to Europeans who come from a very stable society. In China everything changes within a year. Shanghai is unrecognizable from eight years ago – at that time, Pudong did not exist. Contrast that with Rotterdam: since I studied there 14 years ago, nothing has changed. Ten years ago, there were no brands, no supermarkets and no hypermarkets in China. Now hypermarkets constitute more than 30 per cent of the retail scene in Shanghai after just three years. Everything moves extremely quickly.

In Europe you work with innovation cycles of one to two years. In China, however, innovation cycles are between three and six months. If you come to China with European systems and processes, you are heading for trouble because your mechanisms just won't work – they are not fast enough. This pace of change makes China a very different place from Europe. It can be handled, but you have to adapt, to build understanding and capabilities.

These two elements of size and speed make China special and more interesting for me. In terms of competition, there is a lot of it. However, because most industries are young and have not yet consolidated, the competition is somewhat easier to handle. On the other hand, the size of the market means that you don't know much about this competition. That's where the challenge lies. It is not like in Europe where I would have a profile on each one of my competitors.

Brand positioning is critical in China

Positioning yourself as a brand in China has to be done very carefully, especially if you claim that your brand is about understanding local culture and local food habits. One of the limitations will be whether you actually possess the research capabilities and the knowledge to support your claim. For example if your food brand is positioned as 'I'm the expert, I help the Chinese housewife create fantastic dishes', you will face an enormous challenge because you have to develop this expertise for at least 70 distinct regions. If you possess knowledge of Shanghai cooking, this cannot be applied to help a housewife in Changsha. They have different needs and a different food culture.

Wall's learnt this lesson the hard way. There was a period when the local competition started imitating our flavours and mixes and selling their ice creams at one-third of our prices. We responded by making our brand more Chinese and saying that we knew local flavours and culture. We also made the mistake of lowering our prices. Consequently, our differentiation from the competition completely disappeared. We ultimately realized that we didn't have the depth to really be local and close to the consumer.

Now we choose not to position ourselves that way because we know it is just not credible. Our present positioning strategy is as an international premium brand with a focus on innovative, higher-quality products. Wall's is an international brand – that is one of our great assets. Modern Chinese people are proud to be Chinese, but they like to be connected to the rest of the world and things like music, film and international brands such as Wall's give them that opportunity to connect at low cost. In fact, some of our larger local competitors now put their brand names in English on their packaging to create a fake international image.

There is no one governing principle to positioning your brand successfully in China. Let's consider some examples. If, in your industry, you are able to position yourself as the fashion forefront of Chinese youth culture, and if you are at the same time Shanghai-based, this becomes a fantastic advantage because what is cool in Shanghai will definitely be cool in Changsha. This is supported by the reality that Shanghai is the cultural city of China whether in terms of the advertising industry, fashion or night clubs. Things may actually come from Japan, Korea or Taipei but Shanghai is where they start becoming popular in China. When you approach brand positioning in this way, you can create strength from your weakness.

Take Shiseido as an example: it has decided to be really Japanese and it doesn't pretend to be local or Chinese at all. Adopting a positioning that says 'the best of Japan now also available in China' is perfectly valid for the company. 'The best of Japan' can be valid in Changsha and also in Shanghai and, in this way, Shiseido has managed to create a positioning that is credible throughout China.

The people who are responsible for the President brand in China will tell you something completely different. They started their business in Shenyang and it was only after they became very knowledgeable about Shenyang that they moved to Beijing and only then, after becoming very intimate with the Beijing market, did they enter Shanghai. President has a very modular approach. It won't claim that it understands Chinese food culture but it will claim that it understands Shanghai food culture, Beijing food culture and so on. Again, because there is no one Chinese food culture, it's very fragmented to the Chinese as well.

When you look at the brands that are successful in China, I think it becomes clear that success is always due to how you position your brand and how you choose a positioning that fits your overall business system and strategy. Personally I believe that, in China, there is a role for both global and local brands. Wall's business is, and will stay firmly rooted in, China and will be run eventually by Chinese management, but our brand positioning will stay international. I mean, why do we want to be a local hero? There are already so many of them.

A deeper understanding of branding versus local insight

In the ice-cream industry at the moment, local companies are still primarily cost-focused, price-focused and brand awareness-focused. What they presently understand and describe as marketing or branding is limited to building brand awareness or product awareness through advertising. Very few local companies think seriously about brand positioning or about creating a more rounded 360° brand experience in the way we do at Wall's. For instance, we have recently started to open our own branded ice-cream shops in China. The objective is twofold. On the one hand, we wish to develop a profitable

sales channel but, even more importantly, we want to get closer to the consumer and create a more intense and rich brand experience for them.

But this does not mean that international companies have an edge over the
local competition. International companies do understand branding theory
but they have an enormous problem with implementation because of lack of
consumer understanding and insight. Most foreign companies are run by foreigners who, like me, don't have a clue how the Chinese think and act. And
they don't have a clue because they don't speak Mandarin, they don't read the
languages and they don't always have quality marketing resources within their
own businesses. The advertising agencies are full of Hong Kongese and Taiwanese who often don't have a clue either about the hopes and aspirations of
the mainland consumers.

Without decent market research and staff, international companies are
often very much handicapped. We try to limit this handicap by fully localiz-
ing and empowering our marketing and sales staff. Additionally, we have
based our marketing departments in the main cultural centres of the country:
Shanghai, Beijing and Hong Kong. We could have based them in Inner Mongolia or Yunnan where it would have been cheaper but we would have been
further removed from the development curve of Chinese youth and urban
culture.

But, although local companies are not very refined or systematic in their
thinking about marketing issues and brand positioning, they still have the
advantage of better local insights over international companies. And they are
often able to combine these good insights, even if crudely executed, with
superior cost management to successful effect. This, I think, explains why
there has been a huge surge of local companies over the last couple of years in
many FMCG categories in China.

Local insights can make all the difference

The value of local insight should never be underestimated even if you are an
internationally successful brand. When we were developing the advertising
for Viennetta in China, we realized that our standard advertising approach
would not work. The Chinese do not eat desserts. So, instead, we positioned
Viennetta as a snack, the kind of treat you wish to share with your friends. We
set the scene in an aspirational apartment, dressed with IKEA-style furniture
(hugely popular in China now) and a more traditional Chinese-style round
table with a lazy Susan. The cast is very aspirational – good-looking, successful, urban, white-collar Chinese – the sort of people all Chinese mothers hope
their kids will become. The drama is created around the question of which
one of the friends seated round the table will get to eat that last slice of

Viennetta. This is always the moment of truth, the perfect denouement in every Viennetta commercial around the world.

The insight in this advertising that really enabled us to connect at a deeper level with our consumers in China and helped transform their perceptions of this brand was the idea of socializing with friends at home as the new expression of success in life. The lazy Susan centred on the round table with that last slice of Viennetta spinning was another interesting touch. Who is going to be the lucky one? Watching this commercial, you just have to smile.

Harnessing local insight, hiring the right people

It is in order to harness such local insights within Wall's that I hope my successor in the future will be a Chinese person. I will fight very hard for that because I believe that one of the success factors for our business is having local leadership and a local management team. China is too culturally complex and diverse to be managed by foreigners. Presently, I have already replaced every single expatriate in my company with a local Chinese person. This means that there are young members of the company promoted to the board with seven or eight years' work experience instead of the normal 14–15 years. They may have skill gaps but what I get back in return is a reality check and those local insights. If it were a choice between insight and skill, I would, in the fast-moving consumer business, choose insight. Without insight on your target group you will never find the foundations on which to build your brands. And only a brand can help you differentiate and avoid the price wars that are prevalent in most product categories in China.

Wall's is a premium international brand that is all about fun and indulgence. Our vision is to paint a smile on the face of China, to make China a happier place with our brands. Our core target group is the urban middle-class Chinese. When we need to develop sales strategies or when we want to develop advertising or new products, it all needs to be done by people who have an intimate understanding of the target group they are selling to. And what is a better way to make sure of this than to have these very same urban, middle-class Chinese creating your brand portfolio and business strategy? We are all young and urban here at Wall's. That is the interesting thing about our internal culture.

This is a principle that I would apply in any other case. For example, if I were running a business in the US selling to Hispanics I would make sure that I have a representative group of Hispanics running my business because otherwise we would only be second-guessing.

And if we stretch this thinking a little, then it becomes obvious that we also need to recruit people who have the potential to 'be' the brand. Basically, we need to be able to say of any potential recruit, 'Yeah, this could be a Wall's person.' They need to be able to breathe and live the brand. I think that is extremely important because, ultimately, the people within the business need to identify themselves with the brand in order to grow it successfully. And the outside world needs to identify those people with the brand in order to believe in the brand. It is just common sense, but it nevertheless makes a lot of difference to the success of your business, whether in China or elsewhere in the world.

The real battlefield is branding

We have seen a couple of waves hit the Chinese market. The initial surge into China was of the foreign FMCG companies, driven by the demands of curious Chinese consumers who desired the choice and differentiation that these foreign companies offered. The second wave was the rise of local companies who copied most of the marketing approaches (packaging, reliable quality, advertising, distribution) of the international players at much lower cost structures and started selling at lower price levels.

This dealt an enormous blow to the international FMCG players but in the end, as could be expected, the good ones adjusted to the new competitive environment and also adjusted their cost structures. What we will see now is the last wave – those who will survive the branding battle. This battlefield will be a huge challenge to local companies because they are used to selling products on the basis of price only. Unfortunately, this is no longer going to be good enough.

We have made that mistake in the past, believing that the main drivers for success in China are distribution and price. But now we know that, in the end, all decent companies (whether foreign or local) are able to manage cost and build up distribution channels. In the real battle of branding, it will be about how you can sharply position your brand and how you can build up enough magic around it to make it stand out. At Wall's, our brand determines where we are going to sell our products in terms of territories and channels. It drives our innovation and advertising strategies. It steers our supply chain strategies and technologies.

Wall's exists and prospers in China because of its brand. When this is clear, then it also becomes clear that every decision we make in our business is a question of whether we will ultimately create a richer and more satisfying brand experience for our customers.

COMMENTARY

The story of Wall's ice-cream brand in China demonstrates how powerful the combination of local insight with international brand expertise and technology can be for a multinational entering the Chinese market. Chairman, Peter Ter-Kulve's analogy, comparing China to an amalgamation of all the European countries, makes the point vividly that foreign multinationals should not underestimate the complexity arising from the sheer size and diversity of the Chinese market. It is not one market.

When you add to this complexity the fact that Chinese food tastes actually differ widely from region to region, it could be a recipe for disaster for any international food and beverage company. Yet Wall's has succeeded in dominating the key markets of Beijing, Shanghai and Wuhan and is targeting strong growth in Guangzhou and Shenzhen: all this with a product that traditionally has no place in the Chinese menu.

To match the local understanding of its domestic competitors, Wall's bases its key offices in the markets of Shanghai, Beijing and Hong Kong so as to be close to the centres of urban cultural development in China. It also employs within its ranks the very people it is trying to target with its brand. Ter-Kulve makes a very strong point when he talks about his plans to replace the leadership of the company with a full Chinese team in the near future. In fact, he is the last foreigner remaining in the company in China. Having a local indigenous management ensures that the company possesses a deep understanding of the mindset and the needs of its target market and, at the same time, builds loyalty and commitment amongst its local employees to the company's future. Despite these local nuances, Wall's employs a brand positioning that leverages off the appeal that it has to the young modern Chinese consumer as an international brand.

In effect, the company appears less like an arm of a foreign multinational and more like a local player with the advantages of foreign technological capabilities and foreign brand management know-how. With the former, the company manages to introduce innovative ice-cream products ahead of the local competition. With the latter, the company is able to differentiate itself by introducing Chinese consumers to fresh, insightful and engaging expressions of pleasure that in turn mirror the brand experience.

With this strategy, it is hoped that it will be able to sustain higher prices for its premium position in the market, moving away from the effects of the price wars that it has had to suffer in the past years. This will also allow it to protect its brand equity and premier position in China in the long term. Wall's has achieved the perfect marriage for the foreseeable future – bringing together local human capital and supply chain efficiencies combined with international brand and intellectual capital.

Index

3M 19

A

Adams, Douglas 17–18
administration structure 161–2
advertising, television 207
AIG 26
air-conditioners 125, 135
    direct-fired absorption (DFA) 126–7
    gas-absorption 125
    non-CFC/gas-driven 135
alliances
    Legend 148
    Tong Ren Tang 108
America see US
Angong Niuhuang Pill 101, 107, 108
Anheuser-Busch 182
Antaibao Coal Mine 117
AOL 149
Asahi Brewery 182
AsiaInfo Holdings Inc. ix, 5, 25, 153–66, 159
    core values 164
    corporate governance 160–62
    customers 163–4
    growth 159
    innovation 157
    international markets 159–60
    management 158–9
    name 155
    operations 157–8
    social responsibilities 165
    suppliers 163–4
    trust 163–4
    vision 156
Asian beauty 195–6, 205
Asian colouring 198
attitudinal clusters 11

B

B&Q 26
banks 111, 116, 117
Bass Group 182
BDI 154
beauty, Asian 195–6, 205
beer 181–4
    international companies 182

Beijing Changyi Ginseng Drinks Co. Ltd. 184
Beijing Enterprises Holdings 183, 184
Beijing Five Star Brewery 183
Beijing Hangxing Flavoring Limited Liability
    Company 184
Beijing Olympic Games 188
Beijing Shuangyan Colour Printing Works 184
Beijing Three Rings Brewery 183
Beijing Tong Ren Tang 108
Beijing University 165
Beijing Yanda Crown Corks Co. Ltd. 184
Beijing Yanjing Beer Group Corporation
    (Yanjing Beer) x, 4, 183–94
    core values 191–2
    corporate culture 191–2
    customers 192
    future 188
    international market 187–8
    logo 191
    mineral water 189–90
    name 185
    social responsibilities 193
    vision 185
Beijing Yanjing Brewery 181, 182
Beijing's Silk Market 6
Body Shop 12
Bohai Aluminium Smelter 117
boilers 126
Bradley, Kelvin 74
brand awareness 43
brand building 30
    China Mobile 42–4
    Haier 64–9
brand capital 1, 2
brand development 4
brand equity
    Erdos 170
    Legend 147–8
brand goodwill 2
brand image
    Haier 72
    TCL 96
brand innovation 17–21
brand loyalty, Haier 71
brand management
    Erdos 173–4

Legend 143
brand positioning 10–11
    Legend 141
    Wall's 220–21
brand reputation, CITIC 122–3
Brand Shifting™ 49, 87
brand strategy 177–8
    China Mobile 41–2
    Legend 145–6
    TCL 91–2
brand value creation, Legend 143
branding 7
    nation 27–9
    region 27–9
brands 177
    architecture 30
    international 25–7
    strong 3
    value 7–10
Broad AC Co. Ltd xiv, 1, 125–36
    business purpose 128
    competition 134–5
    employees 132
    HR policies 132
    innovation 128
    logo 128
    management 129–30
    names 128
    procedures 130
    vision 133–4
Broad Town 130–31
'The Brothers Haier' 72
Buddhism 213
business purpose, Broad 128
businesses, successful 2

C
Caravan 14
Carlsberg 182
Carrefour 26–7
Carroll, Justine Blair 199
case studies 3–4
cashmere 167
CCTV (Chinese Communist government
    television station) 198
cell-phones 35
censorship 212
CEOs 9
CEqs™ (communication equities) 22–3, 24
chaos theory 18
Chen Lu Yu 210, 211
Chen Wu Lu 214
China 178–9
    brand 28, 97
    change 219
    creativity 31
    customers 177
    demography 15
    diversity 218–20

    education 55–6, 158, 204
    international competition 179
    open-door policy 115
    size 218–20
China Academy of Science 165
China Beijing Tong Ren Tang Group Company
    104
China brand 28, 97
China Central Television 209, 210, 211
China Handicapped People's Committee 214
China International Trust and Investment
    Corporation see CITIC
China Mobile 9, 35–50, 155
    brand strategy 41–2
    co-operation 46–8
    competition 45–8
    corporate culture 38–40
    customers 42, 44
    distribution 44–5
    innovation 41
    partners 47, 81
    PR 41
    price wars 40, 41, 46
    promotion 43–4
    slogans 43
    social responsibilities 48–9
China Netcom 36, 154
China Postal and Telecommunications Ministry
    35
China Resources Enterprises Ltd 182
China Telcom 36, 46, 81, 155
China Unicom 36, 46, 155
'China's Most Famous Trademark' 169
Chinese Academy of Sciences 137
Chinese companies
    disadvantages 162
    global competitiveness 162–3
Chinese Fermentation Research Institute 185
Chinese language 22
CISCO 164
CITIC (China International Trust and
    Investment Corporation) 29, 111–24
    brand reputation 122–3
    cross-selling 118
    employees 121
    financial strategy 121
    future 121
    growth 116–17
    information sharing 118
    innovation 116
    non-financial assets 120–21
    restructuring 117–19
    risk management 118
    social responsibilities 123–4
CITIC Commercial Bank 121–2
CITIC Financial Holdings 118, 119
CITIC Industrial Bank 116, 117
CITIC Ka Wah Bank 117, 118
CITIC Pacific 120

CITIC Prudential Life Insurance Company
  117, 123
CITIC Securities 117, 121
cities 51–2
citizen loyalty 27–8
co-operation, China Mobile 46–8
Cobra beer 183
colour palette 198–200
colouring, Asian 198
communication equities (CEqs™) 22–3, 24
competition
  Broad 134–5
  China Mobile 45–8
  Legend 142
  Shanghai 58–9
  TCL 94–5
  Wall's 220
  Yue-Sai Kan 203
computers 137
construction projects 120
consumers *see* customers
convergence 82
core ideology *see* core values
core values 23
  AsiaInfo 164
  Haier 70–71
  Legend 140
  Sina 83
  TCL 92–3
  Tong Ren Tang 104–5
  Yanjing Beer 191–2
corporate culture
  AsiaInfo 159
  China Mobile 38–40
  Erdos 174–6
  Haier 73–4
  Legend 139–40, 146–7
  TCL 93
  Yanjing Beer 191–2
corporate governance 160–62
corporate social responsibility (CSR) *see* social
  responsibilities
corporate strategy, Legend 145–6
cosmetics 195, 203
Coty 195
counterfeiting 6, 174
creativity, China 31
credit co-operatives 111
cross-selling, CITIC 118
CSR (corporate social responsibility) *see* social
  responsibilities
customers
  AsiaInfo 163–4
  China Mobile 42, 44
  Chinese 177
  Legend 141–3
  Sina 83–6
  TCL 95–6
  understanding 222

Yanjing Beer 192

D
Da Ba 95
'Da Ge Da' 36
Dalian 58
Dell 142
Deng Xiaoping 59, 103, 115, 122
DFA centre 127
dietary trends 17
differentiation 18
  Sina 81–2
Ding, James ix, 153–65
direct-fired absorption (DFA) air-conditioners
  126–7
distribution
  China Mobile 44–5
  Erdos 172
  Legend 144–5
  Tong Ren Tang 106
diversification, Haier 66–7
dolls 204
domestic markets
  Erdos 169–70
  Legend 142
Dou wen tao 211
DreamStorm® 20–21

E
East 81
economic development 48, 97, 105, 112–14
education 19
  Chinese 55–6, 158, 204
electricity generation 133
employees
  Broad 132
  CITIC 121–2
  Erdos 175–6
  Legend 146–7
  TCL 94
energy-saving technology 134
Enron 12
entrepreneurs 29–31
entrepreneurship 54
  Sina 83
environment protection 133
Erdos Cashmere Group xii, 5, 6, 167–80
  brand equity 170
  corporate culture 174–6
  counterfeiting 174
  distribution 172
  domestic markets 169–70
  employees 175–6
  future 176
  international markets 168–9
  joint ventures 176
  logo 172
  management 173–4
  ownership 170–71

price wars 171–2
social responsibilities 173
vision 172–3
Erdos Cashmere Wool Fashion Show 169
Excite 81
export markets 4, 5
Erdos 168
see also international markets
extension, Haier 67–8

F
'Farm Law' 128–9
FedEx 9
Feng Huang (phoenix) 209–10
financial sector 111
financial strategy, CITIC 121
fishing, sustainable 12
focus groups 19
'Forest Law' 132
Founder 142
future
CITIC 121
Erdos 176
Haier 75–7
Legend 148
Phoenix 215
Sina 86–7
Yanjing Beer 188
Yue-Sai Kan 205

G
Ganmao Qingre Granule 101
Ganmao Soft Capsule 101
gas-absorption air-conditioners 125
Germany 68, 150
GITIC (Guangdong International Trust and
Investment Corporation) 112
Glaxo-Wellcome 26
GM 26
Go-Tone 36, 43, 44
Gong Li 204
Great Wall Electronics 90
Grove, Andrew S. 156
growth
AsiaInfo 159
CITIC 116–17
Legend 146
Yue-Sai Kan 204
Guangdong International Trust and Investment
Corporation (GITIC) 112
GuangdongNet 155
Guog ong Liquor 106

H
Hai-O Enterprise Berhad 108
Haidian District, Beijing 164–5
Haier xiv, 4, 5, 25, 63–77, 95, 150
brand building 64–9
brand image 72

brand loyalty 71
core values 70–71
corporate culture 73–4
diversification 66–7
extension 67–8
future 75–7
HR policies 73–4
international markets 68–9
Little Genius 65
market orientation 65–6
partners 76
quality control 65
slogans 72, 74
training 74
US 69, 74
Han International Consulting Company
148
handicapped people 214
He Ji Huang Pu 108
hedonism 16
herbal medicine *see* traditional Chinese
medicine
Hillman, Kevin 18
home appliances 63
honesty, Legend 139
Hong Hai 95
Hong Kong 59, 187, 211, 212
Hood, Gloria 74
Hope Project 165, 173
Hope schools 173
household appliances 67
HP 142, 164
HR policies
Broad 132
Haier 73–4
Huchu Ha 185
Hutchison Whampoa 108

I
IBM 95, 142
ice cream 217
shops 221–2
ideology *see* core values
immigration, Shanghai 57–8
indices of performance 11–12
Industrial and Commercial Administration
Bureau 169
information-based society 48
information sharing 118
Infoseek 81
Inner Mongolia Autonomous Region 167, 168,
170, 173
innovation 17–21
AsiaInfo 157
Broad 128
China Mobile 41
CITIC 116–17
innovation cycles 219
Intel 95

intellectual property 6
Interbrew 182
international brands 25–7, 220
international competition 179, 182
international markets
   AsiaInfo 159–60
   Erdos 168–9
   Haier 68–9
   Yanjing Beer 187–8
international trust and investment corporations
   (ITIC) 111, 112, 113
Internet 5, 60, 79
   evolution 82
   infrastructure 154
   media and entertainment services 79, 81
   users 85
Issey Miyake 204
ITIC (international trust and investment
   corporations) 111, 112, 113

J

Japan 28, 54, 55, 149–50, 150
Jiang Zemin 115, 209
Jin Yongnian 101–9
joint ventures 90
   Erdos 176
   TCL 90
   Tong Ren Tang 108
   Yue-Sai Kan 195

K

Keller, William 60
Kenzo 204

L

leadership, local 223
leasing companies 111
Legend xii, 4, 5, 10, 13, 95, 137–51, 165
   alliances 148
   brand equity 147–8
   brand management 143
   brand positioning 141
   brand strategy 145–6
   brand value creation 143
   competition 142
   core values 140
   corporate culture 139–40, 146–7
   corporate strategy 145–6
   customers 141–3
   distribution 144–5
   domestic markets 142
   employees 146–7
   future 148
   growth 146
   honesty 139
   management 139
   market share 138, 142
   marketing 143, 144
   name 138

   partners 145, 149
   PR 143
   price wars 142
   R & D 144
   service 141, 142
   slogans 147
   social responsibilities 149–50
   technology 148
   trust 139
Legend Group 138
Legend World 145
LG 150
Li Dongsheng x, 89–99
Li Fu Cheng x
Li Jiacheng 108
Liberhaier 72
life cycle 15
Liquan Beer 183
Little Genius 65
Liu Changle ix, 22
Liu Chuanzhi 137, 139, 145
Liu Hai Ruo 213, 214
Liu Hairuo 107–8
Liuwei Dihuang Pill 101, 106
local insights 222–4
local leadership 223
local management 223
local partners 27
logos
   Broad 128
   Erdos 172
   Phoenix 209–10
   Yanjing Beer 191
   Yue-Sai Kan 200
L'Oreal 203
Lu Xiang Dong x–xi, 35–49
Lui Changle 207–15

M

M-Office 43
M-Zone 43
'Made in China' 97, 149, 179
Malaysia 108
management
   AsiaInfo 158–9
   Broad 129–30
   Erdos 173–4
   Legend 139
   local 223
   Phoenix 213–14
   Western 76
Mandarin Oriental Group 22
manufacturing industry 1
   negative perceptions 149, 179
Mao, Daniel 80–87
Mao Dao Lin xi
Marine Stewardship Council (MSC) 12
market orientation, Haier 65–6
market share, Legend 138, 142

marketing
  Legend 143, 144
  Tong Ren Tang 106
  Wall's 222
markets *see* domestic markets; export markets;
  international markets; regional markets
McDonald's 218
media industry 207
media personalities 210–11
medicine, herbal *see* traditional Chinese
  medicine
mergers and acquisitions 5, 67, 148
metaphors 22
mineral water 189–90
mobile phones 35, 90
Monternet 36, 37–8, 43, 45
moral significance, Tong Ren Tang
  104–5
MSC (Marine Stewardship Council) 12
Municipal Sugar, Tobacco and Wine
  Corporation of Beijing 185
Murdoch, Rupert 208

N
names 38
  Broad 128
  Legend 138
  Phoenix 22
  Sina 80
  Yanjing Beer 185
NASDAQ 161
nation branding 27–9
national brands 149
National Herbal Medicine Research Institute
  103
national spirit 150–51
nationalization 103
natural gas 133
Nestlé 7, 26
network solutions 153
News Corps 208, 212
Niuhuang Jiedu Tablet 101
Niuhuang Qinqxin Pill 101
non-CFC/gas-driven air-conditioners
  135
non-financial assets, CITIC 120–21
Novartis 26
NTT Docomo 47
Nyingchi Prefecture 124

O
observational behaviour research 19
One World xiii, 198
OOCL 22
open-door policy 115
operations, AsiaInfo 157–8
outsourcing 134
  partners 76
ownership, Erdos 170–71

P
partners 182, 193
  China Mobile 47
  Haier 76
  Legend 145, 149
  local 27
  outsourcing 76
  Sina 80–82
  TCL 98
Patten, Chris 209
Peng Zhen 103
pension support 14
people
  as ambassadors 53
  Shanghai 56
People's Bank of China 119
Pepsi 218
performance, indices of 11–12
Pfizer 26
pharmaceutical products 101
Philips 98
phoenix 209–10
Phoenix Television ix, 207–15
  future 215
  Hong Kong 212
  logo 209–10
  management 213–14
  name 22
  slogans 211
  social responsibilities 213–14
pollution 133
positioning 10–11
Post-it® 19
power generation 120
PR (public relations)
  China Mobile 41
  Legend 143
presenters 210–11
President 221
price 9, 142–3, 224
price wars
  China Mobile 40, 41, 46
  Erdos 171–2
  Legend 142
procedures, Broad 130
Procter & Gamble 11
promotion
  China Mobile 43–4
  Shanghai 59
psychographic drawing 21–2
public relations *see* PR

Q
Qilu Petrochemical 117
Qingdao Refrigerator Plant 63
quality, Haier 70
quality control
  China Mobile 41
  Haier 65

Quinghua University 165

R

R & D, Legend 144
refrigerator market 64
region branding 27–9
regional markets 106
regulatory environment 47
research 19
Research and Development Institute
190–91
respect, earning 13
restructuring, CITIC 117–19
risk management system, CITIC 118
Roddick, Anita 12
Rong Yiren 29, 114, 122, 123

S

SAB (South African Breweries) 182
Samsung 10, 30, 31, 94, 96, 142, 150
Sankong Brewery Co 183
Sanyo 76
Schwartz, Diane C. 199
service
  Haier 70–71
  Legend 141, 142
Shanghai 16, 27, 51–62, 219, 221
  brand 54–5
  competition 58–9
  people 56
  promotion 59
  urbanization 57–8
Shanghai Fortune Forum 91
Sheehy, Gail 15
Shell 13
Shenzhen 58
Shenzhouxing 36, 43
Shiseido 203, 221
Sina xi, 79–88, 165
  core values 83
  customers 83–6
  differentiation 81–2
  entrepreneurship 83
  future 86–7
  name 80
  partners 80–82
Sina Online 80
Sina.com 5, 79, 80
Sina.net 80
Singapore 59
slogans
  China Mobile 43
  Haier 72, 74
  Legend 147
  Phoenix 211
  Tong Ren Tang 108
Smith, Fred 9
SMS 19, 85
social ideology see social responsibilities

social responsibilities 12–14
  AsiaInfo 165
  China Mobile 48–9
  CITIC 123–4
  Erdos 173
  Legend 149–50
  Phoenix 213–14
  TCL 98
  Yanjing Beer 193
society, change in 14–17
Sohu 81
Sony 10, 30, 31, 94, 95, 96, 142, 150
South African Breweries (SAB) 182
Spain 61
spiritual needs 25
stakeholders, TCL 98–9
Star TV 208, 209, 213
Starbucks 8
Stone 165
Stone Rich Sight 79
Strickland, Ian 26
Studwell, Joe 26
Su Fangwen 63–77
successful businesses 2
Sun Television Cybernetworks Holdings 80
suppliers, AsiaInfo 163–4
sustainable fishing 12

T

Taiwan 188, 211, 214
target groups 42–3
tax incentives 27
TCL x, 5, 6, 89–99, 142, 150
  brand image 96
  brand strategy 91–2
  competition 94–5
  core values 92–3
  corporate culture 93
  customers 95–6
  employees 94
  joint ventures 90
  partners 98
  social responsibilities 98
  stakeholders 98–9
TCL Communications Equipment Share Co.
  Ltd 89
TCL Electronics Sales Company 90
TCL Holdings Corporation Ltd 89
TCL International Holdings Ltd 89
teams 19
  Tong Ren Tang 109
technological innovation 127
technology, Legend 148
telecommunications 35, 36, 37, 47, 89, 120,
  153, 154, 162–3
telecoms network integration 154–5
television advertising 207
television sets 90
Ter-Kulve, Peter xi–xii, 217–24

text messaging 19
Tian, Edward 154
Tian Huning 157
Today's Asia 212
Tokyo 55
Tong Ren Tang 14, 101–10
   alliances 108
   core values 104–5
   distribution 106
   joint ventures 108
   marketing 106
   moral significance 104–5
   slogans 108
   teams 109
Tong Ren Tang Hutchison Pharmaceutical
   Development 108
Tong Ren Tang Ji 108
Toyota 150
traditional Chinese medicine 101, 103, 106,
   107
training, Haier 74
trust 124
   AsiaInfo 163–4
   Legend 139
trust and investment sector 111–12
Tsingtao Brewery 181, 182, 183

U
UNICEF 205
Unicom 47
Unilever Group 11, 12, 217
urbanization, Shanghai 57–8
US 15–16
   Haier 69, 74
   Tong Ren Tang 108

V
values see core values
Viennetta ice cream 18–19, 222–3
Virgin 7
vision
   AsiaInfo 156
   Broad 133–4
   Erdos 172–3
   Yanjing Beer 185
Vodafone 23–4, 47
Vovlo 23
VTech 9

W
Wall's (China) Co. Ltd 5, 16, 26, 217–25
   brand positioning 220–21
   competition 220
   ice cream shops 221–2
   marketing 222
   Viennetta ice cream 18–19, 222–3
Wang Jun 114

Wang Linxiang xii, 167–79
washing machines 65–6
Weaving Import and Export Authority,
   Mongolia 168
Wong, Allan 9
World Exposition 2010: 51, 55, 58, 60
World Wildlife Fund for Nature (WWF) 12
WTO (World Trade Organization), China's
   entry 4, 41, 46, 75, 97, 98, 108, 148, 162, 193
Wu, Shirley 211
Wuming Brewery Co 183

X
Xiao Li 211
Xinjiang 48
Xishuangbanna Autonomous Prefecture 124

Y
Yahoo! 81
Yang, Jerry 87
Yang Lan 208, 210
Yang Yuanqing xii–xiii, 138, 145
Yanjing 185
Yanjing Beer see Beijing Yanjing Beer Group
   Corporation
Yanjing Brewery 10
Yizheng Fiber Optical Plant 117
yoga 24
young people 107
Yue Fengming 102
Yue Hongda 102
Yue-Sai Kan xiii, 6, 195–205
Yue-Sai Kan Cosmetics xiii, 4, 5, 195–206
   colour palette 198–200
   competition 203
   future 205
   growth 204
   joint ventures 195
   logo 200
Yue-Sai Wa Wa 204
Yue Songsheng 103
Yue Xianyang 101–2

Z
Zhang, Professor 162
Zhang Er Jing 183–93
Zhang Jian 125, 126
Zhang Ruimin xiv, 63, 65, 66, 73, 75
Zhang Yimou 204
Zhang Yue xiv, 32, 125–35
Zhongguancun 165
Zhou Hanmin xv, 19, 28, 51–60
Zhou Yunjie 63–77
Zhu Guang 137–50
Zhu Rongii 212
Zhujiang Beer Group 182
Zhunjiang Brewery 181